Dreksler I Härle

1000
keyboard tips

GPAC

Voggenreiter

Cover design: OZ, Essen (Christian & Katrin Brackmann)
Setting-up and Layout: Notengrafik Werner Eickhoff, Freiburg

Original © 1987 VOGGENREITER PUBLISHERS
Complete Revised Edition © 2002 VOGGENREITER PUBLISHERS
International Copyright Secured
All Rights Reserved

VOGGENREITER PUBLISHERS
Viktoriastraße 25, 53173 Bonn/Germany
www.voggenreiter.de
info@voggenreiter.de

ISBN: 3-8024-0417-3

CONTENTS

1 PLAYING WITHOUT NOTES
A quick, "idiot-proof" course which gives you the feel of things

2 KEYS-NOTES-TIPS
Short information for beginners

3 CHORDS
How the hoards of chords came about

4 HARMONIES
Musical etiquette

5 RHYTHMS
From Rock to Pop-Reggae to Alka Salsa

6 IMPROVISATION
About the chances of being hired or fired in Musicland

7 KEYBOARD-STYLES
The most important styles in current pop music

8 PROFESSIONAL TRICKS
Intros, Hammerings, Licks-Riffs, Runs, Tricks

9 ARRANGING AND COMPOSING
From Fuzzy to the first million

10 MIDI AND COMPUTERS
All about MIDIotic masters and slaves

11 THE MAGICAL KEYBOARD TABLES
Everything at a glance: Chords, Harmonies, Scales, Improvisation scales, Intervals – with and without notes

12 KEYBOARD DICTIONARY
From Analogue-Synthesizer, Attack Time and Adagio via MIDI, Master-Keyboard and Mixing Desk to Xylophone

13 CD CONTENT
Listening examples, Improvisation exercises, Keyboard styles

PREFACE AND GUIDE TO USE

A book about learning how to play keyboards has to be good fun, easy to understand for beginners and informative for the more advanced. We would like you to tell us whether we have achieved this aim. If you have any criticisms, praise or suggestions for improvements, simply mail to: JDreksler@aol.com or Quirin.Haerle@t-online.de

The book contains ...

1000 Tips as a Textbook and Dictionary. The book is a textbook and a dictionary at the same time. As a textbook it shows you the current and professional keyboard techniques for all important Pop and Rock styles. As a dictionary it contains scales and chords in all commonly used keys, in addition to rhythm-patterns, specialist terms (and much more).

1000 Tips for Novices and Advanced Keyboarders. The book is made up of modules. Each chapter deals with an important subject as a unit. If, however, you at first want to accustomize yourself with the feel of the keyboard, we recommend that you work through the first four chapters step by step.

1000 Tips in C major. All examples of notes are given in the simplest key C-major/A-minor. If you master chords, scales, riffs, and tricks in C-major, you will have very few problems transposing them yourself into any other key with the help of the Magical Keyboard Tables. Apart from this, most keyboards have an automatic transposing function. Only when you have mastered one key, will an instinctive feeling for the positions of chords and notes ensue.

1000 Tips as Rules and Recipes: It is better to learn structures than non-related details. Wherever it was possible we have indicated regularities; and we have not been afraid to offer a few simple recipes here and there for quick beginner's successes.

Summary

1. Keys-Notes-Tips	2. Keyboard without Notes	3. Chords
First orientation on the keys and in the notation.	You learn how to "see" chords, how to strike and play.	From the common chords to the $Cmaj^{7/-9/+11/13}$ chord.
4. Harmonies	**5. Rhythms**	**6. Improvisation**
The theory of harmony and recipes for accompanying Pop songs.	All the important Pop-rhythms and how to read and learn them.	Scales, recipes, and tips for hot and creative professional solos.
7. Keyboard-Styles	**8. Professional Tricks**	**9. Arranging + Composing**
The most popular Pop-styles built up on a building-brick system.	All fascinating techniques used by the keyboard superstars.	Recipes used by the Head-Chiefs of the Pop-world.
10. Midi	**11. Magical Keyboard Tables**	**12. Keyboard-Dictionary**
The Basics, plus wiring and system sketches.	Chords and scales in all keys at a glance.	Musical and electronic terms explained briefly and clearly.

A KEYBOARD GADGET FOR YOU TO MAKE YOURSELF

This Keyboard gadget helps you to find the right note. Please copy first, than cut it out, stick it together, fold it and place it on the keyboard.

1 C D E F G A B **2** C D E F G A B **3** C D E F G A B

1

fold back

Glue here

C D E F G A B

2

fold back

Glue here

C D E F G A B

3

fold back

C D E F G A B

1 PLAYING WITHOUT NOTES

A quick, "idiot-proof" course which gives you the feel of things

1.1 THE ABC OF KEYS

Is it really possible to tell the difference between the white and the black keys?

sure it is
Orientate yourself on the black keys: they are more clearly recognizable, set out in groups of two or three. The white key to the left of **every** group of two is a "C"!

The ABC of notes and keys

It is used to refer to all white keys.
Just like the real ABC, the ABC of notes begins

A B C D E F G

Earlier, someone came up with the original idea of beginning with the C instead of A. Fortunately this has stayed the same:

C D E F G A B

Natural notes and C-Major scale

The ABC of notes, the notes from C to B are called natural tones. At the same time they are the notes of the C-major scale. The sequence begins from the beginning at every C on your keyboard. The further to the right you strike a key, the higher the sound.

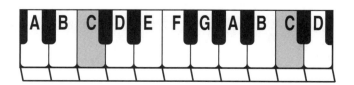

Middle-C

The most important C is the Middle-C. On many keyboards it is exactly in the middle (measure it!). If you don't find a C in the middle, you should take the next to the left of the geometric centre as Middle-C. C is always to the left of a group of two black keys.

This, the Middle-C is the most important orientational aid on your keyboard. To the left thereof, we play **most** of the bass-figures in Pop and Rock (left hand) and to the right we play melodies and chords (right hand) – a rule with many exceptions.

Octave

The distance between two notes (keys) is called the interval (from the Latin "inter" = between; "vallum" = wall).

The distance between two C's (or D's, E's, etc.) always amounts to 8 notes, if you count C (D, E etc) as the first note. This interval of notes is called an octave (from the latin "octavus" = the eighth).

Viewed from Middle-C, we refer to the octaves as first octave left, second octave left, etc.

What about a summary?

Distance of 8 notes from C to C = 1 Octave

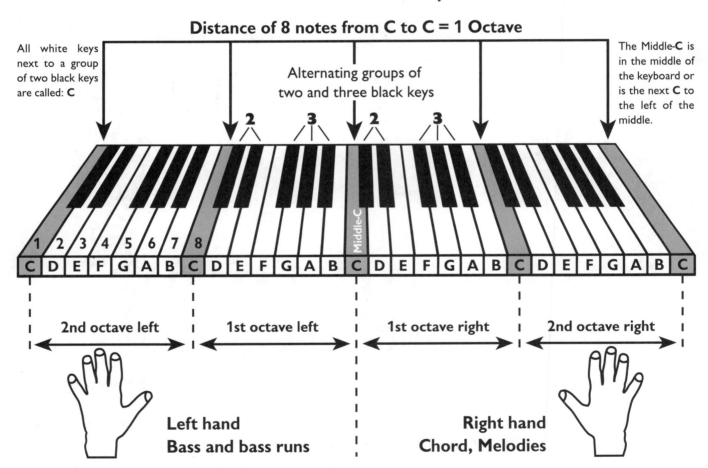

All white keys next to a group of two black keys are called: **C**

Alternating groups of two and three black keys

The Middle-**C** is in the middle of the keyboard or is the next **C** to the left of the middle.

2nd octave left — 1st octave left — 1st octave right — 2nd octave right

Left hand
Bass and bass runs

Right hand
Chord, Melodies

And what about the black keys?

They are named after the white keys. Here, of course, there are always two possibilities of naming a black key: according to the lower white key, or the higher white key. In spite of different names, the note remains the same (musical term: enharmonic change).

Rule: Raised notes from white keys are written with a sharp (♯), lowered notes with a flat (♭). When spoken they are refered as sharp or flat.

Example: The black key between C and D is called either C♯ (C sharp) or D♭ (D flat).

The summary at a glance

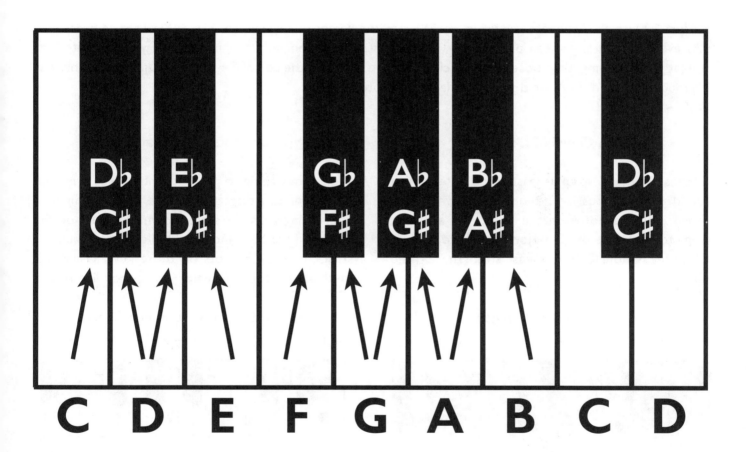

1.2 A CHORD

Occupational therapy for itchy fingers

In this section we will show you how you can play all chords if you have only fully understood **one**; and we provide demonstrations using **one** family of chords as examples. Put concisely: We are going to present a system and its structures so that you don't (as is usually the case) have to learn every chord and its variants individually. You will learn how to play using strike-patterns and chord-symbols – a professional technique. And as "Gimmicks" we are going to show you rock-bass patterns, improvisation scales, harmonies, song-accompaniment techniques and how to transpose – all without notes!

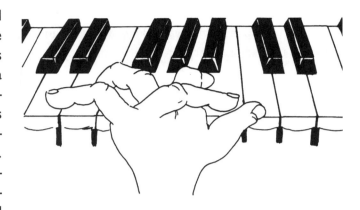

5 Tips: 1) Use the keyboard gadget (p. 8). 2) Learn the names of the keys (p. 11). 3) Please read every line, play everything until you can play fluently, off-by-heart. 4) Buy songbooks which contain **your** favorite hits, and (at the beginning) transpose all of the chords in the books to the key of C-major (p. 50), because this way it's much more fun. 5) After this chapter learn the notes.
O.K. – off we go!!

The Chord of C-major

Chords are made up of at least three notes which sound simultaneously. The simplest form is the chord of three notes or the triad. We are now going to introduce the **C-major triad**. It consists of the notes **Middle C, E, G**. Please strike these three notes.

... and its chord diagram

We are not going to illustrate the chords using the usual confusing diagrams, but we will use simplified **chord-diagrams**. In scaled-down sketches of the keyboard we have indicated which keys should be struck by drawing dots on those keys. Using this method, the chord C-major would look like this:

The Chord of C-major

Middle C

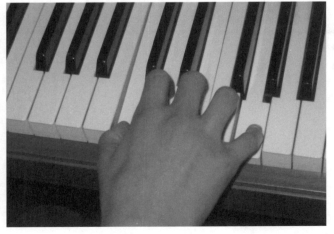

Chord Diagram – C-major Chord

Middle C

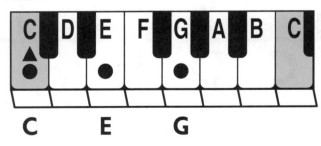

You now know **where** to strike the notes which go to make up the chord C-major; but you don't know **how**: i.e. with which fingers and in which order. To be able to show you this we have developed a **new system of keyboard symbols** (keyboard tablature).

Fingering

The fingers of your **right** hand are given the following symbols:

TH = Thumb: strikes key once
IF = Index: finger strikes key once
MF = Middle: finger strikes key once
RF = Ring finger: strikes key once
SF = Small finger: strikes key once

Fingering for the Chord of C-major

The black dots tell you which key you strike, the letters in the dot tell you with which finger. Please never change the fingering shown! To help you find your way, we have emphasized all C's and marked Middle-C with a triangle

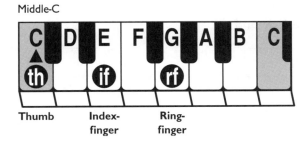

Ways to play

When playing the three notes you basically have three possibilities.

Closed

The fingers all strike the notes/keys at the same time. We show this in our notation system as three fingering symbols, written above another. For the chord C-major, TH, IF and RF strike Middle-C, E and G simultaneously.

|
RF
IF
TH

Broken/Arpeggio

The fingers strike the keys successively. We show this in our notation system as three fingering symbols written separately one after the other. For the chord C-major, TH, IF and RF strike Middle-C, E, G successively.

| | |
TH IF RF

Mixed

This occurs when closed and broken methods are mixed together. To the right you can see an example. The way of notating such a form of fingering for C-major would look like this:

| | | |
  RF   RF
TH IF TH IF

The thumb (TH) strikes Middle-C, then the ring- and index-fingers (RF, IF) strike the E and G keys simultaneously. And, as you can see: The same again from the beginning.

Strike-Patterns

The secret of being able to play the keyboard well is being able to hit the right key with the right finger at the right time. The best way of achieving this at the beginning is by using strike-patterns; if you tend to impatiently tap with your finger at the wrong time, you should use such a pattern – the fingers then strike in a specific order, which is repeated continuously. Important: These patterns have to be played at such a regular rhythm, as if you had a drummer behind you.

The built-in drummer ...

... and your right hand

within the strike-patterns is the count-bar which contains the main counts "1, 2, 3, 4" and the sub-counts "+", which are to be spoken as "and". The best way to work with these patterns is to count out loud when practising them ...

strikes the key with the **fingering** which is notated above the count-bar. If nothing is written there, your right hand may have a break. In the example below you count "1" while striking a closed C-major chord, on the counts "+ 2 +" you do nothing and on the count "3", you strike the chord again ... etc.

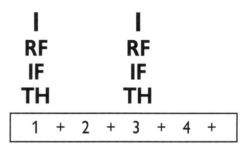

Count: one and two and three and four and

| 1 | + | 2 | + | 3 | + | 4 | + |

Our strike-patterns are one bar long (more about that on p. 24/25). In connection with a chord or its **letter-symbol** (the C-major chord has the symbol "C") this tells you: 1. which keys you strike, 2. in which order, 3. that you repeat the patterns of notes until a new chord appears and that you repeat the notes in the same patterns until a new chord appears suggesting that you play other notes for a change using the **same finger-strike-sequence**.

The C-major chord ...

and the strike-pattern 1 ...

are played as follows:

On every whole count the thumb, index-finger and ring-finger strike the 3 notes of the C-major chord simultaneously.

The C-major chord ...

and the strike-pattern 2 ...

are played as follows:

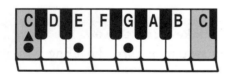

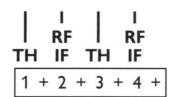

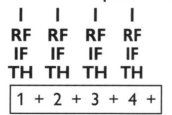

On the count of one, the thumb-strikes the Middle-C. On the second count the ring and index-finger strike the notes E and G simultaneously ... and then the same again.

Strike-patterns are one bar long (see page 26). Please play these patterns 20 to 50 times until they become automatic. Don't forget to always emphasize the first count.

1.3 MAJOR AND MINOR

Big and small in the music world

In Human biology there are two sexes: male and female. People of both sexes are built-up in very much the same way, but there is one, well-known little difference. This is exactly the same where notes and chords are concerned. There are two musical sexes - major and minor. These are also made up in very much the same way, and yet again there is one small difference here. Here is the principle behind all major and minor triads (before this please read "Octave" on p. 10).

The Intervals of the C-major Triad

A **triad** consists of three notes from one scale: the first note of the scale (keynote) the third note of the scale (third) and the fifth note of the scale (fifth). **All white keys** are notes in the C-major scale. The first note is C. If you build a triad up on this note, the triad is named after this note. This letter is also the triad's **Chord Symbol**.

Keynote (= KN): This is the foundation of the chord and gives it its name. The major triad which is built up on the note C is therefore called C-major. Numerical symbol: 1 = first note.

Third: Three notes above the keynote C (when counting C as the first) is the note E. This part of the triad, is called the **"Third"**. Its numerical symbol is 3 = third note.

Fifth: Five notes above the keynote is the note G. This part of the triad is called the **"Fifth"**. Numerical symbol: 5 = fifth note.

C = chord symbol for the C-major chord

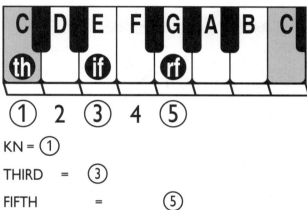

The musical distance from one note to the next (whether it be black or white) is always **half a tone**. The small difference between major and minor triads is that the **"Third"** in a minor triad is **a semitone deeper** than in the major triad – keynote and fifth are the same.

Example: C-major and C-minor

The C-major triad consists of the notes C-E-G, the C-minor triad consists of the notes C-E♭-G.

C-major

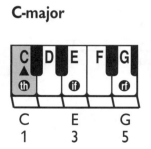

C-minor
(Third semitone deeper)

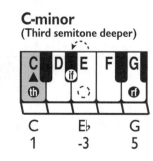

What does major and minor mean?

Major comes from the Latin "maior" and means greater. Minor also comes from the Latin and means smaller. Minor chords sound somewhat softer and a little sad – perhaps because they are a little smaller.

Therefore: Please remember the Keynote, Third and Fifth of **every** triad, you will then automatically be able to play a minor-triad in that you play the Third a semitone deeper **and vice-versa!**

1.4 THE C-MAJOR-CHORD FAMILY

1 scale and 6 chords

You can build up a triad upon every note in the C-major scale according to the pattern which we have just described. The triads built up on the first note C, on the fourth note F and the fifth note G are all major triads, the others are minor (more about this on p. 70). Every triad is given the name of its keynote as **chord symbol**. Instead of C-major, F-major and G-major we use the symbols C, F, and G; instead of D-minor, E-minor and A-minor we write Dm, Em, Am. **All triads are struck in the same way**. Eighty percent of all Pop and Rock music is based on the six triads of such a **chord family**; you can therefore do a lot with these.

The Triad-Elephant-Crib

Please learn the notes of every chord and which is the keynote, the third and the fifth. We have developed a crib for the notes in a chord, it is made up of the (okay we admit it ... the somewhat stupid) sentence:

Clever Elephants gain brilliant directions from anteaters ...

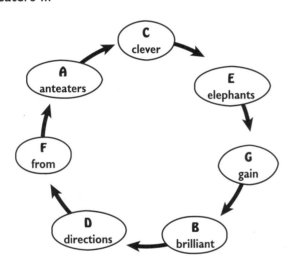

The first letter of each word represents the notes of the triads in groups of three. Mumble this crib until you arrive at the letters of the triad which you want to know; for example:

C: **C**LECER **E**LEPHANTS **G**AIN (C-E-G)

Dm: (Clever Elephants gain brilliant ...) **D**IRECTIONS **F**ROM **A**NTEATERS (D-F-A)

Am: (Clever Elephants gain brillliant directions from ...) **A**NTEATERS **C**LEVER **E**LEPHANTS (A-C-E), etc.

The C-major-Chord-Family

C
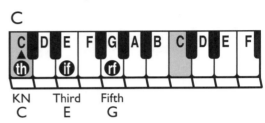

KN   Third   Fifth
C   E   G

Dm
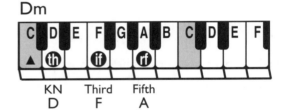

KN   Third   Fifth
D   F   A

Em
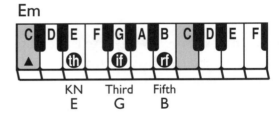

KN   Third   Fifth
E   G   B

F
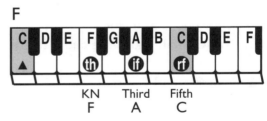

KN   Third   Fifth
F   A   C

G
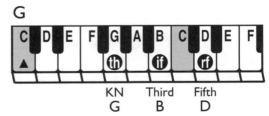

KN   Third   Fifth
G   B   D

Am
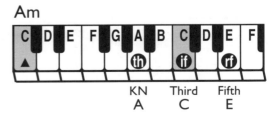

KN   Third   Fifth
A   C   E

KN = Keynote

Chords and Strike Patterns

Here we assume that you have mastered the two strike patterns on page 14 using the C-major chord (if not: GO AHEAD!). In the exercises below we use both patterns, BUT: from now on you are going to play the patterns with several chords. This is really not a great problem, because the fingers on your right hand do exactly the same thing – irrespective of which chord you play. Here's an example of the principle again:

Chord changes with Strike patterns

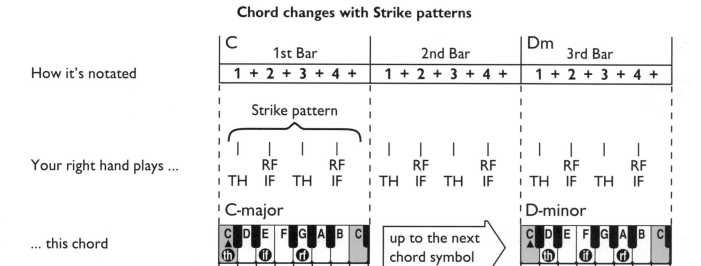

Successions of chords

Here are five typical successions of chords, which you will recognize from hundreds of Rock- and Popsongs. Please practise them using the strike-patterns from page 27, until the successions can be played without you having to cheat ... or ... change the tempo.

Typical Rock-Pop Successions of chords

① C — Dm — F — C
| 1 2 3 4 | 1 2 3 4 | 1 2 3 4 | 1 2 3 4 | 1 2 3 4 | 1 2 3 4 | 1 2 3 4 | 1 2 3 4 |

② C — F — G — C
| 1 2 3 4 | 1 2 3 4 | 1 2 3 4 | 1 2 3 4 | 1 2 3 4 | 1 2 3 4 | 1 2 3 4 | 1 2 3 4 |

③ C — Em — Dm — C — C — Em — F — C
| 1 2 3 4 | 1 2 3 4 | 1 2 3 4 | 1 2 3 4 | 1 2 3 4 | 1 2 3 4 | 1 2 3 4 | 1 2 3 4 |

④ C — F — Dm — G — C — Dm — G — C
| 1 2 3 4 | 1 2 3 4 | 1 2 3 4 | 1 2 3 4 | 1 2 3 4 | 1 2 3 4 | 1 2 3 4 | 1 2 3 4 |

⑤ Am — F — Dm — G — Am — G — F — C
| 1 2 3 4 | 1 2 3 4 | 1 2 3 4 | 1 2 3 4 | 1 2 3 4 | 1 2 3 4 | 1 2 3 4 | 1 2 3 4 |

1.4 CHORD INVERSION

Turn around before its too late!

"Chord Inversion" means: You don't, for example, always have to play the C-major triad in the order C-E-G. The keynote **doesn't always have to be the deepest note**, even the Third and the Fifth can be "below" the others. Chord inversions are the most important aspect of keyboard playing and consequently we ask you to thoroughly work through this section. Once you have mastered the system of inversion, you will no longer view your keyboard as a mere collection of black and white keys, but as a collection of chord-structures – just as if you had stuck dots on the keys. On these two pages we explain the principle of chord inversion using C-major as an example. Please do us – no! – do yourself a favour, and buy some sticky dots. You will need three different colours (you can even colour them yourself). Now stick the red dots on the five C's in the two octaves to the left and the right of Middle-C, the green dots on the four E's and black dots on the four G's.

The C-major-Triad (basic form) in 4 Octaves

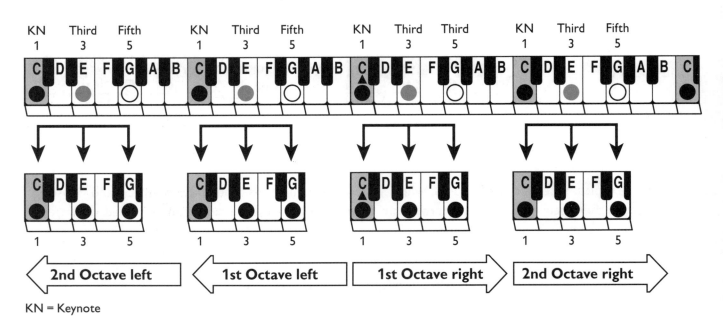

KN = Keynote

Change of position

Now you can see graphically where C-major is positioned in all four octaves.

Please, play now these 4 C-chords using both strike patterns (p. 14) in all octaves (from the left to right and from right to left). This tip could also be expressed as follows: please play the C-major chord **in all four positions**.

Please note that no lengthy pauses occur when the position is changed.

A little story

Many years ago in Soundland the Keynote-tyrants ruled over the subjugated Fifths and Thirds. The Keynotes were always the lowest notes in a chord. If a Third ever stood up and said: "I want to be the lowest note too!", it would be insulted and degraded (by a semitone!). Soon the quest for freedom could no longer be kept down: "Down with the Keynotes!" echoed through the scales. All hell was let loose, I can tell you! The Keynotes let it be known that the triad was only a real triad if they were at the bottom. The other intervals, however, overthrew the tyrants and from this point on, the Thirds and Fifths could also be at the bottom. This is why nowadays every triad has one primary form and two inversions. Today we know that regardless of the order of notes, the triad remains the same triad: **its all a matter of the combinations!**
Your main goal – your fingering remains unchanged!

C-major Triad Inversions

Primary form – Sequence of notes:
Keynote - Third - Fifth
Optically: Equal distance between notes.

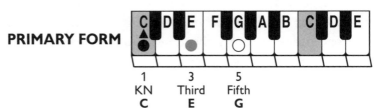

1st Inversion. Sequence of notes:
Third - Fifth - Keynote.
Optically: Distance of one key below and two keys above.

2nd Inversion. Sequence of notes:
Fifth - Keynote – Third.
Optically: Distance of two keys below and one key above.

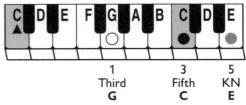

The C-major Triad (Inversions) in 4 Octaves

Now please play all inversions again, in all positions, using the strike patterns.

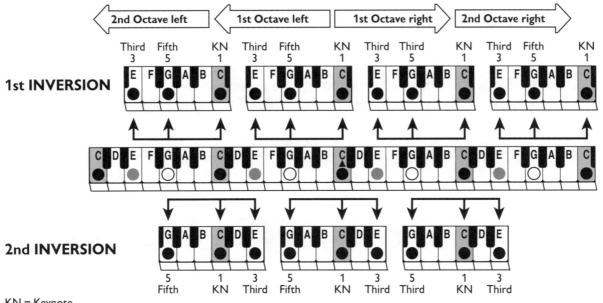

KN = Keynote

And now we have some good news and some bad news for you. First the bad: There is no point in looking at these two pages if you can't already do the following:

1. Find the primary form of the C-major chord and both inversions in all positions straight away (okay – almost straight away).
2. Play the primary form and both inversions of the C-major triad in the following order (and relatively fluently at that): Primary form – 1st Inversion – 2nd Inversion – Primary form – one octave higher – 1st Inversion (also higher) etc. – and then the same again **backwards**!

If you can't do this, go directly one page back and learn the technique, do not pass go and do not collect ...

Before we dish you up the good news, we have another tip for you: learn the 19 Inversions in the C-major family of chords. Good keyboarders always play using a mixture of primary forms and inversions. If you don't want to get lost in the confusion of inversions, you always have to know which finger strikes the keynote, which finger the third and which the fifth. Theoretically this would mean that you have to learn the position of every interval in every chord inversion **by heart** – shock – horror! Unfortunately many keyboarders learn to play in this way. They learn every chord **individually**. We go about this business in a different way: We are going to reveal to you the simple system behind our method. You must, however, know which intervals you are playing. So that you don't give up all hope – we have invented a **new rule** for you. With this rule everything becomes easy.

The Interval rule
(The gap between the keys-rule)

Note: In the primary form of the triad, the keynote is always the deepest note which is struck with the thumb. After this the third and fifth follow from left to right.

Note: In the **primary form** of the triad, the keynote is always the deepest note which is struck with the thumb. After this the third and fifth follow from left to right.

1. With **inversions** it is always the **finger to the right** to the largest gap between the keys which plays the keynote.

2. With **inversions** it is always the **finger to the left** of the largest gap which plays the fifths.

All that is left is the Third. **Remember:** If you know the name of the **keynote**, you know the name of the chord!

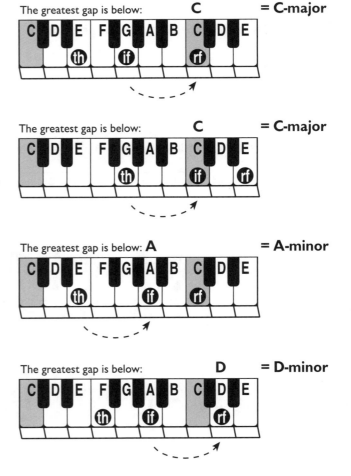

And now the good news: With the primary form of the C-major triad and its two inversions – with these three chords – you can produce all primary forms and inversions of all the triads belonging to the C-major family (i.e. Dm, Em, etc.)

How? Well – by simply **shifting the C triad** along the C-major-scale (white keys) we have created the following sequence of chords: C - D - Em - F - G - Am. If we shift the first inversion of the C triad according to this pattern, we obtain all inversions of the other triads in the C-major family. If we shift the second inversion in the same way, we obtain the second inversions as well. Basicly you can play a primary form or an inversion, then freeze this position and by shifting your right hand you get the other chords. Here is the system:

First inversion of C-major
and the chords obtained by shifting

Second inversion of C-major
and the chords obtained by shifting

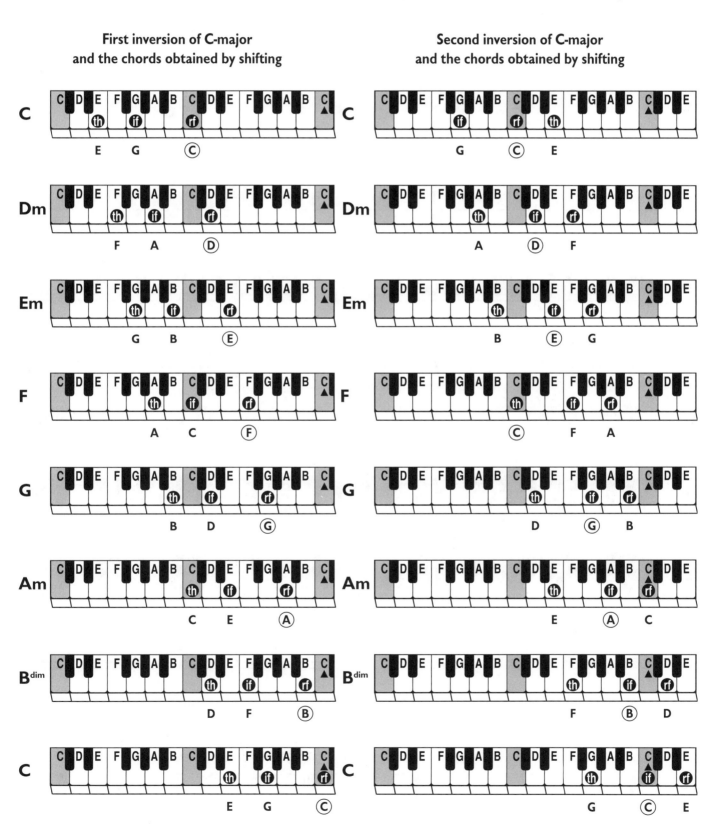

The Practical Side of Chord Inversions

They make it easier to play sequences of chords and help them to sound better and more logical. To this point another rule, which should not be adhered to vehemently:

Rule for the Succession of chords

The greater the number of common notes in a succession of chords, the better the sound!

Play the successions below using both strike-patterns. In the first vertical row the succession contains only primary forms; in the other two rows you have the same chords but this time with inversions. They sound much better! Have fun!

Practise Program

The three exercises below contain all primary forms and inversions which are to be found in the C-major chord family. They are typical successions of Rock and Pop chords. Please learn them by heart (play each approx. 100 times) – if it is necessary, learn them bar-by-bar (page 17). Please stick to the fingering TH, IF, RF and be sure about which inversion and which chord you are playing by checking with the interval rule on page 20.

Exercise 1

C	Primary form	G	1st inversion	Dm	2nd Inversion	Am	2nd Inversion
1 2 3 4		1 2 3 4		1 2 3 4		1 2 3 4	

C	2nd Inversion	G	Primary form	F	Primary form	C	1st Inversion
1 2 3 4		1 2 3 4		1 2 3 4		1 2 3 4	

Exercise 2

C	Primary form	F	2nd Inversion	Dm	Primary form	G	2nd Inversion
1 2 3 4		1 2 3 4		1 2 3 4		1 2 3 4	

Em	Primary form	Am	2nd Inversion	F	Primary form	C	1st Inversion
1 2 3 4		1 2 3 4		1 2 3 4		1 2 3 4	

Exercise 3

C	Primary form	Am	1st inversion	Em	2nd Inversion	Dm	2nd Inversion
1 2 3 4		1 2 3 4		1 2 3 4		1 2 3 4	

F	1st Inversion	Em	1st Inversion	Dm	1st Inversion	C	1st Inversion
1 2 3 4		1 2 3 4		1 2 3 4		1 2 3 4	

1.6 BASS NOTES

The storming of the Basstille

"Hey! Wake up left hand!" – "Who? Me? – I wasn't asleep, I was just hanging cool!" – "Don't answer back!"– "Okay, okay ... What's goin' down?" So that chords sound fuller, the **Keynote (= 1)** is often also played in the bass region – below Middle-C – using the left hand. Just as there are three typical **chords for the right hand** (primary form, 1st and 2nd Inversions), there are also **bass chords** for the left hand. Here two keynotes are played simultaneously at a distance of one octave (p. 10) using the thumb and the small finger. An example for the C-major chord is ...

The Bass-Octave Chord: Example chord – C-major

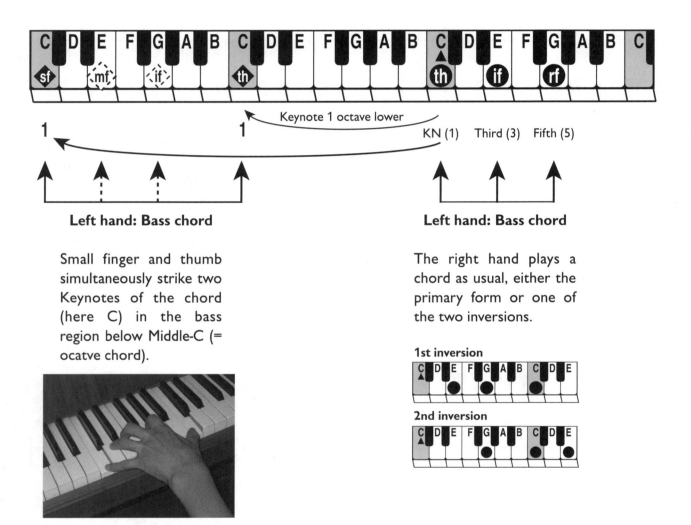

Left hand: Bass chord

Small finger and thumb simultaneously strike two Keynotes of the chord (here C) in the bass region below Middle-C (= ocatve chord).

Left hand: Bass chord

The right hand plays a chord as usual, either the primary form or one of the two inversions.

1st inversion

2nd inversion

Fifth (5th) in the Bass chord

The dotted arrows and triangles on the keyboard show you how you can play the Fifth and the Third in the bass-octave-chord. Try it yourself: If you play the two C's in the bass octave chord, your index-finger is already **hovering** above the Fifth - G like a very violent Venezuelan vulture, which ... but that's another story !

New System of Tablature for two-handed Strike-Patterns

In the preceding strike-patterns, the right-hand action was notated above the count-bar – this remains the case. The strikes for the left hand are notated below the bar. The octave bass-chord is indicated using the letters "SFTH" (= Small finger + Thumb simultaneously play the keynote (1) in the bass region), which are written under the count-bar. If you should play the fifth with your index finger, we write IF below the count bar. All other rules remain the same. If something is notated above and below the count bar, both left and right hands play at the same time, if there is only notation below the count bar and nothing above it, only the left hand plays. Here is a detailed example.

The Octave-Bass chord and other chords

In the diagram below you have a complete view of things. When playing C-major you play the keynote C as an octave-bass-chord, when playing Dm you play D, and with Em you play E, etc. Now try the following: Play both C's in the octave-bass-chord a few times, freeze the position of your hand and move up to the next key and play the D's, then the E's up to the B's and then back again. Using this style you should play the exercises on pages 35 and 40.

The C-major Triad (primary form) and appropriate Octave-Bass-chords

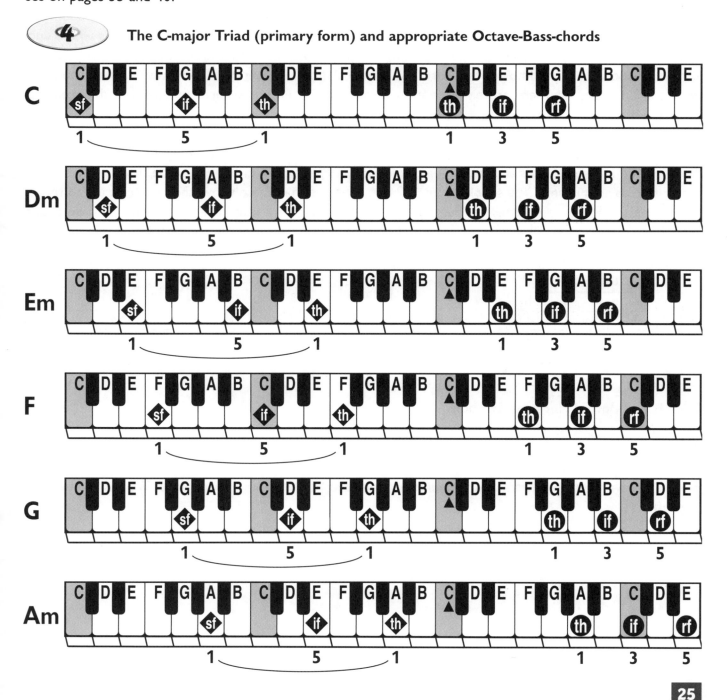

1.7 RHYTHMS

What the word that nobody can spell really means

On the next two pages we have listed 33 great strike-patterns for two-handed rhythms. Most of them are very easy and some are a little complicated (i.e. patterns 8-16), but these are the most interesting and the rockiest of all. There is a simple method of practising two-handed strike-patterns which can be employed at any time, any place and on any surface (table, knee etc.): The "tapping technique". Here you tap the strikes below the count bar with your left hand, and those above with your right and while doing this you count out loud, start slowly and then increase the speed.

Types of bars

Bars are sections of identical length in a piece of music. Our strike-patterns are all one bar long. A piece of music is made up of a multitude of bars which are all joined together.

Up to now you have learnt the most common bar time which is used in Pop- and Rockmusic: The four-four time. What does this mean? Let us assume that the bar is a unit of time and that we divide this whole unit into four: we could say that four quarters go to make up a whole: hence four four. These four quarters also form our main counts. And now for a short fraction calculation ... 4 fourths = 8 eighths ... so we could say that in a four-four bar, there are eight notes – these would then go to form our main- and sub-counts (1+2+3+4+).

We have also written down two other types of bars for you, three-four-time and six-eight-time. You will know three-four-time from Waltzes and the um-pa-pa of German Music. Even in the Pop scene there are many pieces written using this time. You simply count 1+2+3+. Six-eight-time doesn't have the same relation to three-four-time as eight-eight-time does to four-four-time. The "feeling" is a little different. That's why we count 1-2-3-4-5-6. Here are all 3 bar timings again and how to count them in a simple diagram. Please note the emphasized parts!

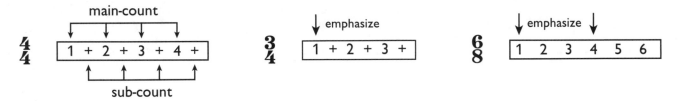

Triplets and dotted Fingering Symbols

You will find these in patterns 8, 14 and 16. In pattern 8 you must play three strikes instead of two for every main- and sub-count. It's easy to count: One-a-day, two-a-day, three-a-day etc. In pattern 14 and 16 you count in the same way, but only strike on the counts of "one" and "day". There is more about Triplets and bars on page 104.

Pop and rock Rhythms in 4/4 time (closed action)

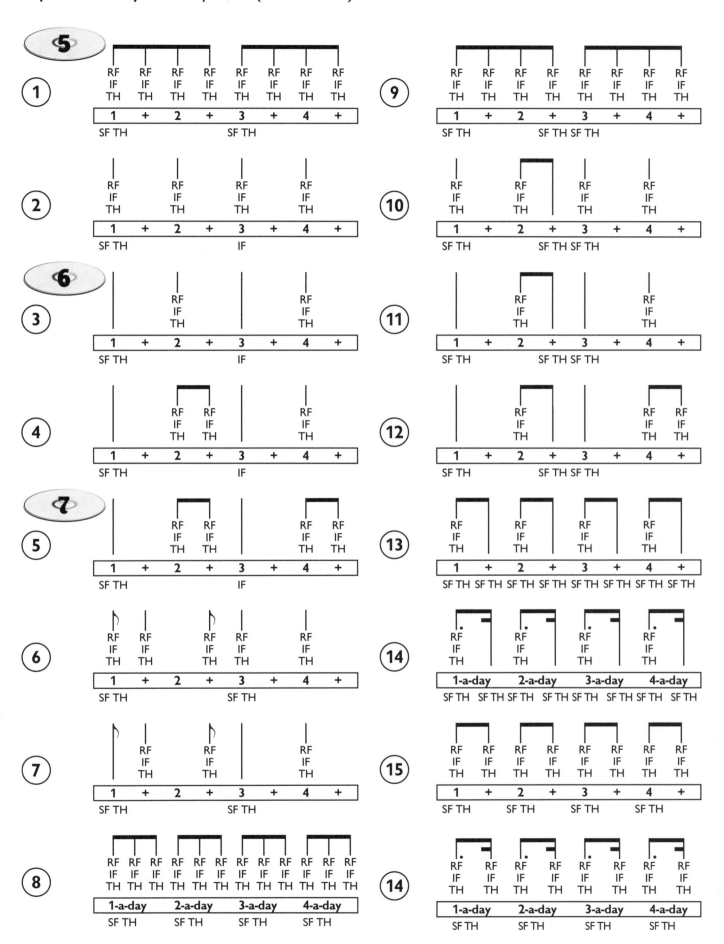

Pop and rock Rhythms in 4/4 time (broken and mixed action)

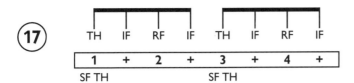

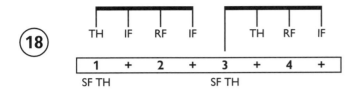

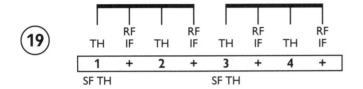

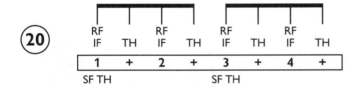

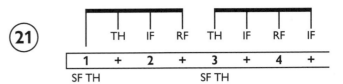

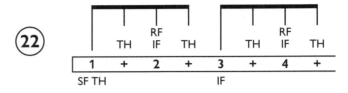

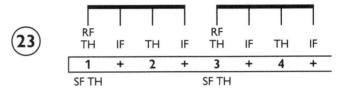

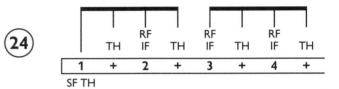

Pop and rock Rhythms in 3/4 and 6/8 time (all actions)

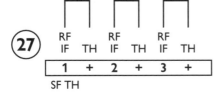

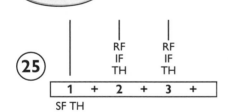

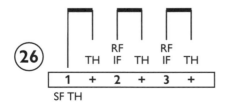

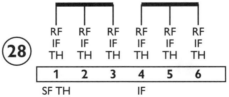

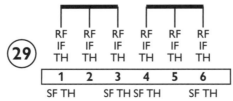

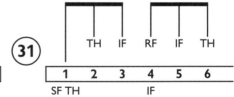

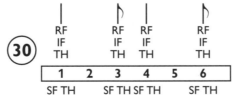

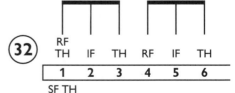

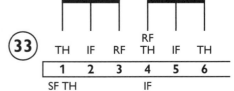

1.8 Triad Variations

Why don't you triad?

Up to now you have learnt 6 triads from the C-major chord family. We are now going to show you the 54 other triads which are possible within one octave. No! Don't run away: They are all based on one single blueprint. To be able to show you this we need the interval names of some notes in our basic key, C-major, which we have not used until now. As usual we use the C-major triad for all examples. All other major triads function in the same way.

Half tones and whole tones

The interval between one key and the next amounts to a semitone. The distance (interval) between C and C sharp is a semitone. From C sharp to D, from D to D sharp, from D sharp to E and **from E to F the distance (interval) is also a semitone**. Two semi-tones are one whole-tone. The interval from C - D is therefore a whole-tone (The names of the black keys are on page 11 by the way!)

The new intervals

Two new intervals are now added to the keynote (1), the third (3) and the fifth (5): these are the second (2) and the fourth (4). These are derived from the latin "secundus" and "quartus" which mean second and fourth, respectively.

The third which you know from the Major-Triads is known as a **major third**. If this is lowered by a semitone it is called a **minor third**.

The fifth which is lowered by a semitone is known as a **diminished fifth** (-5). When it is raised by a semitone it is known as an **augmented fifth** (+5). **The keynote is never changed in this way, otherwise it would be a new chord!**

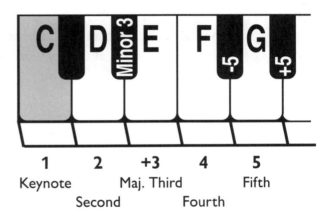

The amazing Augmentation of Triads (Part 1)

We are now going to make 5 triads out of one and we are going to use the C-major triad in our examples. Of course the following is also true for all other major and minor triads.

1. Major Triads: This is the C-major triad – hard, pure and large just like a hero of Greek mythology. He was created by the music gods and they called him "major" which is latin for larger. He really does sound larger and brighter. The name even appears in other walks of life. There are majors in the army, there's a major suit when playing bridge and there's even an Island named Majorca.

Formative Rules:
Keynote – major Third – Fifth

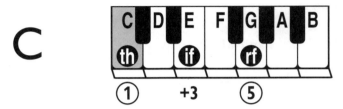

2. Minor triads: In the last great battle of the thirds, somewhere between Majorca and Minorca, half of the major triads fought like lions, the other half like lambs. "Weaklings" cried the brave triads, and as a punishment lowered the others' thirds by a semitone. Since then they have been called minor triads – from the latin minor: smaller, and that is exactly how they sound, smaller and sadder, because they were so degraded that day.

Formative Rules:
Major Triad with third (semitone lower)

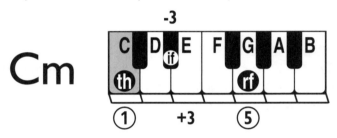

3. Diminished Minor Triads: The two "sound sexes" have lived together in peace since then. It should only be mentioned in passing that during the Middle Ages a few minor triads became so degenerate that King Henry was forced to degrade their most prized possession, the fifth, by a semitone. These inferior companions with their mini, minor thirds and diminished fifths have since then been referred to as diminished (Minor-5) Triads.

Formative Rules:
Minor Triad with fifth (semitone lower)

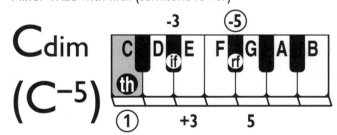

4. Augmented Major Triads: With malicious glee the major triads watched as the minor triads suffered these heavy blows. Some were so excessively proud that they still had the major third and their fifth that they loudly cheered "Long live Henry the Fifth!" As a reward their fifth was raised by a semitone in such a way that their fifths became augmented. Remember what they look like: These augmented arrogant dandies have a plus sign in front of the fifth!

Formative Rules:
Major Triad with fifth (semitone higher)

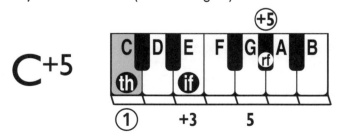

5. Diminished Major Triads: Not so very long ago, a few drunken augmented triads were swaying through the narrow streets of London bawling the National Anthem "God save the Queen" with the slightly bowdlerized text "God shave the fifties Queen". The monarch heard this from the palace and passed a royal decree that the fifths in these inferior triads should be diminished – to make them truly sorry! This is how the diminished major triads came to be.

Formative Rules:
Major Triad with fifth (semitone lower)

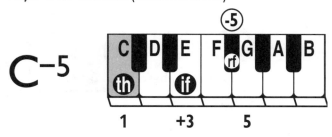

6. Suspended Triads: We have already mentioned the Balearic islands of Majorca and Minorca as a well-known musical trouble spot. Well, many years after the great battle of the thirds, trouble flared again. A group of four major triads on Majorca started fifth column activities for the enemy Minorca. The Majorcan authorities were soon hot on their tails so the fifth columnist Majorcan triads had to flee. They grabbed what they could and left, leaving their thirds behind. They were left with only keynotes and fifths. "What shall we do now without the thirds which tell us apart from the minor triads?" asked the first triad. "We need a third dimension" said the second, "let's use another interval as a replacement!" – "You mean a fourth dimension ... that's it: the fourth!" said the third triad "Just a second!" said the second triad "I was thinking more of the second". They began to quarrel, until they agreed that both were possible. "But what shall we call them?" asked the fourth triad. "Jesus, that's a big problem!" said a D-major chord. "No!" said a C-triad, "Not Jesus, but C-sus! We'll call ourselves suspended chords and say that we threw the thirds out of our own free will." They all cheered "Hooray! C-sus-factor positive!"

Formative Rules:
Sus 4: Major Triad. Third goes, fourth comes in.
Sus 2: Major Triad. Third goes, second comes in.

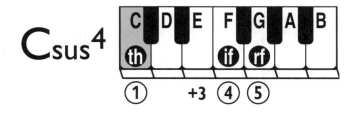

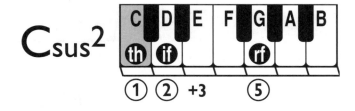

The Inversions of the variations

Of course you don't learn them all off-by-heart individually. On page 19 you learnt the positions of the keynote, third and fifth in the primary forms and inversions of the triads. Turn to page 18: Play all of the C-major inversions again, strike all notes individually and say which interval you are playing! Then do the same again with the inversions on page 20. **And now the last step: Change the notes in the triad according to the formative rules – which you have just learnt and you have C sus, plus, minus and all that slush, and on the next page there's a visual summary!**

THE C-MAJOR FAMILY OF CHORDS

Form:
Cm
C dim
C+5
C−5
Csus4
Csus2

C

Chord shown here:
C maj

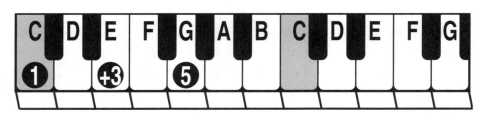

Form:
Dm
D dim
D+5
D−5
Dsus4
Dsus2

D

Chord shown here:
D m

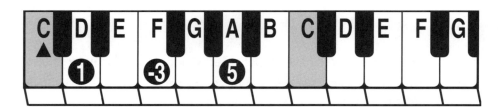

Form:
Em
E dim
E+5
E−5
Esus4
Esus2

E

Chord shown here:
E m

Form:
Fm
F dim
F+5
F−5
Fsus4
Fsus2

F

Chord shown here:
F maj

Form:
Gm
G dim
G+5
G−5
Gsus4
Gsus2

G

Chord shown here:
G maj

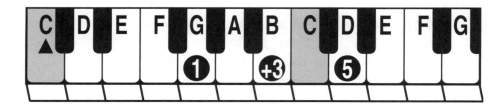

Form:
Am
A dim
A+5
A−5
Asus4
Asus2

A

Chord shown here:
A m

Form:
Bm
B dim
B+5
B−5
Bsus4
Bsus2

Attention! The shifted C-major triad produces a diminished triad in B.

B

Chord shown here:
B dim

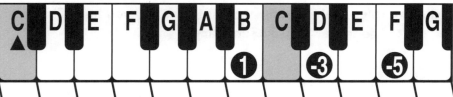

1.9 BLACK TRIADS

No room for prejudice on the keyboard!

You now know all triads and their variations which have a white key as keynote. All that is missing now are those which have a black key as keynote, i.e. C#/D♭, D#/E♭, F#/G♭, G#/A♭ and A#/B♭. See page 11 for a description of the black keys.

You have already seen how easily the primary forms of the white-keyed triads (and their inversions) can be produced by simply shifting the C-major triad along the natural notes. So far as the black-keyed are concerned we also use the C-major triad and shift it so that the thumb strikes a black key as keynote. This does cause us a little problem, however so we are going to make a ...

Triad Ruler

Please use a ruler or a piece of paper of about 2 x 0,8 inch and lay it on the keys so that it covers the keys of the C-major triad.

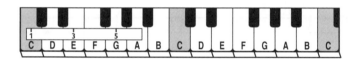

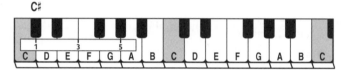

1. Please mark the centres of the keynote key (C), the third key and the fifth key of the C-major triad as exactly as possible on the top edge of the ruler.

2. Now shift the ruler in such a way that the keynote mark now points exactly at the middle of the black C# key. The third mark now points at E and the fifth mark at G#. Play C#-E-G#: Hmmm – wasn't that a C# minor triad? – It certainly was!

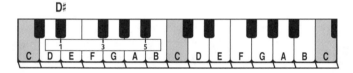

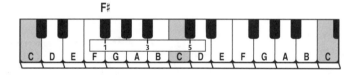

3. Now shift the ruler so that the keynote mark points at the black key D#. The third mark now points at the F# key and the fifth mark points at A#. Play D#-F#-A#. Now you can hear how the D# minor triad sings: "Thanks for listening in !"

4. Now shift the ruler so that the keynote mark points to the middle of the F# key. The third mark is now pointing towards the edge of the A and A# keys ... but more towards the A. The fifth mark is pointing to C#. The F# minor triads begs you not to play, but you do all the same!

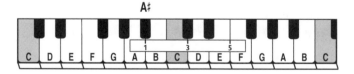

5. Please shift the ruler so that the keynote mark is pointing to the middle of G#. The third mark is pointing between the B and C keys ... but more towards the B. The fifth mark is pointing towards the D#. Play G#-B-D# – voila: the G# minor triad!

6. Now shift the ruler so that the keynote mark is pointing to the middle of the A# key. The third mark points at the right hand side of the C# key, the fifth mark is pointing at the F key (just about!); here F is the same as E#. A#-C#-E# form the A# minor triad (=B♭m).

Results of our measurements: If you shift the **frozen C-major chord**, so that your thumb strikes a black key you strike the fifth with your ring finger (with a little practise); with your middle finger in most cases you strike the minor third in the triad, but sometimes also the major third – what the heck! You can hear the minor differences between major and minor by now! If you want to play a major third and play a minor instead your middle finger simply has to move one key higher up and vice versa. Practise makes perfect!

The Black-keyed Triads and their variations

You should now please play the "amazing augmentation of triads" again, using our little black-keyed monsters. Learn the names of the triad notes and work the inversions out yourself. Take your time, you don't need all chords at once anyway. The important thing is that you learn the primary forms! Using your knowledge about the variations rules (page 30), the interval rules (page 20) and the inversion rules (pages 21) you can **work out everything at the keyboard, without the book, any time you need! Have fun!**

Form:

C#m	=	Db
C#dim	=	Dbdim
C#+5	=	Db+5
C#−5	=	Db−5
C#sus4	=	Dbsus4
C#sus2	=	Dbsus2

Chord shown:
C#/Db

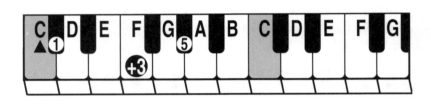

Form:

D#m	=	Eb
D#dim	=	Ebdim
D#+5	=	Eb+5
D#−5	=	Eb−5
D#sus4	=	Ebsus4
D#sus2	=	Ebsus2

Chord shown:
D#=Eb

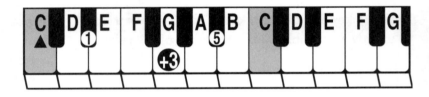

Form:

F#m	=	Gb
F#dim	=	Gbdim
F#+5	=	Gb+5
F#−5	=	Gb−5
F#sus4	=	Gbsus4
F#sus2	=	Gbsus2

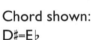

Chord shown:
F#=Gb

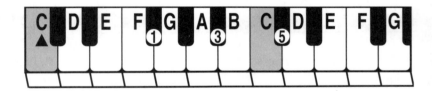

Form:

G#m	=	Ab
G#dim	=	Abdim
G#+5	=	Ab+5
G#−5	=	Ab−5
G#sus4	=	Absus4
G#sus2	=	Absus2

Chord shown:
G#=Ab

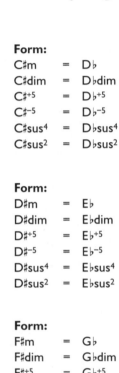

Form:

A#m	=	Bb
A#dim	=	Bbdim
A#+5	=	Bb+5
A#−5	=	Bb−5
A#sus4	=	Bbsus4
A#sus2	=	Bbsus2

A#/Bb

Chord shown:
A#=Bb

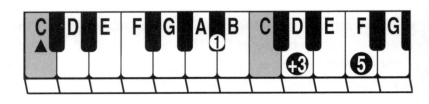

Rock-Pop Successions of chords with the Black-keyed Triads

Play the exercises as usual, using strike-patterns of your choice. They sound good using all patterns. You can of course play in three-four or six-eight time, but then you have to remember that the count bar ends after 3+. It also sounds good if you only play each chord once or twice per bar using the closed technique (both hands) – perhaps with a brass or string setting (if you have a synthesizer etc). Again, have fun!

Exercise 1

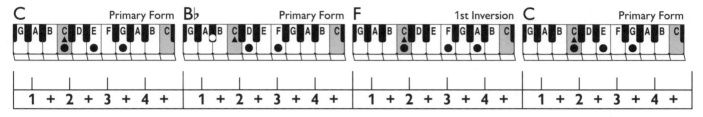

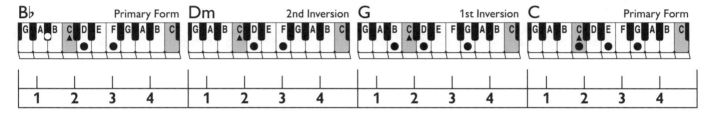

Exercise 2

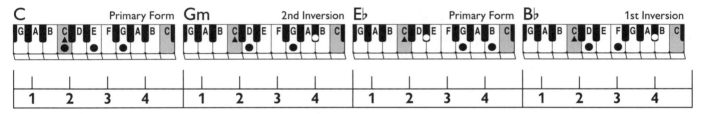

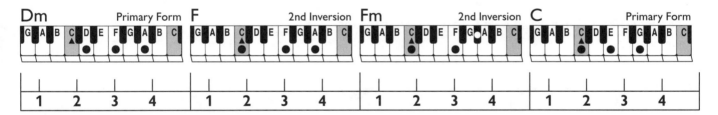

Exercise 3

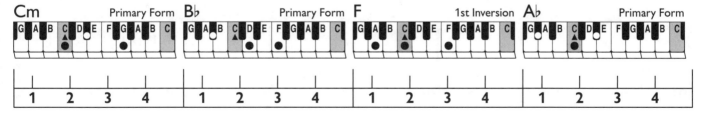

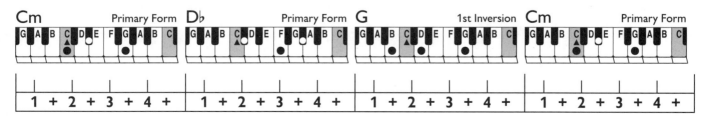

1.10 Four Note Chords/Tetrads

How to make a fourtune

Tetrads, or chords of four notes are nothing more than **our good old triads with an extra note**, so that they sound more colourful and interesting. What is new, is the fingering. The new fingering is made up from a simple rule for the right hand – the left hand stays the same.

A word about the new fingering

Viewed from left to right you play the first note with your thumb, as usual. The second note is played with your index-finger, the third with your middle finger and the fourth note can be played with your ring or small finger – whichever can do it better (fingering symbols page 13).

New intervals

Where tetrads are concerned, an extra note is stuck onto our old triad, a note from the scale from which the triad is derived. We again use the C-major triad as basis for our examples. It is possible to add the following ...

> **The sixth**, the sixth note in the scale. The numerical symbol is 6. In C-major it is the note A.
>
> **The minor seventh**, the seventh note in the scale lowered by a semitone. Numerical symbol: m7. In C-major it is the note B♭ – a black key.
>
> **The major seventh**, the seventh note in the scale. Numerical symbol: maj7. In C-major it is the note B.

The octave, the eighth note in the scale (8th = 1st !!!) is often added to the triads so that they sound fuller and so that they harmonize better with the other tetrads. From the chord-symbol, however, you are not able to see whether a C-maj. triad or a C-maj. tetrad is meant.

Visual summary: The old and new intervals

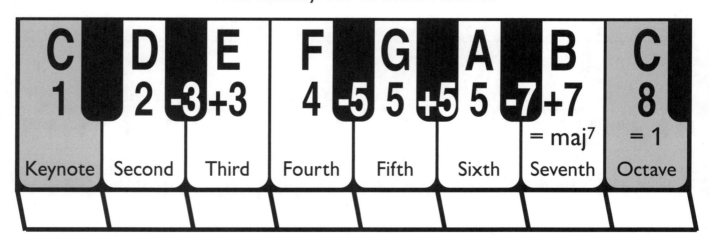

C-MAJOR TETRADS (PRIMARY FORM)

METHOD OF FORMATION	CHORD SYMBOL	TETRAD (please play!)

C-maj triad + octave of the keynote (1)

C

C-maj triad + 6th note of the scale (sixth)

C^6

C-maj triad + 7th note of the scale, lowered by a semitone (minor 7)

C^7

C-maj triad + 7th note of the scale (major 7)

$Cmaj^7$

maj^7 = +7

C-MAJOR TETRADS (1ST INVERSION)

C

Method of formation

Don't get confused! Simply play the 1st inversion of the C-major-triad:

= 3 5 1

C^6

Then you add the additional notes from the scale: sixth, minor 7 or major 7.

C^7

Then you add the additional notes from the scale: sixth, minor 7 or major 7.

$Cmaj^7$

C-Major Tetrads (2nd and 3rd inversions)

Method of formation

Triads have two inversions – Tetrads of course have three inversions, since each of the four notes will be at the bottom: keynote, third and addition.

With the **second inversion** it's just like with the first: To begin with you play the normal 2nd inversion of the C-major triad and add the extra note. Later you have to strike them all together.

The **third inversion** only looks a little unusual. You play the additional note with your thumb and with the rest ... you play the normal primary form of the C-major triad, one octave higher!

2ND INVERSION   ## 3RD INVERSION

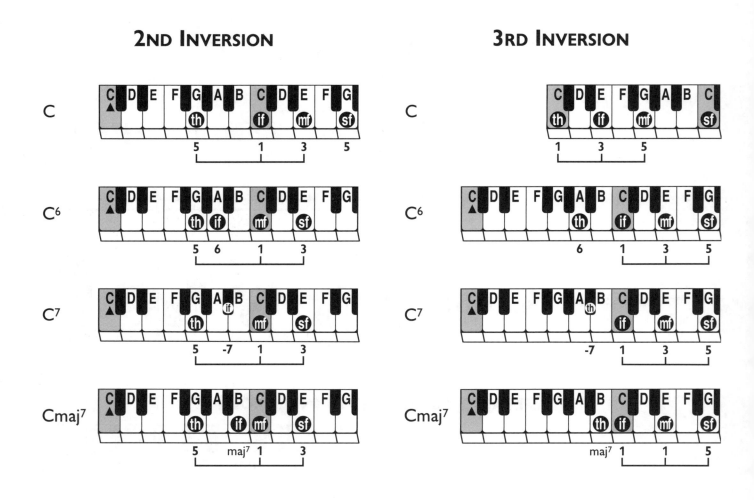

The Tetrads of the remaining chords in our C-major Chord Family

As usual it's up to you to work them out for yourself or if you need to, turn to pages 209 to 233! We do, however, recommend that you spend a lot of time working on the primary forms and inversions of the tetrads in our C-major chord family – these are the chords which you need the most in Pop and Rock (of course not just the chords in the C-major family, but also the others, above all those in the D-, E-, Eb-, F-, G-, A- and Bb families; but for now study the relationships using only one chord family as example).

THE C MAJOR CHORD FAMILY

Please form:
C
C6
C7
Cmaj7

The primary form of the C-maj. triad is shown here.

Form:
Dm
Dm6
Dm7

The primary form of the Dm triad is shown here.

Form:
Em
Em6
Em7

The primary form of the Em triad is shown here.

Form:
F
F6
F7
Fmaj7

The primary form of the F-maj. triad is shown here.

Form:
G
G6
G7
Gmaj7

The primary form of the G-maj. triad is shown here.

Form:
Am
Am6
Am7

The primary form of the Am triad is shown here.

Form:
B
B6
B7
Bmaj7

The primary form of the B-maj. triad is shown here (exception).

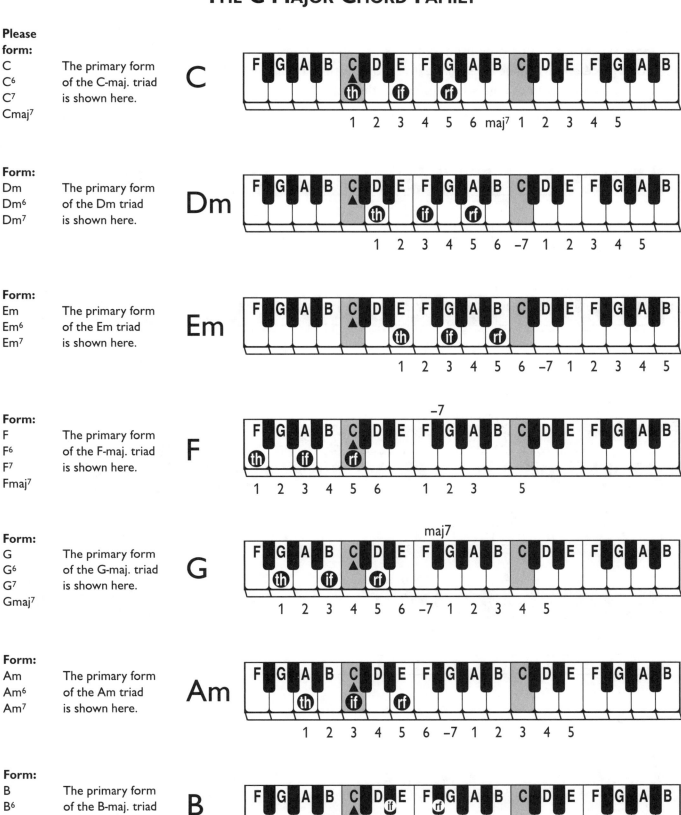

Successions of chords with Tetrads

Note here **how few notes** you have to change when changing chords if you choose the correct inversion. Play the same successions using **only** primary forms and you will hear and feel how hectic such successions are if you don't place enough value on suitable inversions. Just to remind you, here is the inversion rule from page 22: the fewer notes you change when inverting, the better.

Exercise 1

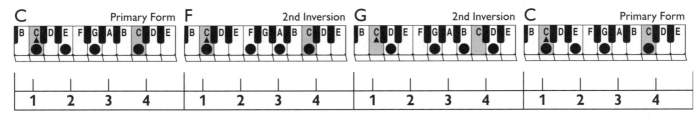

Exercise 2

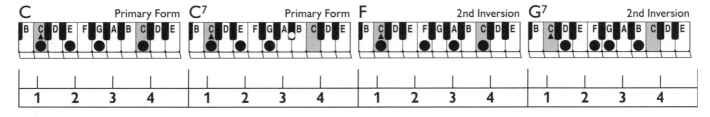

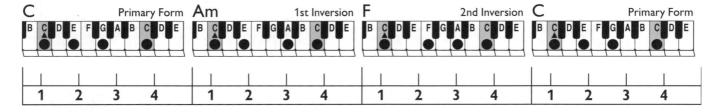

Exercise 3

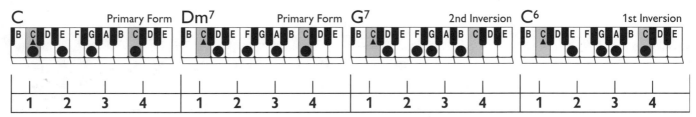

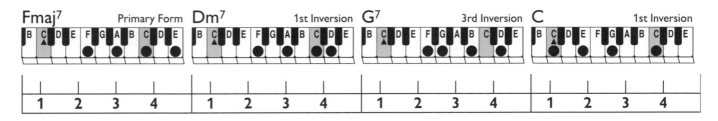

1.11 CHORDS OF FIVE AND SIX NOTES

The chord monster attacks

Before you shrug your shoulders and mumble "I don't want to have anything to do with these chord monsters" – you should know that chords of five and six notes are played like tetrads in Pop and Rock music. How can that be? You simply throw intervals out, which are **relatively** unimportant for the desired sound. More about that soon. At first we are going to show you the new intervals in a visual summary.

This really does contain all intervals, even those which the professionals themselves only seldom use. Of course we have again used the chord of C-major for all examples.

All Intervals at a glance

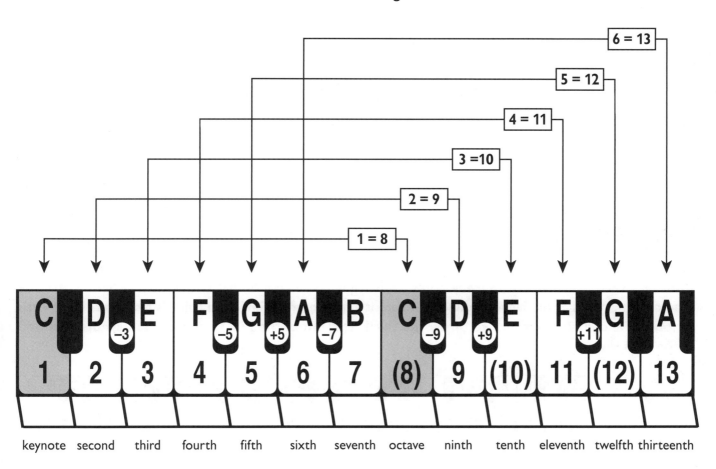

Interval rule

You can see that the ninth has the same note as the second – only it is one octave higher just as the eleventh corresponds to the fourth and the thirteenth to the sixth. All you need to do, therefore, is to count seven keys further to obtain the parallel interval in the next octave up, or to count seven keys down to the left and know which note it corresponds to. Furthermore, these higher intervals are mostly only played within the range of one octave, because most keyboarders can perhaps manage to reach a ninth and play both notes simultaneously, but when it comes to the tenth most of them throw the towel in.

Chord structure and Chord symbols

The chords which are mostly used in Pop and Rock Songbooks are (using C-major as an example) chords such as $C^{7/9}$, $C^{7/9/11}$ and $C^{7/9/13}$. They sound terribly complicated but they are nothing more than sheep in wolves' clothing, since apart from the major triad they only contain the extra two or three intervals which are written behind the chord symbol. We have shown you the names of the chords in their correct and complete versions. You will, however, often find them in shortened versions. The 7/9 chord can, for example, be written as C^9, the 7/9/11 chord as C^{11} and the 7/9/13 chord C^{13}, more about this on page 74.

The 7/9th Chord

This chord of five notes contains the intervals 1-3-5 + m.7-9. We can dispense with the keynote on the right hand, since we play it in the bass region anyway. Thus the right hand plays the remainder – the tetrad 3-5-m.7-9. If you want you can even play the fifth in the bass region so that you are left with the following three note trunk-chord: 3-m. 7-9.
Here is an example of the 7/9 as a C-major tetrad. You can of course by now form the right-hand inversions yourself.

$C^{7/9}$

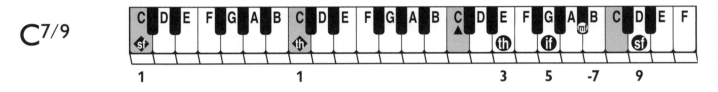

The 11th Chord

This chord of six notes contains the intervals 1-3-5 + m. 7-9-11. To reduce it to a tetrad we have to shift the keynote and the fifth to the bass region. Then this monster looks a lot less dangerous. You have to be careful with the inversion. There are so many notes sounding in these chords that one normally tries to have the characteristic notes as the highest sounding – here it's the eleventh. **Since the third is near to the eleventh (= fourth) and clashes with it, we throw the third right out of the 7/9/11 chord, the keynote is played in the bass region.**

$C^{7/9/11}$

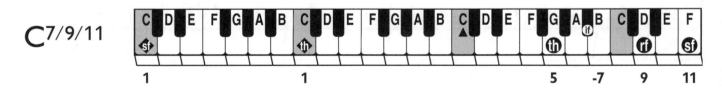

The 13th Chord

is also a chord of six notes, which contains the triad notes 1-3-5 and in addition mm. 7-9-13. The process is the same as with the 11th, we play the 13th as high as possible and **send the keynote and fifth to the bass region**. Here you go ...

$C^{7/9/13}$

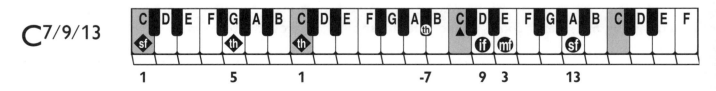

1.12 BASS VARIATIONS

Basstardized chords

These are successions of chords in which the bass notes form independent (simple) melodies. In exercise 1, the bass travels backwards along the C-major scale, in exercise 2 it takes descending semitone steps. Try it, it sounds great !

This technique is notated as follows: **You distinguish between the chord and the bass symbol.** If (as up to now) the keynote should be played in the octave bass chord you simply write the chord symbol down. If another note should form the bass chord, you write the new note behind the chord symbol, separating them with a diagonal stroke. Let's go through the first exercise.

1st Bar: Play 1st Inversion of C with right hand, normal C Bass chord with left hand. **2nd Bar:** Right hand plays 2nd Inversion of G, left hand plays B as octave bass chord (is directly below the C just played). **3rd Bar:** Right hand plays 2nd Inversion of Am, left hand plays the A which is one key below the B, as bass chord. **4th Bar:** Right hand plays 2nd Inversion of G again, left hand also plays G – directly below the A which has just been played. **5th Bar:** Right hand plays 2nd Inversion of G⁷, left hand plays F (the G seventh) etc. Practise each fifty times please ... well, okay, ten then!

Exercise 1

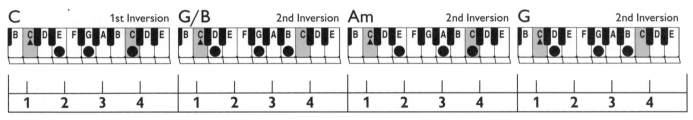

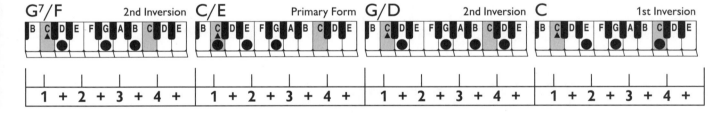

Exercise 2

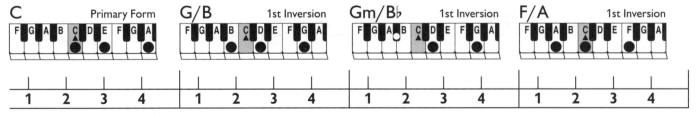

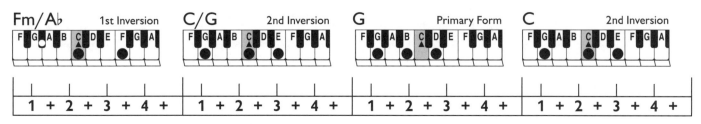

43

1.13 ROCKBASS-PATTERNS

That's the way to do it ... but don't try to cut them out!

Now that we've baked the chord cake – it's time for the icing – just like on a real cake. You use these rockbass patterns instead of the octave bass chords. This means: For each chord you have to play different notes in the bass region, but – as usual – the same intervals. To accompany these rock patterns you can play normal chords with your right hand – i.e. in strike patterns 1, 2 or 8 on page 27 or you improvise (see next page).

The intervals which are to be played are written under the count-bar. Fingering is generally: Keynote (1), as usual with the small finger, all others are played with the thumb. Numbers which are written above each other should be played simultaneously. **The intervals are valid for every chord.** Of course you have to play the interval which belongs to the chord in question. In the example on the right you play the **C-major:** The keynote C (1), with your small finger on the first count together with the fifth – G (5) with your thumb! In **G-major** you play keynote G (1), fifth D (5).

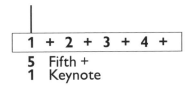

are played so ...

Rockbass Patterns

So that you can start straight away: Play the patterns in this bar sequence (1 chord symbol = 1 bar): C - C - F - C - G - F - C - G ... and again.

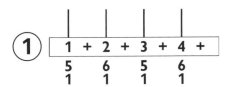

C

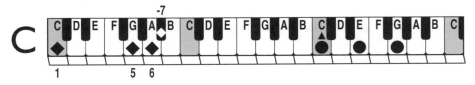

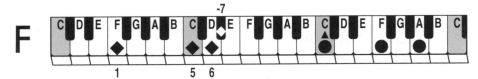

F

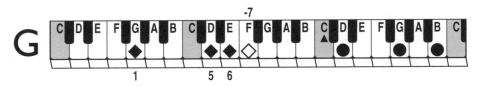

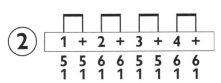

G

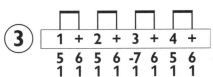

1.14 ROCK AND POP IMPROVISATION

Oh, solo mio

Improvisation scales are special scales with which you can play non pre-determined melodies using a chord scheme. With some types of scales you can improvise using several chords – the blues scale on the right is one of these. With other types of scales you have to change scale when changing chord – the pentatonic scales belong to this group. They consist of five notes (greek – "penta" = five). You can play this scale over C, F, G and even G^7. It is best if you learn the blues scale first. This is suited to the chords C - F - G as well as G^7. Practise this until you can play the notes quickly ascending, descending and mixed. Before you do anything with the pentatonic scales, have a good look at them. The notes in all three scales are natural notes (C-major-scale). Each initial note is the keynote of the chord. More about this in Chapter 6.

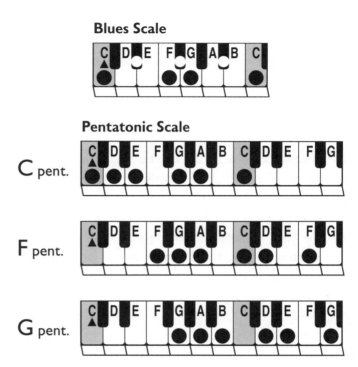

Blues Scale

Pentatonic Scale

C pent.

F pent.

G pent.

The Improvisation scheme

This consists of a **fixed** succession of chords. Here we have notated the famous **Blues-scheme**. Not only is Blues based on its successions of chords, but also a large amount of Rock and Pop music. You have two possibilities:

1. Play the rockbass patterns from the previous page using the successions of chords in this scheme with your left hand, and then use the blues scale to improvise with your right hand with all chords.

2. You continue with the rockbass according to this scheme, but you improvise pentatonically and change the scale with every chord. In C you play the pentatonic C scale, in F the F scale, in G^7 the G scale.

If this is too complicated for you, just use the C pentatonic scale throughout the whole chord progression.

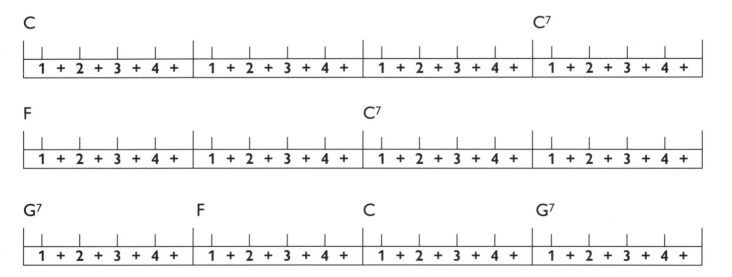

1.15 HARMONIES

It's not my money, it's harmoney!

So many triads, tetrads and chords of who knows how many notes?! Is there a system at the heart of all these chords and if not – why not? Now, there is such a system, but without using notes we can only explain the basic outline to you. If you want to know more, learn the notes (page 57) and acquaint yourself with this chapter on "harmonies".

Scales

Every note (key) in a scale can be the initial note in a diatonic scale. This is a scale with a pre-determined sequence of whole tones or semitones – i.e. our C-major scale. All twelve major scales in an octave are formed according to this pattern: Between all notes there are steps of one whole note, except between the third and the fourth and the seventh and eight notes.

	C	C#/Db	D	D#/Eb	E	F	F#/Gb	G	G#/Ab	A	A#/Bb	B	C	C#/Db
Chromatic Scale	C	C#/Db	D	D#/Eb	E	F	F#/Gb	G	G#/Ab	A	A#/Bb	B	C	C#/Db
C-maj. Scale	C (1)		D (2)		E (3)	F (4)		G (5)		A (6)		B (7)	C (8)	
C#-maj. Scale		C# (1)		D# (2)		F (3)	F# (4)		G# (5)		A# (6)		C (7)	C# (8)
D-maj. Scale			D (1)		E (2)		F# (3)	G (4)		A (5)		B (6)		C# (7)

The Basic Triads

In our musical civilisation there are three types of chords which we regard as "related" and which are harmonies when combined – just like some people who find that hamburgers, chips and Coca Cola are related and harmonic in taste. This is the reason why many Folk-, Pop- and Rock songs are only made up of these three chord types. In the theory of harmony these are called **Basic Triads**.

Let's look at them using the C-major scale as an example (white keys) over a span of two octaves. The rules are valid for all other scales and keys.

The first triad is built up on a mid-point note (here C). This basic triad is called the **tonic**.

This is the central chord. Five notes of the scale above it is the **upper-dominant**, mostly refered to as the dominant. Five notes below it is the **lower-dominant**, mostly refered to as the **sub-dominant**. These three chords are the basic triads in the key of C-major. They are formed from the first, third and fifth notes of the scale which is named after their keynote. Dominant and sub-dominant have the aim to return to their musical resting place – the tonic.

The Basic Triads

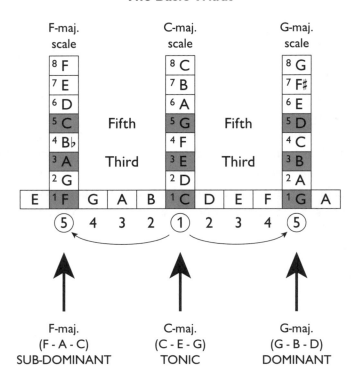

F-maj. scale	C-maj. scale	G-maj. scale
F-maj. (F - A - C) SUB-DOMINANT	C-maj. (C - E - G) TONIC	G-maj. (G - B - D) DOMINANT

System of basic and secondary triads in two octaves

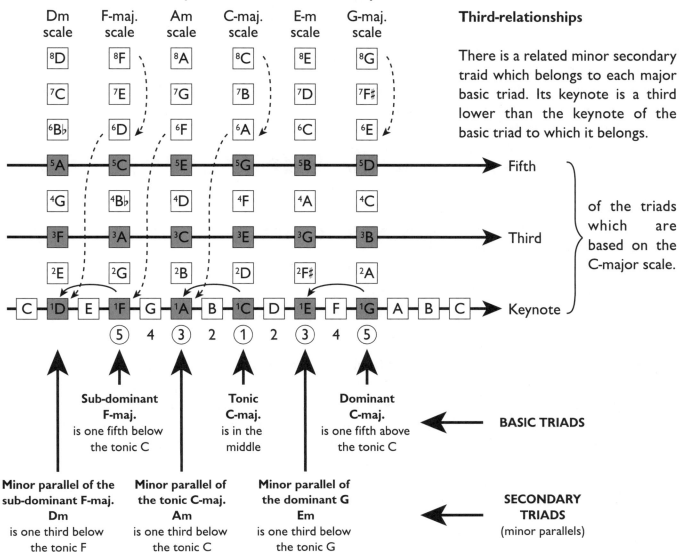

Third-relationships

There is a related minor secondary traid which belongs to each major basic triad. Its keynote is a third lower than the keynote of the basic triad to which it belongs.

of the triads which are based on the C-major scale.

BASIC TRIADS

SECONDARY TRIADS
(minor parallels)

The Secondary Triads

In addition to the major basic triads there are three secondary triads in the minor key. They may also be called substitute or parallel minor triads. Each belongs to a basic triad and uses the same scale – the difference is that the keynote of the minor scale is three notes deeper than the keynote in the major dominant scale. In some musical situations they can assume the tasks of their basic triads. You can see the whole system above:

Chords as degrees

Practically the basic and secondary triads are ordered in **one octave** and assigned to the notes of the tonic's scale, which are refered to as degrees C-major is the chord of the 1st degree, Dm the chord of the second degree etc.

The degrees are represented by Roman numerals, instead of saying "play C - Dm - G - C in C-major", you could also say "play I - II - V - I in C".

The system of basic and secondary triads within one octave

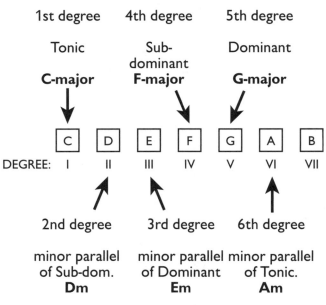

The Parallel Minor Key

Just as there are minor and major chords there are also major and minor keys and therefore chord systems or chord families. The parallel minor scale to C-major is A-minor. The first, third and fifth notes of this scale go to form the triad A-minor. If you use it as the tonic, you have a sub-dominant, the chord which is built up on the note D, which is five notes deeper. According to our system, E would really be a minor chord, but when playing it as a dominant for a minor tonic one plays the major version. There are many chord-relationships which shift from the note, Key-note major key (i.e. C-major) into the minor key (here: A-minor), and mostly via the dominants of the parallel minor key. Play: C - F - C - E - **Am** - Dm - G - C!

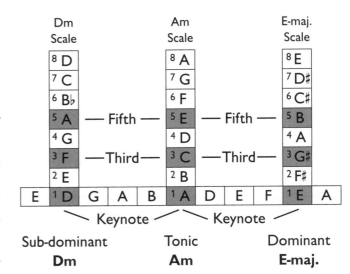

Dominant and Sub-dominant chains

In this chapter we have presented the C-major family of chords, and only the basic and secondary triads and some of their chord variations. In the C-major family, the tonic is of course C-major. Each of the twelve semi-tones in the chromatic scale in one octave, however (black and white keys), can be the keynote of the tonic. Two such characteristic notes are the keynotes of the sub-dominant and the dominant. Assuming that the chord G played in the key of C-major were the tonic, then C would be its sub-dominant and D its dominant, second degree. If we were to take D as the tonic, G would be its sub-dominant and A its dominant – and so on! We can build similar chains on the sub-dominant side. If C is the tonic, F is the sub-dominant. If F is the tonic, B♭ is the sub-dominant. Here is everything again in a visual summary ...

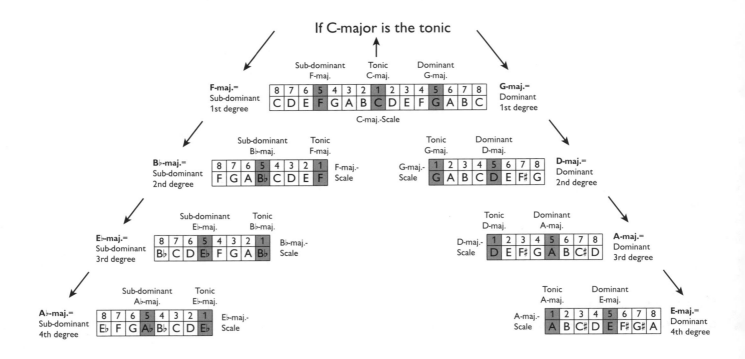

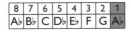

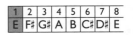

1.16 CIRCLES OF FIFTHS AND FOURTHS

Don't make squares out of my circles.

We have summarized all information in our diagram below, which is of practical importance for Pop- and Rock-keyboarders – the harmonic relationships in the C-major family, or if you want: the C-major chord clan. The hub of the family are the basic triads C, F and G – to a certain extent "Mummy, Daddy and offspring". Joined to these are the closest relations – the secondary triads of Dm, Am and Em.
The distant relations, the dominants and sub-dominants of differing degrees, are the next stage in the family. Finally we have the parallel minor key of Am and the diminished chord B, the black sheep of the family, which is formed on the seventh degree, and which neither basic nor secondary triads want to adopt.
The triads are in the circles, the connecting channels between them and the routes for possible successions C-major and A-minor of chords. It is not always the case that all successions sound equally as good: Just like in a real family-life, sometimes distant relations get on really well together, whereas close relations are always fighting. If there is no connecting channel between two chords it does not mean that they may never be played successively, this happens only occasionally.
The diminished chord of B has a dominant effect and forces the musical occurrences in the direction of the tonic.

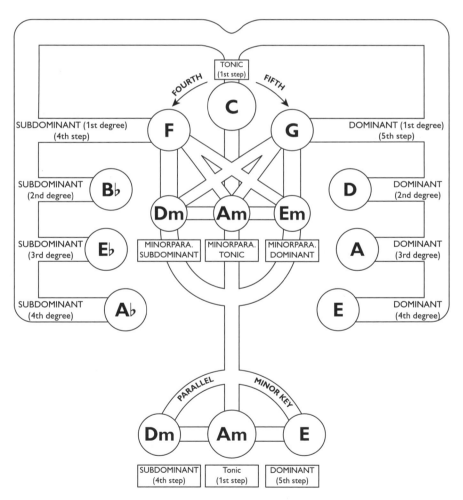

Instead of the triads mentioned here, you can also use the chords of four, five and six notes.

Try these successions of chords:

1. C - Am - F - Fm - C - Am - Dm - G^7 - C
2. C-maj^7 - Am^7 - Dm^7 - B - Cmaj^7
3. C - E^7 - A^7 - D^7 - G^7 - C

1.17 TRANSPOSING

Chord transport

"Transposing" (from the latin "transponere" = to carry over) in music means: to convert a piece or a song from one key to another. In this chapter we have used the C-major chord to explain all chordal and harmonic relationships because it is the easiest chord and because we believe that it is better to have learnt one key properly than five badly. **Of course a good keyboard player must have equally perfect command over all usual keys.** It will, however, certainly take some time for you to learn them all.

Up to then you will surely want to be able to play current hits or your favourite oldies from songbooks. You buy a book, open it up and ... BANG ... the song you want to play – your favourite number "Shooby-Dooby" is notated as follows:

SHOOBY-DOOBY

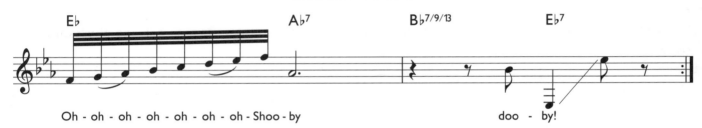

Oh - oh - oh - oh - oh - oh - oh - Shoo - by   doo - by!

Shock, horror! What do I do now? Do I learn all of the chords which I don't know and then play the song? Good idea! That's the quickest way to learn. But you know how it is ... I'll do it tomorrow ... the next time ... etc! You'll still, however, want to play this super-hit – and not only that, but also in the only key you know – in C-major! Now, it is possible to help you – using the transposing-table on the next page. This contains 12 chromatic scales in the horizontal lines, beginning with twelve different notes (in the vertical lines, too)!

It's best if you proceed step by step.

Step 1: You find out which key the piece is written in. You can tell this from the sharp and flat signs at the beginning of the system of notation (more about "signatures" on pages 11 and 60). In our example (above) there are three flat-signs.

Step 2: You look for this number of sharp or flat signs in the left margin of the transposing table. Make a note of the horizontal line – in our example it is the fourth line.

Step 3: Locate the horizontal line of the key into which you want to transpose the piece. In our example it's line 1.

Step 4: Take the first chord in the song. In our example it would be the chord E♭7. Forget all of the additional indications other than the perfect chord symbol itself (such as 6, 7, maj7, or m for minor). Look for the chord symbol E♭ in the line which corresponds to the key in which the song is written. In our case: 4th line, 1st row.

Step 5: Move up, or down the table to the chord into which you want to transpose – for us it is C-major. Take the letter which is in the corresponding position and insert it in the song instead of the original chord. So in our example you have the chord C instead of E♭.

Step 6: Assume all additional indications. In our case you play C7 instead of E♭7.

Additional Tip:
If a chord symbol is written in the lower part of a square which is divided diagonally, you also take the lower symbol in the corresponding square in the new key. If there's only one chord there – take that one of course. If the symbol is in the upper part, you take the upper symbol in the new key, etc.

Now transpose all other chords from the original Eb-maj. of "Shooby-Dooby" in the same way into chords in the key of C-major. The result should look like this:

Eb^7 becomes C^7, Ab^7 becomes F^7 and Bb$^{7/9/13}$ becomes G$^{7/9/13}$!

By the way: the technique of transposing is not just there for keyboard-players, who can only play one or a few keys. A piece of music often has to be transposed into another key, be it higher or lower, because it is too high or too low to sing.

Transposing table for the most important keys

Row / Line	Signature	Key	1	2	3	4	5	6	7	8	9	10	11	12
1	–	C	C	C#/Db	D	D#/Eb	E	F	F#/Gb	G	G#/Ab	A	A#/Bb	B
2	♭♭♭♭♭	Db	C#/Db	D	D#/Eb	E	F	F#/Gb	G	G#/Ab	A	A#/Bb	B	C
3	♯♯	D	D	D#/Eb	E	R	F#/Gb	G	G#/Ab	A	A#/Bb	B	C	C#/Db
4	♭♭♭	Eb	D#/Eb	E	F	F#/Gb	G	G#/Ab	A	A#/Bb	B	C	C#/Db	D
5	♯♯♯♯	E	E	F	F#/Gb	G	G#/Ab	A	A#/Bb	B	C	C#/Db	D	D#/Eb
6	♭	F	F	F#/Gb	G	G#/Ab	A	A#/Bb	B	C	C#/Db	D	D#/Eb	E
7	♯♯♯♯♯♯	F#	F#/Gb	G	G#/Ab	A	A#/Bb	B	C	C#/Db	D	D#/Eb	E	F
8	♯	G	G	G#/Ab	A	A#/Bb	B	C	C#/Db	D	D#/Eb	E	F	F#/Gb
9	♭♭♭♭	Ab	G#/Ab	A	A#/Bb	B	C	C#/Db	D	D#/Eb	E	F	F#/Gb	G
10	♯♯♯	A	A	A#/Bb	B	C	C#/Db	D	D#/Eb	E	F	F#/Gb	G	G#/Ab
11	♭♭	Bb	A#/Bb	B	C	C#/Db	D	D#/Eb	E	F	F#/Gb	G	G#/Ab	A
12	♯♯♯♯♯	B	B	C	C#/Db	D	D#/Eb	E	F	F#/Gb	G	G#/Ab	A	A#/Bb

1.18 SONG ACCOMPANIMENT

We're of one achord in the singing hoard!

At first we thought: Here we will print a good collection of current super-hits. While we were working on this book those super-hits became yesterday's snow! Then we thought: We'll print some Rock- and Pop-Oldies but what's a golden memory for someone, is a group of Grandfathers and tear-jerkers for others. So **for the first practise-sessions** we have notated a few simple Folk-songs which almost everybody knows.

The system of song accompaniment is simple: You proceed as in our exercises. Choose a suitable strike pattern and stick to it. When singing, play the chord in the text until another appears. So that you can find the first note in the song, we have written it down for you.
We wish you much success and lots of fun!

ROCK MY SOUL (Initial note E)

C
Rock my soul in the bosom of Abraham,
G7
Rock my soul in the bosom of Abraham,
C
Rock my soul in the bosom of Abraham
G7   C
oh, rock – a my soul.

HE'S GOT THE WHOLE WORLD IN HIS HANDS (Initial note G)

        C
He's got the whole world in his hands
        G7
He's got the whole world in his hands
        C
He's got the whole world in his hands
        G7   C
He's got the whole world in his hands

WHEN THE SAINTS (Initial note C)

C
Oh, when the saints go marching in
        Am   Dm G7
Oh, when the saints go marching in
   C C7   F   Fm
I want to be in that number,
      C   Am F Fm C
When the Saints go marching in.

AMAZING GRACE (Initial note G)

     C B° F   C
Amazing grace, how sweet the sound,
      Em Dm G7
that saved a wretch like me.
 C   G F   C
I once was lost, but now I'm found,
   Am   Em,G7,C
was blind but now I see.

GREENSLEEVES (Initial note A)

```
  Am      C      G      Em
Alas, my love, you do me wrong
   Am            E7
to cast me off discourteously
    Am      C      G      Em
and I have loved you oh, so long
   Am     E7      Am
delighting in your company.
   C            G
Greensleeves was all my joy
   Am                 E7
Greensleeves was my delight.
   C            G
Greensleeves was my heart of gold
    Am       E       Am
and who but my lady has green sleeves.
```

MY BONNIE (Initial note G)

```
C F C
My Bonnie is over the ocean
C D7 G7
my Bonnie is over the sea
C F C A7
my Bonnie is over the ocean,
F G7 C
oh bring back my Bonnie to me.
C F
Bring back, bring back,
G7 C G7 C
oh bring back my Bonnie to me, to me.
C F
Bring back, bring back,
G7 C
oh bring back my Bonnie to me.
```

MICHAEL ROW THE BOAT ASHORE
(Initial note C)

```
         C                      F C
Michael row the boat ashore, halleluja,
         Em        Dm      C  G7 C
Michael row the boat ashore, hallelu - u - jah.
```

2 KEYS - NOTES - TIPS

Short information for beginners

2.1 A SENTENCE ABOUT FINGERING

Hey, why can't I strike all of the keys with my agile little index finger?

Well of course you can – if you are happy with the sound which results! If not, you can always come back to our suggestions for fingering. **Fingering** means: which finger strikes which key. To make this easier to understand, each finger is given a number. These numbers are written next to the notes, and show you which finger you should use to play that particular note.

This is what it looks like in the music ...

this is how the fingers are numbered ...

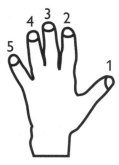

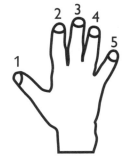

Left hand   Right hand

and this is how the fingering is played!

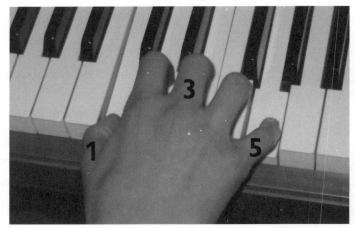

Tips for positioning

1. Do what you want – the main thing is that the sound is okay!
2. Many professionals hold the back of the hand horizontally.
3. Try to form a reasonably straight line with your lower arm and the back of your hand. Some people achieve success when playing using this method (this is of course not suitable if you have to play three different keyboards, one above the other, in your band).
4. Do not place your fingers completely flat or vertically on the keys; do not paw with them, do not bend them inwards, and they should not be elegantly propped up either. Otherwise: Refer to point 1!

Anything else?

If you play scales ... what? ... what did you say? ... oh! you don't want to play scales. The best thing for you to do is to skip this page, and the chapter on "Improvisation" as well, for example.

As much as we regret it: even improvisation-scales are scales. Good, let's try it again: If you want to play sequences of notes and want to bridge large gaps between notes and therefore keys ... (better?) ... and if you want to combine these notes without any pauses, you are going to have trouble when using only five fingers. Let us suppose you play the sequence C-D-E-F-G, beginning by playing C with your thumb and ending by playing G with your small finger. What do you do if you then want to play A, without a pause? You could let go of the G and jump to A with your thumb, but as a consequence you have an unwanted pause. Therefore we have the techniques of putting under and putting over. Here they are ...

Putting the thumb under

When playing an ascending sequence of notes, the thumb is passed under the other fingers to the next key. In our example, however, this shouldn't happen after the third finger has played E, but while the second finger is striking the D!
Don't turn the hand outwards, you should turn it inwards a little:

Putting the finger over (the thumb)

When playing a descending sequence of notes, one finger is passed over the thumb to the new key (in our example it is the third finger). This happens while the first finger is striking F. Here you should also turn the hand slightly inwards, and not outwards.

2.2 TIPS FOR PRACTISING

Practise?

This isn't about you, it's about your fingers! Between the two of us, Fingers have the I.Q. of an untrained cucumber and the sense of direction of a hen which went blind too early. When you already know what is going on, these little brain-boxes are still tapping around on the keys somewhere, totally confused, and crying: "Where ... where am I?" With good persuasion and a little clip behind the ear now and then, this lack of sense of direction soon disappears, and then they have reached the next stage. You will recognize this next stage when one of the ten little devils shouts: "Hey, you lot, here's one of those black keys again, who wants to have a go? Thumb?" – "No, don't want to." – "Index Finger?" – "No! I've enough to do with my white key!"" – "Middle Finger?" – "Why do I always have to? Let's have a vote!" If you continue to educate them according to our special training programme they will soon be jumping across the keyboards like panthers with the ape-like elegance of a nimble gazelle.

Finger-training

1. Don't try to run before you can walk. Let your fingers proceed beat by beat - if necessary half beat by half beat. Then play the whole bar, then the next, then both together etc.

2. Tempo: The little beasts always want to play faster than they can. At the beginning let them work at a speed at which they play everything without mistakes and without hesitating. Then speed it up gradually.

3. Stay in Beat: be careful! The clever little clumsy louts play more quickly during easier sections and really put the brakes on for difficult sections, but often with such subtlety, that you don't notice the change in pace, which gives you the impression that they can play the piece. When called to account, they deny everything. In this case only a slave-driver can help, one just like the man on the ancient galleys who unperturbedly signalled the beat, BOOM-BOOM-BOOM! for example the built-in rhythm function on an electric organ or a predecessor of the rhythm-computer: the metronome (available cheaply in every music shop). The metronome does not have a bass-drum or a snare-drum sound but a clicking sound which drives the fingers on mercilessly when they become slap-dash and slovenly.

4. Direction: You can show your little blind worms where to go, using our keyboard gadget on page 8. Another tip: At the beginning mark all of the C's (and all of the E's and G's if you can't memorize them) by fixing different-coloured labels on the keys (Stationer's Shop!). You should, however, gradually **remove all initial aids as quickly as possible** – ending with the C's!

5. Notes: The little brain-boxes can never learn notes. You have to patiently explain to them what is contained in the sheet music and then let them a) practise, b) repeat and c) start again from a. Do not ever listen to them when they start complaining "I'm never going to be able to do that!" and be gentle when they forget something which took a long time to learn (this happens again and again). Show them how to play it again, and we wish you luck!

2.3 THE SYSTEM OF NOTATION

Lines with personal notes

There are top-keyboarders, who cannot read notes but who can still produce great sounds with their keyboards. You even find these keyboarders now and again amongst studio musicians. We have nothing against talent and a good ear, but we shouldn't kid ourselves: Notes are the simplest way for musicians from different countries to communicate amongst themselves, 95 percent of all pop- and rock-music (even your favourite hits!) are recorded in note-form in songbooks. Do you want to dispense with this? And why? Learning to read notes is no problem whatsoever. So, let's get to work!

The System of notation for the Keyboard

A stave consists of 5 lines and 4 spaces; if there were any more lines everything would be too unclear, therefore we expand on this by using two ledger lines above and below the stave. Middle-C is located on one such ledger line. Clefs are directional aids. Where keyboards are concerned we need two clefs. The violin-clef or G-clef is nothing more than a heavily decorated "G" which clearly says: "The loop of my stomach engulfs the G-line." The bass-clef or F-clef is a highly stylized "F" which has been written the wrong way round and which says: "My dot is exactly where the F-note is positioned in the bass system."

1. One stave is not sufficient for the keyboards – this would only be enough for the notes above the middle-C.

2. We write the deeper notes on a bass stave which joins directly onto the other stave. Middle-C is exactly between these two staves.

3. So that the two staves do not encroach upon one another, we separate them. Middle-C, and the ledger line it is on, can be used by both staves.

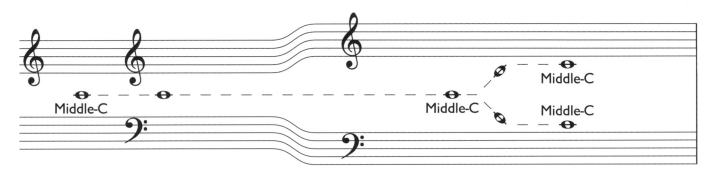

All notes at a glance

All right! So there are more notes on ledger lines above and below both staves. In this book, however, we do not need any more little black dots! In the diagram below, we have pushed both staves back together again so that you can see the ascending sequence from the deepest to the highest C.

You can see that our keyboard notation system is symmetrical when folded. If the notes in the lower stave were small rubber stamps and we folded the page along the middle C line, the deepest C would leave a mark in the upper stave which would look like the highest C in the upper stave.

The Division of the Notation system into octaves

Please re-read the section "The ABC of Keys" on page 9. We have accentuated all of the C's so that you can also see how the division into octaves works. Our names for the octaves, which were given on page 10 are sufficient for our use. In the interest of completeness we have also provided the classical terms for the divisions.

Tip: Try to remember the positions of the C's (2 ledger lines, the second space from the top in the upper stave, and the second space from the bottom in the lower system ... Middle-C – where else but in the Centre).

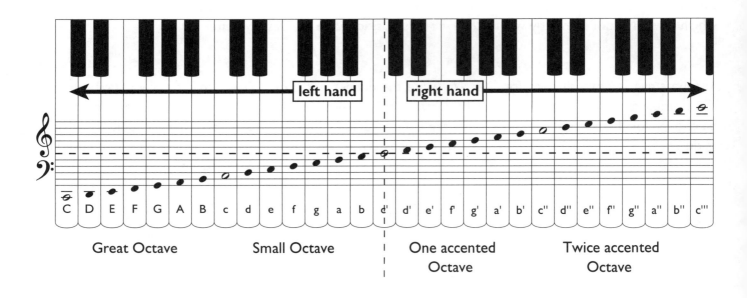

When the right hand becomes a left hand

Notes for the right hand are written in the upper stave whereas those for the left hand are written in the lower stave. If the right hand has to play notes which are deeper than Middle-C, it "breaks" into the bass stave and steals lines there. So that is not noticeable, the lines are only drawn as ledger lines. However, what is stolen, is stolen, as you can clearly see with the note F.

The Names of the notes

The first hurdle when learning notes is to associate names with the multitude of black dots in the staves. We have thought out three new cribs (mnemonics). Even if they sound a little stupid – they do help. Try them!

Cribs for the Names of notes

1. You can remember the positioning of the C's by using the crib: "C" as in "C"econd – the note C is always on the second ledger line above or below the stave or in the "C"econd space. Middle-C is in the "C"entre.

2. The G-line (G-clef) and the F-line (F-clef) are easy to remember. For the others use the crib "D" as in "Down under" (below the fifth line).

3. If you don't like these cribs, the only one left is our Elephant-crib which we use to remember the notes of a triad (see also page 16). Simply remember the sentence CLEVER ELEPHANTS GAIN BRILLIANT DIRECTIONS FROM ANTEATERS. You should read from the bottom to the top if you are using it in both staves. The differences between notes on the lines (staves) and notes in the spaces: with notes on the staves the system begins with C and with notes in the spaces, with D.

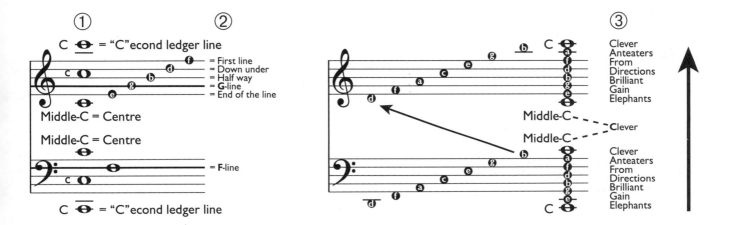

Reading music ...

The best way to learn this is by doing it. By the way, you will of course forget notes repeatedly – simply look at page 58 if this happens; and please don't forget the cribs and elephant-crib!

2.4 ACCIDENTALS

Has it all to do with "noughts and crosses" and "silly b's"?

Not at all! Please read the section "The ABC of Keys" on page 9 again. In this section we will now show you how to express what was said there in notes.

Sharp: If a note should be raised by a semi-tone, a sharp sign is written in front of it (♯); when we refer to the name of the note, the sharp sign is added behind the name. A 'C' becomes C♯ etc. When we speak we simply add the word 'sharp' to the name of the note i.e. 'C'-sharp.

Flat: If a note should be lowered by a semi tone, a flat-sign is written in front of it (♭). The name of the note itself is written with the flat-sign behind it. When spoken we simply add the word 'flat' to the name of the note i.e. B-flat.

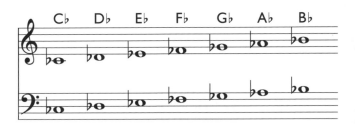

Natural sign: Sharp and flat signs are valid for all notes of the same name within one bar. If, for example, a 'C' within the bar which has been raised to a 'C-sharp' should be played as a C again, the accidental has to be cancelled with a natural sign (♮) in the next bar, none of the accidentals are valid anymore.

2.5 SCALES

Fishy business!

Notes are arranged in tone-series, which are called scales. The whole scale is named after its deepest tone, the keynote. Just as in the case with us humans there are two sexes of scales: Major and Minor.
The similarity doesn't end here. Just as we can tell by the way somebody takes a step whether this person is masculine or female, we can tell by the individual steps within the scale, whether it is a major or a minor scale. We will now show you this by using the C-major and the A-minor scales:

1. Major-Scale: Every major-scale consists of two "equal" parts, so-called Tetrachords. Each of these consists of two whole-tone-steps (WT) and one half tone-step (HT).

Put in another way: Every major-scale consists of whole tone-steps; only between the third and fourth, and the seventh and eighth step is there a half-tone-step.

C-major scale

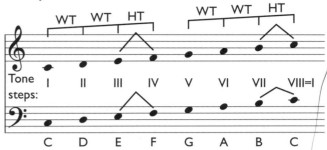

2. Natural-Minor-Scale: The natural minor scale begins at step 6 of a major-scale. The same notes are used as in the major-scale and it is consequently called a parallel-minor scale. This also consists of whole-tone-steps, but the half-tone-steps are located between the second and the third as well as the fifth and the sixth step.

A-minor scale ("natural", "pure" or "aeolian")

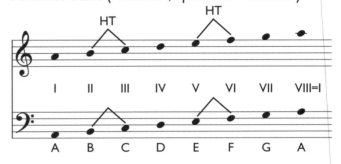

3. Harmonic Minor-Scale: A half-tone step between the seventh and the eighth step is called a leading tone because it (musically) leads to the eighth step (= first step) as is the case in the major scale. In order to attain this effect in the minor scale, the whole tone between steps 7 and 8 is increased by a half-tone. Voila! The harmonic minor scale.

A-minor scale (harmonic)

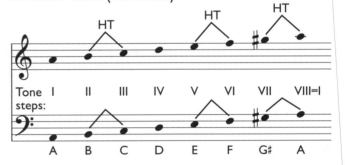

4. Melodic-Minor-Scales: By raising the seventh step, a step of one and a half tones arises between the sixth and seventh steps which cannot be sung easily. This is why the sixth step is also raised to obtain the "melodic-minor-scale". The leading note step is only needed when playing upwards, it is played "naturally" when descending.

A-minor scale (melodic)

2.6 SIGNATURES AND KEYS

This has nothing to do with signing the rent contract

Chromatic Scales and the Keys.

If you systematically strike the white and the black keys one after the other, you will be playing chromatic scales. This means: you are playing steps of half a tone. Using the rules for forming major and minor scales you can derive all other scales from the chromatic scale. We have derived the C- and D-major scales on the right. The C-major scale has no accidental, the D-major scale has two, F sharp and C sharp. Try to build the C#-Major scale yourself, starting on C#.

Result: This little beast has seven sharp signs! So that you don't have to write the sharp signs and flat signs in front of every note, you revert to a little trick ...

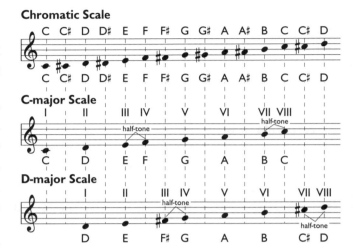

Chromatic Scale

C-major Scale

D-major Scale

From accidentals to Signatures

All accidentals are collected at the beginning of every accidentals line in the stave. They are on the line upon which the note to be raised occurs in the order they occur in the scale and are valid for all notes on that line. On the right, for example, D-major.

D-major scale with accidentals

... and with signatures

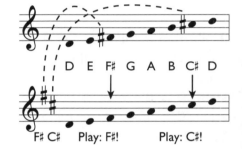

Signatures for all keys

Of course you don't have to learn them all at once. You can refer to them here at any time. Probably the best thing to do is to learn the signatures for the keys which are used most often and the parallel minor keys underneath them: G-, D-, A-, E-, F- and Eb-major. As you can see the parallel minor-keys have the same signatures as the equivalent major-keys. This is obvious, since they consist of the same notes and only have a different keynote.

Sharp Keys

C# is usually enharmonically changed to Db-major, A#-minor to Bb-minor and D#minor to Eb-minor.

G-maj.	D-maj.	A-maj.	E-maj.	B-maj.	F#-maj.	C#-maj.
Em	Bm	F#m	C#m	G#m	D#m	A#m

Flat Keys

Cb-major is usually enharmonically changed to B-major.

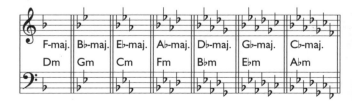

F-maj.	Bb-maj.	Eb-maj.	Ab-maj.	Db-maj.	Gb-maj.	Cb-maj.
Dm	Gm	Cm	Fm	Bbm	Ebm	Abm

2.7 INTERVALS

You always have to keep your distance

"Interval" means "distance between two tones" (lat. "inter" = between; "vallum" = wall . . . therefore the distance between two tone walls). Here we have noted all intervals which are used in Pop and Rock using the C-major key. Intervals are always calculated from the deepest to the highest note, the deepest note counts as the first note. You must be able to work with intervals in your sleep. There is an understanding between Pop and Rock musicians which often leads to the following: ... "play me a C-major chord ... no, no move the fifth down and add a seventh and a ninth ... okay, that sounds great!"

Intervals and Degrees (Roman numerals)

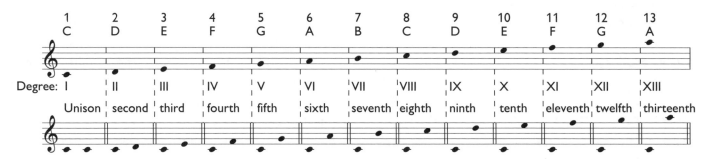

Interval-variants

Now a few lines of theory. If you strike a string on a guitar, the sound you hear is the prime. If you then place your finger on the string so that an exact ratio of 1:2 occurs you hear the eighth. If you place your finger on the string so that a ratio of 2:3 occurs you hear the fifth and with a ratio of 3:4 you hear the fourth. The ancient Greeks were so happy about these whole number methods of division, that they called them "perfect". All other intervals have more complicated proportions. For practise: strike all of the intervals which are on the right of the keyboard. You will see that if perfect or major intervals are raised by a semitone, augmented intervals are created. Also if minor intervals are lowered by a semitone, diminished intervals are created. If minor intervals are raised, major intervals are created – and vice versa. You can learn more about intervals and their function in chords, without being confronted with seventh notes on pages 12, 16, 33 and 36, and on page 68 with notes.

Interval \ Size	perfect	major	augmented	minor	diminished
unison	♪		♪♯		
second		♪	♪♯	♪♭	♪
third		♪	♪♯	♪♭	♪
fourth	♪		♪♯		♪♭
fifth	♪		♪♯		♪♭
sixth		♪	♪♯	♪♭	♪♭
seventh		♪	♪♯	♪♭	♪♭
octave	♪		♪♯		♪♭

2.8 NOTE VALUES

Full and empty heads

Note values tell you two things: when you should strike the keys and how long the note should sound. Now strike any note on the keyboard and count from the moment you strike the note 1-2-3-4 and keep the key depressed whilst doing this – you have now played a whole note. Now strike the key again, but this time count to two and then let the note go – you have now played a half note. Now count 1-2-3-4 and strike the key with each number – you have now just played four quarter notes. Now we are going to tell you the rest ...

Note and rest values

The shape of the note determines the length of the note. A whole note lasts as long as it takes to count 1+2+3+4. Through division, smaller values are always produced.

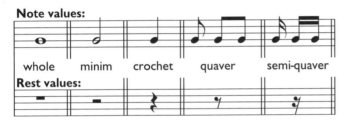

The Lengthening of a note

This is done with a dot or a tie. The full-stop says: lengthen the note by half again. The tie means: strike the first but not the second note, and add the value of the second note to the first.

Triplets

If instead of halving the value of the note, you divide it into three, triplets are formed.

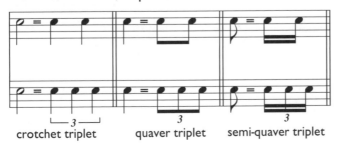

Counting notes

Linear distances are measured in metres. The length of notes are measured in times or **beats**. The tempo of the beats is variable. The best way to count notes is in time with the **smallest note value** in the bar. If you only have whole notes, minims and crotchets it's best to count in quarter-feeling 1-2-3-4 and so on. If you also have quavers you should count everything in quaver-time 1 and 2 and 3 and 4 and. If semi-quavers appear everything should be counted in semi-quaver-time 1-a-and-a-2-a-and-a-3-a-and-a-4-a-and-a! Triplets are counted as follows: 1-a-day-2-a-day-3-a-day-4-a-day.

2.9 Time and Bars

Time ladies & gentlemen please!

Bar: Pieces of music are divided into sections of equal length using bar-lines. Behind the clef there is a fraction, the denominator of which indicates whether we are to count in, for example, crotchet time or quaver time; the numerator tells us how many counts there are in each bar. In **simple** bars the numerator contains two or three counts, in **mixed** bars two or more simple time forms are combined.

Accentuation and counting: Each bar has accented and unaccented beats, which you should learn together with the typical way of counting. In four-four time, the most common time in Pop and Rock music, there are two variants of accentuation: a "european", which places accent on the first and third beat, and an "Afro-American" which places accent on the second and fourth. In Rockmusic, this accentuation of the "2" and "4" is commonly referred to as "backbeat"

The Upbeat is an incomplete bar at the beginning of a piece of music, with which you literally take a "runup" at the piece of music. The final bar is shortened by the value of the upbeat. When the final bar and the upbeat are added together, the result is a complete bar.

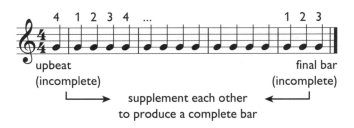

The Syncope: This occurs if you shift an accent in the bar so that a beat which isn't really accented suddenly is. There are three ways to play syncopes. a) you bind over the unaccentuated beat to the accented beat, b) you pause on the beat which is usually accented, c) you play the unaccented beat louder than usual.

Beat and Off-Beat: The beat has the function of emphasizing the beat-times of the bar, i.e. 1-2-34. The vocalist or instrumentalist can stay in beat, but can also place emphasis before or after the beat: "off the beat".
The emphasis of the "and" counts is often referred to as off-beat.

2.10 Signs and Abbreviations

But we'll take a short cut

1. Repeats: The double dot at the end of a bar section means: "Play everything again which is written before this sign". If bars are **enclosed** by repeat signs only that which is **between the signs** should be repeated, irrespective of what precedes it (here bars C and D).

You play: AB-AB-CD-CD

2. Closing-Brackets: Using the double dot repeat, everything which precedes this sign is repeated. Sometimes, however, we only want to repeat a large part of the preceding piece – without the final bars. Here we use the closing-brackets and the double dot. At first you play everything normally, even that which is under the brackets up to the double dot, then you repeat up to the point where the first bracket begins and play the section which is enclosed by the second bracket.

You play: ABCD-ABC-E

3. D.C. al Fine: Spoken: Da Capo al fine. "Da Capo" means "repeat from the beginning". "Al Fine" means "up to the word Fine". Really what this tells you is: Play everything from here on again, up to the word "Fine" ... and that's that!

You play: ABCDE-ABC

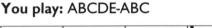

4. D.S. al fine: Spoken: dal segno ("senyo") al fine. If you don't want to repeat everything again from the beginning, as is the case with D.C. al fine, you insert the sign at the place where the repeat should begin. So you go back to the sign (= "segno") and play up to the word "fine".

You play: ABCDE-BC

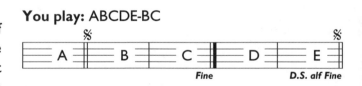

5. D.S. al ⊕ – ⊕ coda: Coda comes from the Italian word for tail. What is meant is the final part of a piece of music. The symbol ⊕ means "head". D.S al ⊕ ⊕ coda is used if you want to repeat a part of a piece of music and then go on to a suitable part which is in the closing section. When this sign appears you go back to the ℅ sign, play up to the head ⊕ jump the rest and continue playing the coda at the second head.

You play: ABCDEF-BCD-GH

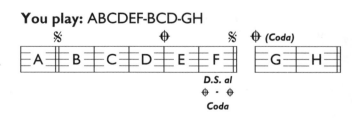

Pedals: The two most important pedals are: the sustainpedal: If you depress this the note played continues to sound after you have released the key. Softpedal: here the notes sound dampened.

Notation: Notes on or above the third line from the bottom have their stems pointing downwards all others point upwards. If the right hand is playing the solo part and the accompaniment, the solo part is written with the stems pointing upwards and the accompaniment stems pointing downwards.

Holds: Allow the notes with this sign to sound as long as you want.

Transposing in an octave above or below. (top) Play one octave higher than is notated (bottom) play one octave lower. From the "loco" symbol onwards, you play as notated.

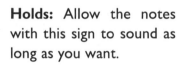

Metronome: Set the given number and the metronome will provide the correct tempo. M.M. means "Mälzels" Metronome (the inventor).

M.M. ♩ = 108

Long appoggiatura: Ornamental note which is played to the length notated prior to another note, the value of which is subtracted from the ornamental note.

Short appoggiatura: Ornamental note. This is struck shortly before or exactly on the count of the note which is ornamented.

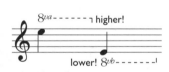

Arpeggio: Italian "arpa" = Harp. You don't play a chord which is written with this sign as a closed chord, but you strike the notes quickly, one after the other, just as if playing a harp.

Dynamics: forte = loud, piano = play softly. The more signs you see, the louder you play, the fewer signs you see, the quieter you play. "Crescendo" means gradually becoming louder, "decrescendo" means gradually becoming softer.

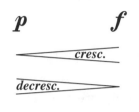

Tremolo: Lat. "tremolare" = to shake/shiver. You play both notes several times whilst quickly alternating between notes.

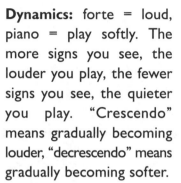

Changes in tempo: The tempo of a piece of music can remain the same, become slower (= ritardando) or become faster (= accelerando). A return to the old tempo is indicated by the term "a tempo".

Glissando: Right hand: You slide from left to right with your angled index-fingernail, or from the right to left with your angled thumbnail, across either the white or the black keys.

Sluring the notes: A slur above or below the notes says: Play the notes joined by this slur in the most flowing way possible. Professional term: "legato". You can also play "Staccato" (= separate). Here the note is only struck for a very short time.

3 CHORDS
How the hoards of chords came out

3.1 Intervals

Double trouble?

Chords are the basis of Pop-Rock keyboard playing: if you don't want to learn loads of individual chords, it's important that you learn how to form them and that you learn their names – the chord symbols. We will show you how chords are formed, inverted, varied and expanded using the C-major scale and the C-major chord which is derived from this scale. The blue prints and rules can then be applied to all other scales and chords. You can find these in the "Magical Keyboard Tables" at the end of the book.

If you still haven't much experience you should, to gain your direction, first read about notes, their names, scales and intervals in the first chapter because this chapter is based on the first.

Intervals – Building bricks for chords

Chords are, quite simply, made up of two or more intervals. To be able to form them you have to be able to tell which interval is the 1st, 3rd, 5th or 9th note of the scale in your sleep. Here is a diagram of the intervallic relationships using the C-major scale.

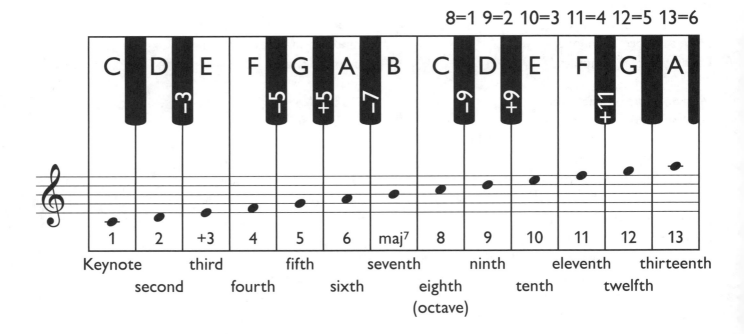

The Major Triad

1. Formation: The simplest form of a chord is the major triad. It consists of 3 notes: The keynote of the scale (1), the major third (3) and the fifth (5). The chord is named after its keynote. This name is also called the "Chord Symbol". The C-major triad therefore has "C" as chord symbol.

2. Inversions: The keynote doesn"t have to be the lowest sounding note in the chord. Even the third and the fifth can be at the "bottom". The order in which the notes of the chord are played is not important, it is only the combination which counts. In the primary form of the chord the keynote is at the bottom. In the 1st inversion the third is at the bottom. Where triads are concerned there are only two inversions – the 3rd inversion would be the primary form of the same chord, one octave higher.

3. Bass: So that chords sound "fuller" one often likes to play the keynote in the bass region. Even with chord inversions you should, as a rule, play the keynote in the bass region and not the lowest sounding note in the inversion.

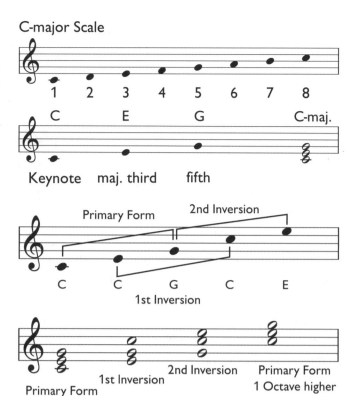

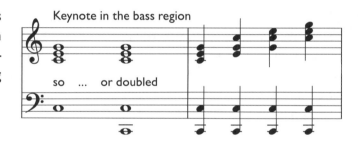

Exercises with the C-major Triad

The following exercises with the C-major triad are fundamental for your orientation on your keyboard. Start slowly and gradually increase the tempo, and play the exercises until you can play them quickly and **off-by-heart**. A rhythm-machine or a metronome can bring more fun and also help to increase the tempo gradually and in a controlled manner.

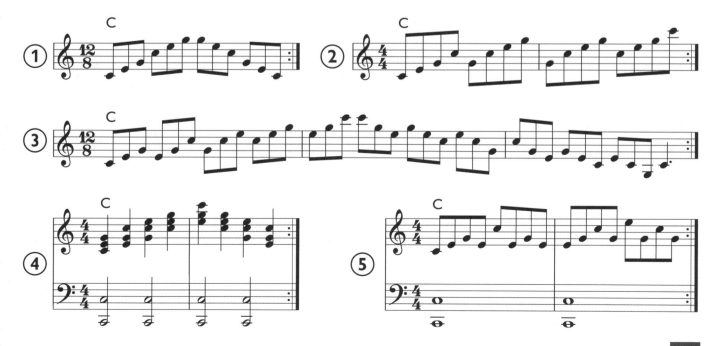

3.2 Triads

Three wise men

With the major triad and its two inversions you almost automatically have 6 triad variations, in which – with one exception – only one note is different to those in the major triad. It is always the third and the fifth which are changed – never the keynote – otherwise we would be left with a completely new chord. Therefore the letter of the chord symbol remains the same; to this we add signs which show which intervals we have changed by a semitone.

1. The minor triad: Major and minor are the two musical sexes (see p. 15). The major triad consists of the intervals: Keynote (1), major third (3) and fifth (5). The minor triad only differs from the major triad in that the third is a semitone deeper – and is known as a minor third – m3.

Chord symbol: Cm (spoken: C-minor)

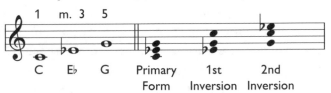

2. The diminished triad: A minor triad in which the fifth has been diminished by a semitone. It therefore consists of the keynote (1), minor third (m3) and a diminished fifth. If an interval is diminished by a semitone, the interval number symbol (here 5 for fifth) is given a minus sign at the front – in this case -5.

Chord symbol: Cm⁻⁵ (spoken: C-minor minus five) or Cdim (= diminished)

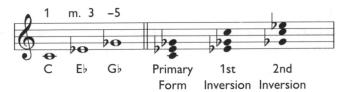

3. The diminished major triad: A major triad with keynote (1) and major third (maj. 3) but the fifth has been diminished by a semitone – therefore a minus sign is set before the number symbol: -5. Of all 6 triad variations this is the least used.

Chord symbol: C⁻⁵ (spoken: C minus five)

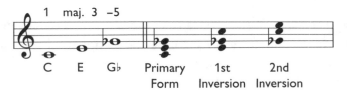

4. The augmented Major triad: A major triad with keynote (1) and major third (maj. 3) and where the fifth (5) has been raised by a semitone – therefore + 5. It has a somewhat stronger sound, but in the right chord combination it flowers in its acrid beauty like a wall flower which has been asked to dance by Rod Stewart.

Chord symbol: Cm⁺⁵ (spoken: C plus five)

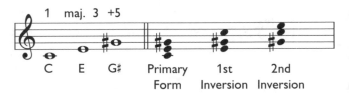

5. The sus4 triad: This consists of, as in the case with major triads, of keynote and fifth, but the third is suspended. As a replacement for the third, the fourth is brought in, which lends the triad a hovering, somewhat undefined sound. This chord sounds like across between C and F: It contains two notes of the C chord (C and G) and two of the F chord (C and F).

Chord symbol: Csus⁴ (spoken: C sus four)

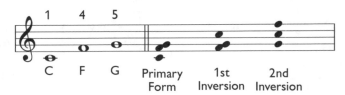

6. The sus2 triad: Even this triad consists of the key-note (1) and the flfth (5) and even here the third is sent packing! As a replacement the second is brought in (2). This triad also has a hovering sound; you often hear them in the combination C – Csus4 – Csus2 – C. Try it yourself, it sounds good! This chord sounds like a cross between C and G: It contains two notes of the C chord (C and G) and two of the G chord (C and G).

Chord symbol: Csus² (spoken: C sus two)

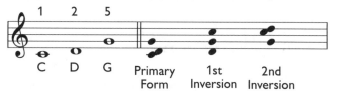

Exercises with the Variations of the C-major Triad

We admit that these exercises are not exactly mind-blowing; but they do deepen your basic orientation on the keyboard which you have attained in the exercises with the C-major triad and its inversions. Perhaps we can motivate you a little with the following argument. Through the previous restriction to one chord, it's variations and extensions, your keyboard no longer consists of faceless black and white keys. Whilst you are playing these exercises your keyboard will gain **structures**. Suddenly you see many C-, Csus and C+5 chords in front of you in all octave positions. If your keyboard at first has a basic structure, it is a lot less problematic to learn new structures in addition.

71

3.3 CHORDS OF FOUR NOTES (TETRADS)

A striking keyboard foursome!

You can now play seven triads and their inversions. If you add a new note, a new interval, you are left with tetrads.

The tetrads are also called "chord extensions" or "chord colourations". The new note lends the triads a new and interesting tone colour; it is to a certain extent the salt in the triad soup.

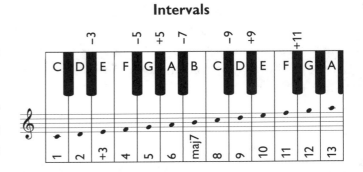

Intervals

In the summary on the next page you will find the construction formulae for the new chords and their chord symbols. As a rule the number symbol of the new interval is added to the chord symbol of the old triad. Exceptions: Cadd9 and Cmadd9 and C°. We will talk about the "add 9" exception on the next page, accept it as it is for now. C° is really a Cm−5 with an additional double diminished seventh (enharmonically newly interpreted as sixth). So as to avoid the notational head-aches it is simply called C°.

Another tip: so as not to get lost in the mass of inversions, you must always keep in mind that basically you are still only concerned with one simple C-major triad and its inversions. Tips for learning tetrads, and on fingering can be found on page 36.

Exercises

Here are a few suggestions to help you come to terms with tetrads and their inversions. Invent a few similar exercises for yourself using other tetrads. Good news: Once you have conquered inversions practically 50 percent of your work in learning to play keyboards has been done. We wish you success, fun and – remember – be patient!

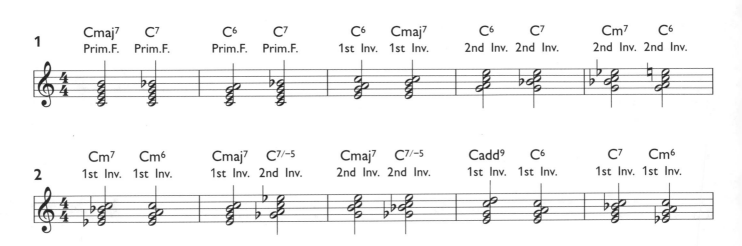

3.4 CHORDS OF FIVE AND SIX NOTES

Chord giants hit out

Lots of keyboard novices are very scared of these gigantic chords. This is totally unnecessary. They are dragons, from which we can extract the teeth before they have a chance to bite – we simply reduce them to tetrads and triads. How? We simply throw the intervals out which are relatively unimportant for the sound as a whole, or we play them in the bass region. Let's consider which intervals we can best throw out. **The keynote** is taboo! So we can't throw it out, but we can move it into the bass region, there it gives our

Intervals

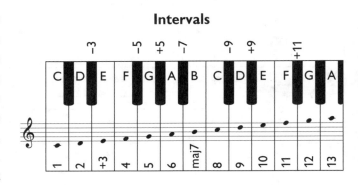

chord a solid basis. The third is also (almost) taboo: It decides whether the chord is a major or a minor chord. Exceptions: If third and fourth appear in a chord at the same time, we leave the third out because a certain friction in sound is caused by the proximity of the two intervals – friction is not wanted! This is the case with $C^{7/9/11}$ so: the 11 corresponds to the 4, and that is right next door to the 3 so – out with the third in the 7/9/11th chord.

The fifth doesn't do much for the sound so we banish it to the bass region or throw it out completely.

The minor or major seventh is one of the most important intervals in the area of Pop, Rock and Jazz. We can't generally do without it. It is even the case that higher intervals such as the ninth, eleventh and thirteenth only appear in a chord when one of the two sevenths are there. Therefore, if you see a chord symbol C^9 what is really meant is $C^{7/9}$. It goes without saying that the seventh is there. If the ninth should be added to a chord without the seventh we use the expression "add" to express this. $Cadd^9$ is therefore a C-major triad with ninth but without seventh. In the summary on the following page you will find all usual chords of four, five and six notes and the ways in which they are formed. Here we are now going to show you how the transformation of a chord of five or six notes into a tetrad or a triad really works.

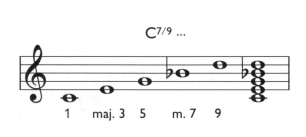

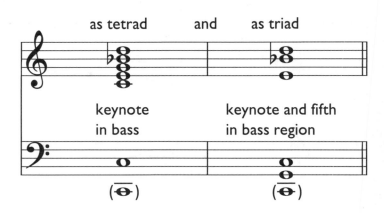

Hint: Notes in brackets can be left out.

C6 | C maj. | + sixth (6) | C6 | 1st Inv. | 2nd Inv. | 3rd Inv.
C7 | C maj. | + m seventh (7) | C7 | 1st Inv. | 2nd Inv. | 3rd Inv.
Cmaj7 | C maj. | + maj. seventh (maj7) | Cmaj7 | 1st Inv. | 2nd Inv. | 3rd Inv.
Cadd9 | C maj. | + sixth (6) | Cadd9 | 1st Inv. | 2nd Inv. | 3rd Inv.
C7/+5 | C+5 | + ninth (9) | C7/+5 | 1st Inv. | 2nd Inv. | 3rd Inv.
C7/−5 | C−5 | + m seventh (7) | C7/−5 | 1st Inv. | 2nd Inv. | 3rd Inv.
C7/4 | Csus4 | + m seventh (7) | C7/4 | 1st Inv. | 2nd Inv. | 3rd Inv.
Cm6 | Cm | + sixth (6) | Cm6 | 1st Inv. | 2nd Inv. | 3rd Inv.
Cm7 | Cm | + m seventh (7) | Cm7 | 1st Inv. | 2nd Inv. | 3rd Inv.
Cmmaj7 | Cm | + maj. seventh (maj7) | Cmmaj7 | 1st Inv. | 2nd Inv. | 3rd Inv.
Cmadd9 | Cm | + ninth (9) | Cadd9 | 1st Inv. | 2nd Inv. | 3rd Inv.
Cm7/−5 | Cm−5 | + m seventh (7) | Cm7/−5 | 1st Inv. | 2nd Inv. | 3rd Inv.
C° | Cm−5 | + sixth (6) | C° | 1st Inv. | 2nd Inv. | 3rd Inv.

3.5 Chords and Symbols

We make a symbowl of chord punch

Chord symbol	spoken	Notes and Intervals	Other Names
C	C-maj		Cmaj, CMAJ
C^6	C-six		$Cmaj^6$, C^{add6}
C^7	C-seven		C^{7b}
$Cmaj^7$	C-major 7		CMA7, $C^{\Delta 7}$, $C^{7\sharp}$, Cmj^7, Cj^7
C^{+5}	C five plus C plus five		C^+, C^{aug5}, $C^{(\sharp 5)}$
C^{-5}	C five minus C minus five		Cdim., $C^{(b5)}$, C^{5-}, Cdim5
$Csus^2$	C sus2		C^2
$Csus^4$	C sus4		Csus, C^4, $C^{s/4}$
$C^{7/4}$	C four, seven		C^{7sus4}, C^4, $C^{7/sus}$
$C^{7/+5}$	C seven, plus five		$C^{7/aug}$, C^{+7}, $C^{7/\sharp 5}$
$C^{7/-5}$	C seven, minus five		$C^{7/b5}$, C, $C^{7/dim5}$
$C^{6/9}$	C six, nine		–
$C^{7/6}$	C seven, six		–
$C^{7/9}$	C seven, nine		C^9
$C^{7/+9}$	Cseven, plus nine		$C^{7/\sharp 9}$

Chords and Symbols

Cmaj$^{7/9}$	C major seven, nine		C$^{j7/9}$, C$^{\Delta7/9}$
C^{add9}	C add nine		C$^{\Delta add9}$, C^{9}
C$^{7/9/11}$	Csevne, nine, eleven		C^{11}, C$^{7/11}$
C$^{7/9/13}$	C seven, nine, thirteen		C^{13}, C$^{7/13}$
Cmaj$^{7/+11}$	C major seven plus eleven		C$^{\Delta7/\#11}$, C$^{j7/11\#}$
Cm	C minor		C^{-}, Cmin, Cmi
Cm^{6}	C minor six		C^{-6}, Cmin^{6}, Cmi^{6}, Cm add^{9}
Cm^{7}	C minor seven		C^{-7}, Cmin7, Cmi^{7}
Cm^{maj7}	C minor, major seven		C^{-7}, Cm7, Cm$^{\Delta7}$
Cm^{-5}	C minor minus five		C$^{-\flat5}$, Cm$^{\flat5}$
Cm$^{7/-5}$	C minor seven minus five		C, C$^{-7/\flat5}$, Cmin$^{7/\flat5}$
Cm^{add9}	C minor add nine		C^{-add9}, Cmi add^{9}, C^{9}
Cm$^{7/9}$	C minor seven, nine		C$^{-7/9}$, Cmi$^{7/\flat9}$, Cmi$^{7/add9}$
C$^{7/-9}$	C minor seven minus nine		C$^{-7/-9}$, Cm$^{7/\flat9}$
C$^{\circ}$	C zero (C diminished)		C dim, C$^{\circ7}$

3.6 CHORDS IN FIVE LANGUAGES

In case you're speechless

English	Italian	French	German	Spanish
c major	do maggiore	ut majeur	C-Dur	do mayor
a minor	la minore	la mineur	A-Moll	la menor
g major	sol maggiores	sol majeur	G-Dur	sol mayor
e minor	mi minore	mi mineur	E-Moll	mi menor
d major	re maggiore	re majeur	D-Dur	re mayor
b minor	si minore	si mineur	H-Moll	si menor
a major	la maggiore	la majeur	A-Dur	la mayor
f sharp minor	fa diesis minore	fa dièse mineur	Fis-Moll	fa sostenido menor
e major	mi maggiore	mi majeur	E-Dur	mi mayor
csharp minor	do diesis minore	ut dièse mineur	Cis-Moll	do sostenido menor
b major	si maggiore	si majeur	H-Dur	si mayor
g sharp minor	sol diesis minore	sol dièse mineur	Gis-Moll	sol sostenido menor
f sharp major	fa diesis maggiore	fa dièse majeur	Fis-Dur=	fa sostenido mayor
g flat major	sol bemolle maggioresol	bemol majeur	Ges-Dur	sol bemol mayor
d sharp minor	re diesis minore	re dièse majeur	Dis-Moll=	re sostenido menor
e flat minor	mi bemolle minore	mi bemol mineur	Es-Moll	mi bemol menor
d flat major	re bemolle maggiore	re bemol majeur	Des-Dur	re bemol mayor
b flat minor	si bemolle minore	si bemol mineur	B-Moll	si bemol menor
a flat major	la bemolle maggiore	la bemol majeur	As-Dur	la bemol mayor
f minor	fa minore	fa mineur	F-Moll	fa menor
e flat major	mi bemolle maggiore	mi bemol majeur	Es-Dur	mi bemol mayor
c minor	do minore	ut mineur	C-Moll	do menor
b flat major	so bemolle maggiore	si bemol majeur	B-Dur	si bemol mayor
g minor	sol minore	sol mineur	G-Moll	sol menor
f major	fa maggiore	fa majeur	F-Dur	fa mayor
d minor	re minore maggiore	re mineur	D-Moll	re menor

4 HARMONIES
Musical Etiquette

4.1 SCALAR CHORDS

"Who's who" in the C-major royal household

The word "harmony" comes from the Greek "harmonia", which means to fit together, to agree or to concord. In a narrow sense, harmonies are notes or chords which sound good together, in a broader sense they are also successions of chords.

In our small section on the theory of harmony we want to show you how and why certain chords and successions fit together well and how you can play boring run-of-the-mill successions in a more interesting way.

Chords live and work in more or less solidly combined chord families, in which every chord has a fixed place and (at least) one task which it fulfils within the family. Instead of the horribly complicated word "task", we like to use the word "function".

We are now going to reveal the chord-family relationships of the famous blue-blooded C-major chord family and we are going to be brutally honest in several very indiscrete gossip-columns. With the help of the magical keyboard tables at the end of this book you can employ all you have learned on all keys and their chord families. We have already dwelled on some of the family gossip (without notes) on page 12. By now you should be able to read (and play) notes; it wouldn't be bad if you have already dealt with the chapter about "chords" (p. 68) either. And now: Have fun with the royal C-major-clan from the country of Harmonia ...

The history of the house of C-major

In the field of harmony the notes of a scale are referred to as **"degrees"** and are numbered using Roman numerals. The VIIIth degree corresponds to the Ist degree (Example A). Triads can be formed, based on every degree of the C-major scale. The notes in these triads all come from the C-major scale. They are therefore known as "scalar chords". Here the thirds are simply layered above the degrees which themselves serve as keynotes. In this way a family of musically closely related chords is produced for every scale. The triads for the degrees I, IV and V are major triads because their first interval is a major third; the triads for the degrees II, III, VII are minor triads, since their first interval is a minor third. A diminished minor triad results from the VIIth degree (Example B).

Scalar Chords in C-major

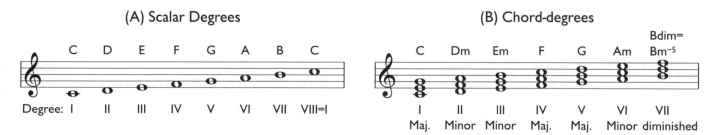

(A) Scalar Degrees

(B) Chord-degrees

4.2 THE TONIC

Her royal highnote

Head of the Royal Triad Family is the triad based upon the keynote of the scale, on the Ist degree: Queen "Tonic" (from the Italian "tonica" = keynote). The whole chord family, including the royal household and servants are named after her. In the Kingdom of Harmonia, most musical developments originate from the Tonic (as some people, irreverently refer to her), and also return to the tonic. Most songs, for example, begin and end with the tonic.

Chord symbol	C						
Degree	I	II	III	IV	V	VI	VII
Function	Tonic						

Sensational revelation: Queen incompetent!

This most closely guarded secret of the Royal Household of Harmonia became known during a royal ball. The pop-song "Help", made famous by the Beatles and Tina Turner, bowed respectfully before Queen Tonic and asked: "Could your Royal Highness accompany me a little?" She shamefully admitted: "I alone, unfortunately not!" As Lord Yesterday and Lady Madonna posed the same question and received the same answer, a somewhat cheeky individual, who had just graduated from the Video-Clip-School shouted: "And what can you accompany your Royal Highnote?" Queen Tonic became as pale and wishy-washy as a "Modern Talking" song and was forced to admit: "Okay, purely on my own I can just about accompany a few children's songs." Then the somewhat rotund court friar Frere Jacques stepped up, offered the Queen his arm and saved the embarrassing situation with the words "Would you care to accompany me, your Majesty?" The court scribes recorded this historical moment in music ...

Tip for playing: Strike a C-major chord on every main count and sing along in a rocky fashion.

Frere Jacques (accompanied by Her Royal Highnote Tonic C-major)

Frè - re   Jac - ques,   Frè - re   Jac - ques,   dor - mez   vous,   dor - mez   vous?

Son-nez les mat - ti - nes?   Son-nez les mat - ti - nes?   Ding, dong, ding,   ding, dong, ding!

4.3 DOMINANTS AND SUBDOMINANTS

Rulers without crowns

Now, good old Queen Tonic is in a similar position to that of her colleague – the King of the chess-board. On their own they are nothing more than pitiful little sausages. A poor start! However, as we so often say: You can start weak, but you should go out with a bang! You have almost certainly seen the scene in a hundred films – where there is a weak queen there is always one, maybe two powers behind the throne in the background who really have the say. In the royal court of Harmonia there are two ladies of differing rank who are lusting for power. The first is the triad on the VIth degree – the **dominant** G-maj (from the Italian "dominante" = ruling) and the second is the triad on the IVth degree – the **sub-dominant** (sub = under). Voila: Countess Dominant and Baroness Sub-dominant and their official positions in the royal court .

Dominant (Degree V) and Sub-dominant (Degree IV)

Chord symbol	C			F	G		
Degree	I	II	III	IV	V	VI	VII
Function	Tonic			Subdominant	Dominant		

The relationship of these two to the tonic becomes somewhat clearer if we look at their position in **two** octaves instead of **one**.

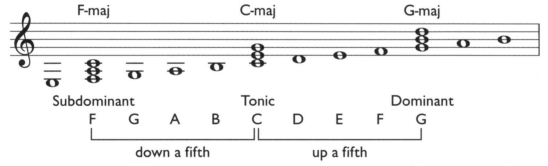

The dominant is a fifth below the tonic (precisely termed this is the upper-dominant),
a fifth below is the sub-dominant (lower-dominant).

The two ladies put an end to affairs

The most important task (function) for both ladies is to lead all of the splendour in the musical happenings at the court to the tonic. Neither the Countess (V) nor the Baroness (IV) can exist on their own. Both build up a musical tension to the tonic which is only relieved when the tonic is played. If you end a piece of music by playing V or IV it has the same effect as not finishing a ...

If a musical section is ended with the chord sequence "dominant tonic" (V–I) we call this an **"authentic ending"**. The ending with "sub-dominant-tonic" is known as a **"plagal ending"**.

So, as you can see, there is a small, but clear difference in importance between Countess Dominant (IV) and Baroness Sub-dominant (IV). If, at the end of a section of music, Baroness Sub-dominant sways through the crowd, graciously greeting as she goes, one tends to hear the murmor "If the Queen Tonic came in now it would be a great ending to things!" If, however, Countess Dominant storms through the crowd with an arrogant expression on her face, the cry goes out "Mercy! Mercy! We can't take it any longer! We pray that Queen Tonic soon turns up to save us!"

Cancellation of musical tension in the Tonic

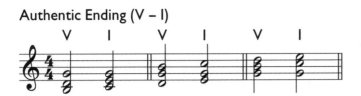

Authentic Ending (V – I)

Plagal Ending (IV – I)

You can considerably increase the effectiveness of this relaxation of tension if you add the minor seventh to the dominant and the sixth to the sub-dominant (from their own scale), therefore making tetrads. The dominant increases the effect of leading to the tonic, in that it receives the additional note F, the keynote of the sub-dominant (and therefore some of its power); and the sub-dominant gains a somewhat "dominant" air through the sixth D, since D is the fifth of the dominant-triad G-major. Listen to it yourself …

G^7

1 3 5 –7

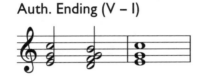

Auth. Ending (V – I)

F^6

1 3 5 6

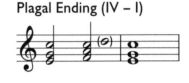

Plagal Ending (IV – I)

Two unequal pairs

Let's summarize: Queen Tonic alone is a pitiful picture: You can't do anything with her on her own. The arrogant countess Dominant alone is an absolute nothing (only with great difficulty can she manage to hide the fifth's wrinkles under her make-up). Baroness Sub-dominant on her own is a sweet nothing (around the key-note she tends to fill out a little). What happens if they both get on friendly terms with the tonic?

Tonic and Dominant (I – V)

Some simple Pop, Rock and Folk-songs can be played and accompanied using the two ladies. Here is a selection:

1. Tulsa Time (Eric Clapton)
2. Rock My Soul (Aretha Franklin)
3. Banana Boat Song (Harry Belafonte)
4. Tom Dooley (Kingston Trio)
5. Pick A Bale of Cotton (Johnny Cash)

The combination V – I is also suitable for simple intros (p. 174).

Intro: G G^7 C

G   C

In many rock numbers there is a bridge, which produces tension for the tonic in the refrain.

F   G   C G^7 Refrain: C

Tonic and Sub-dominant (I – IV)

Many Songs can be accompanied using only the combination I – IV. Beside Beatles-Songs like *Get Back* there are a lot of Soul numbers. Here is an example from us …

In many Pop and Rock numbers you hear a typical quick change between I and IV. In songbooks only the tonic is written in such cases; the change is a form of embellishment, hardly a harmonic function.

4.4 THE BASIC TRIADS

Together they stand strong!

Normally it is the case that if you put a three incapable persons together in a group, shove sticks in their hands and let them shout "All for one and one for all!" – you're a long way from having the three musketeers. In music that's different. Tonic, Dominant and Subdominant form a devilishly strong team of chords, with which you can play and accompany more than half of all Pop and Rock songs. On the right is a selection of famous Oldies, playable using basic triads.

Because they are so good and so important we also call the scalar chords derived from the degrees I, IV and V **"Basic-Triads"**. At the bottom of this page you will find some typical chord-combinations using the I, IV or VI, which are as old as Pop music itself but which still produce fresh sounds.

**Rock and Pop Classics
playable using Basic-Triads**

1. Jailhouse Rock (Elvis Presley)
2. Blowing In The Wind (Bob Dylan)
3. Bobby McGee (Kris Kristofferson)
4. Proud Mary (Tina Turner)
5. Satisfaction (Rolling Stones)
6. Hey Jude (The Beatles)
7. Sloop John B. (Beach Boys)
8. WhenTheSaints (LouisArmstrong)
9. Be-Bop-A-Lula (Gene Vincent)
10. Mr. Tambourine Man (Bob Dylan)
11. Matilda (Harry Belafonte)
12. Summertime Blues (Eddie Cochran)
13. The Gambler (Kenny Rogers)
14. Sylvia's Mother (Dr. Hook)
15. Swing Low (Traditional)
16. My Bonnie (Traditional)
17. Plaisir d'amour (Judy Collins)
18. Guantanamera (Pete Seeger)
19. Amazing Grace (Rod Stewart)
20. Auld Lang Syne (almost everybody)
21. When you say nothing at all (Ronan Keating)

C^7 and F, we enforce the change from C to F

We have reinforced the step from V to I by playing the V as a seventh chord (G^7). You can also reinforce the step from I to IV by playing the I as a seventh chord, too (C^7). To reinforce the step from I to V you have to play a diminished or Zero chord, the zero chord on the VIIth degree (F#) of the scale pertaining to the dominant (G), therefore: F#°.

Chord Pace-Maker

Chord-Combinations with I – IV – V

4.5 THE SECONDARY TRIADS

Minor relations

Every blue-blooded Major-lady has a little sister in the Minor walks of musical life – they are called the Minor parallels, since their sister-scales consist of the same notes. They are also very similar in other ways: Major triads and the accompanying Minor parallels have two identical chord notes. The minor parallel of the tonic is the triad on the VIth degree, that of the dominant is the triad on the IIIrd degree and that of the sub-dominant is the triad on the IInd degree. Here is a visual summary:

The Position of the Secondary Triads (Degrees II, III, VI)

Chordsymbol	C	Dm	Em	F	G	Am	Bm⁻⁵	
C major Scale								
Degree	I	II	III	IV	V	VI	VII	
Function	Tonic	m. Parallel IVth degree	m. Parallel Vth degree	Sub-dominant	Dominant	S. Parallel Ist degree	Chord on leading note	

Parallel scales

A scale is referred to as "parallel", if it uses the same notes as the original scale. For every Major scale there is a (natural) Minor scale, the keynote of which is a third lower than the keynote of the major scale. So there are also minor Scales for the Scales of our basic triads ...

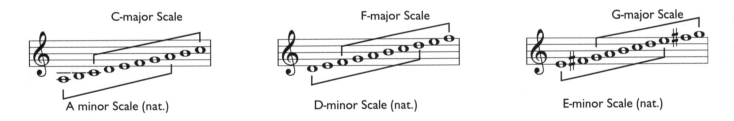

C-major Scale / A minor Scale (nat.)   F-major Scale / D-minor Scale (nat.)   G-major Scale / E-minor Scale (nat.)

A System with system

You can see more clearly how regular the whole system of Basic and Secondary triads is, if the Queen, Countess, Baroness and their minor sisters are spread over two octaves.

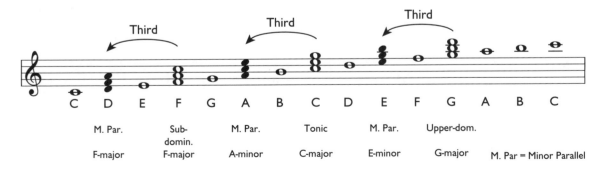

The Revolt of the Minor parallels!

As is generally the case with those in a position of power, the only thing that they are willing to share with you are opinions (their own). In the Royal Court of Harmonia this isn't any different. If it's a matter of accompaniment, the basic triads display an arrogance, which can only be surpassed by insolence: They are of the opinion that they can fulfil all harmonic tasks themselves. Recently Countess Dominant went so far as to claim that the three could even accompany Beethoven's Ninth without difficulty.

When the parallel minor-triads arrived and claimed that they could each substitute for their equivalent basic triads (not always, but in many musical situations), the basic triads started to become very wild. When the minor triads then provided three good examples of their theory, the basic triads were virtually having heart-attacks. Play the three examples (below) in both versions, then you will know why ...

Examples for Secondary Triads as Parallel Substitute Triads

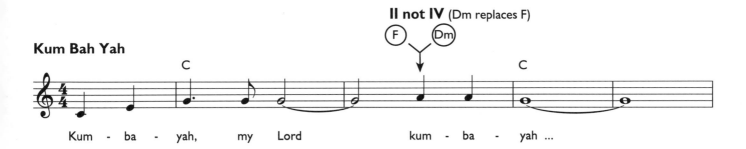

And then the "minor" ladies proved their point further ...

by presenting Rock and Pop songs, which not only sounded better with their help, but which also couldn't be played without it.

As we have already said: The minor-parallels can substitute for "their" basic triads only in certain musical situations and they then show what they can really do! However, the same is true in reverse: The basic triads are absolutely unable to master many musical situations and have to depend on their minor parallels. After the songs you can find a few exercises which sound really good and which are a part of the crucial evidence.

Pop and Rock songs playable with chords from Degrees I – IV – V and VI

1. Sailing (Rod Stewart)
2. Proud Mary (Tina Turner)
3. Candle In The Wind (Elton John)
4. Let It Be (The Beatles)
5. Country Roads (John Denver)
6. Ev'ry Breath You Take (Police)
7. Sounds of Silence (Simon & Garfunkel)

Pop and Rock songs playable with chords from Degrees I – IV – V (VI) and II

1. The Boxer (Simon & Garfunkel)
2. One More Night (Phil Collins)
3. Jump (Van Halen)
4. Islands In The Stream (Kenny Rogers)
5. Ev'rytime You Go Away (Paul Young)
6. Lucille (Kenny Rogers)
7. El Condor Pasa (Simon & Garfunkel)

Pop and Rock Songs playable with Chords from Degrees I – IV – V (VI – II) and III

1. In The Ghetto (Elvis Presley)
2. It's A Heartache (Bonnie Tyler)
3. Suzanne (Leonard Cohen)
4. A Whiter Shade of Pale (Procul Harum)
5. Morning Has Broken (Cat Stevens)
6. Puff The Magic Dragon (Peter, Paul and Mary)
7. Homeward Bound (Simon & Garfunkel)

Typical Rock and Pop Chord-Successions with Basic and Secondary Triads

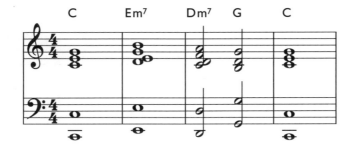

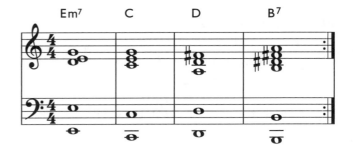

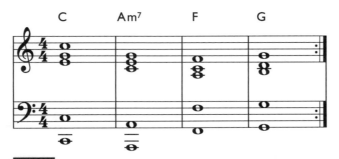

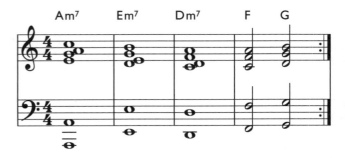

4.6 COUNTER – TRIADS

Mysterious counter-attacks

Up to now the basic triads have kept an eye on the minor thirds deeper down in their minor parallels since they cast some doubt on part of their supposed tasks. What they have forgotten to do, is to keep a look-out for what lurks behind the next major third higher up: lying in wait for the basic triads here, is a counter-triad, which has only one thing on its mind: to take over part of the tasks assumed by the basic triads. What is strange is that two counter-triads are at the same time the minor parallels of other degrees ... strange strange.

The counter-triads of basic triads are a major third above the basic triad

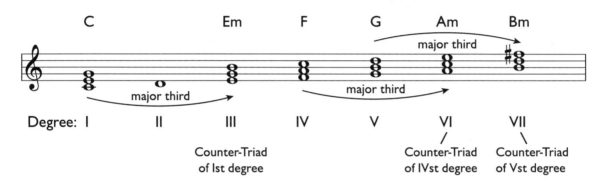

The basic triads – their minor parallels and counter-triads

The Harmonic Function of the Counter Triad

Even these are chords with a substitute-function—in certain musical situations they can substitute for "their" basic triads. Which chord is chosen depends on the respective melody note, which should as a rule be a chordal note. Exception: Passing notes (p. 189) and suspensions (p. 190).

Make note of this in the following:

Counter-Triads in practice

1. Substitution of I by III: The melody of "Help me now" consists almost entirely of E's. In the C-major family there are three chords which contain an E: C (third), Am (fifth), Em (keynote). We have played around with these three possibilities in the 4 suggestions for accompaniment: 1. Harmonisation only with major triads; C sounds a little bit suspect in bars 3-7 but it's not too bad. 2. Instead of C (1) use the minor parallel Am (VI). Up to bar three this doesn't sound too good, but thereafter it's okay! 3. Instead of C we take the counter triad Em (III) – not bad at all! 4. This is how it sounds the best and that's how John and Paul might have arranged it ...

Help me now

1. C (I)			F	C
2. Am (VI)			F	Am
3. Em (III)			F	Em
4. C (I)	Em (III)	Am (VI)	F	C

2. Substitution of IV by VI: The Am in "Don't kick me" looks like the minor parallel of C (I), but it's the counter-triad of F (IV). You could – in an emergency – use the F here; but it's impossible to keep playing C.

Don't kick me

3. Substitution of V by VII: Of course you could play the basic triad G (V) instead of the counter triad Bm (VI I) in the song "Before today" but it sounds – Yuck!

Before today

4.7 THE DIMINISHED TRIAD

Cousin with diminished responsibility

In the royal hierarchy the basic and secondary triads occupy the degrees I to VI; what is missing is the triad on the VIIth degree – the diminished triad. It is the black sheep of the family, somehow it doesn't fit into the system and is viewed as being an inferior relation by the arrogant wenches on degrees I to VI. This is perhaps due to the fact that it is much less used for harmonic functions. Here is the position it occupies in the system of scalar chords in the key of C-major.

Position of the Diminished Triad

Chordsymbol	C	Dm	Em	F	G	Am	Bm^{-5}	
C major Scale	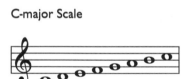							
Degree	I	II	III	IV	V	VI	VII	
Function	Tonic	m. Parallel IVth degree	m. Parallel Vth degree	Sub-dominant	Dominant	S. Parallel Ist degree	Chord on leading note	

The Leading-note Triad

Leading notes are notes which are a semitone above or below and which "lead to" a final note. The most important leading note in a scale is the leading note to the keynote – in C-major the B. Play the C-major scale and finish by playing B: Here you will notice a musical tension which somehow cries out "Play C!"
Bm^{-5} has the same effect. In a succession of chords it has a strong tendency towards the tonic C – because of the leading note. Therefore Bm^{-5} has a similar effect to the dominant – which is no wonder since Bm^{-5} has the same notes as a G^7 chord with the exception of the keynote.

C-major Scale

Example

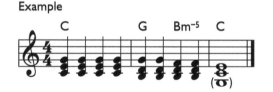

Bm^{-5} = G^7 without keynote

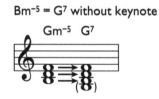

Semi and fully diminished chords

Practically Bm^{-5} is normally played as seventh chord Bm$^{7/-5}$ (with the minor seventh of its own B-major scale = A). For some stupid reason we refer to Bm$^{7/-5}$ as "semi-diminished". If you diminish the minor 7 (A) by another semitone to A♭, the chord is referred to as being fully diminished and is called B° (B zero). B° has an even more dominant effect because it not only contains the leading note (B) to the keynote C – the tonic in C-major, but also the leading note (A♭) to the fifth G in the chord C-major.

B-major Scale

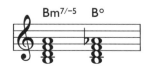

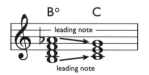

4.8 MEDIANTS – VARIANTS – SHIFTS

Shifty characters moving in various circles

In the royal court of Harmonia there are a few pitiful characters who aren't really noticed by anyone, but who provide colour and variety. We like these little whipper-snappers who lead their pitiful existence in the shadow of the greater personages and carry out their respectable work. We are now going to present them to you, one after the other, in the great stateroom. The folding doors open, the Stateroom attendant calls for attention ...

Mediants

Mediants are related chords which contain a major third above or below the initial chord. If the initial chord is a major chord the mediants are also major chords. Mediants are only formed on the degrees I, IV and V.

Example

Fancy that!

Variants

If you transform a major into a minor chord (or vice-versa) you create a variant. They are used to make a succession of chords more colourful (Example A). The variant of the IVth degree is often used to make the lead back to the tonic more emphatic (Example B). Many like to play a minor tonic at the end of a succession of chords as major variant (Example C).

Example

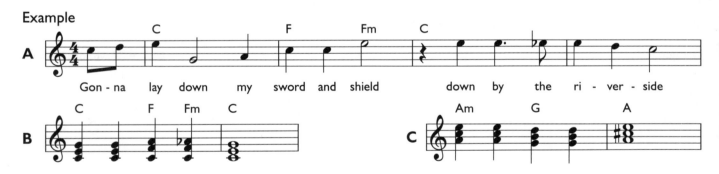

Chord Shifts

Here a chord is shifted by a semitone or a wholetone between two degrees to bridge the gap. This can sound good as an upbeat (Example A) or when narrow gaps (Example B) or broad gaps (Example C) have to be bridged.

Example

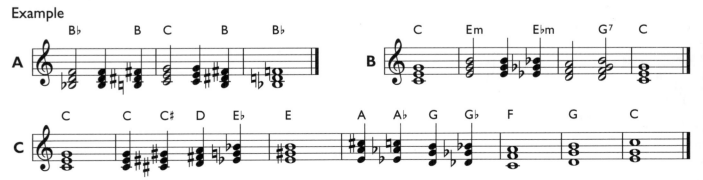

4.9 THE CIRCLE OF FOURTHS AND FIFTHS

Lord Tetrachord reporting

One day the Queen summoned old Lord Tetrachord to the throne.

"I have heard Lord Tetrachord from a member of a royal board that some fifths and also fourths move in strange circles – without remorse!"	Tell me, Lord Tetrachord, could this be true?" "T'is indeed true your Majesty. I'll show you where this place doth be. One of the most secretive places Where circles of fourths and fifths show their faces."

Lord Tetrachord keeps his promise

Tetrachords (p. 72) do not only have the quality of dividing scales into two equal parts; they also order the scales (and the chords derived from them) into "dominant" and "sub-dominant" varieties. Look at the C-major scale in the sharp keys below. It consists of two tetrachords whereby the second tetrachord is, at the same time, the first tetrachord of the G-major scale. The second tetrachord in the G-major scale is, at the same time, the first tetrachord in the scale D-major etc. This functions analogously where the flat keys (below) are concerned.

Let's go back to the second tetrachord in the C-major scale. It starts with G, the fifth note of the C-major scale – the keynote of the dominant. This G is of course the keynote of the chord G-major. Now if G-major were to be the tonic the keynote of the dominant chord would have to be the fifth note in the scale again (this time G-major) which is D. This D is again the dominant of G etc. This works in exactly the same way with the flat keys – but in the direction of the sub-dominants. Here is a summary for you ...

How sharp keys originate

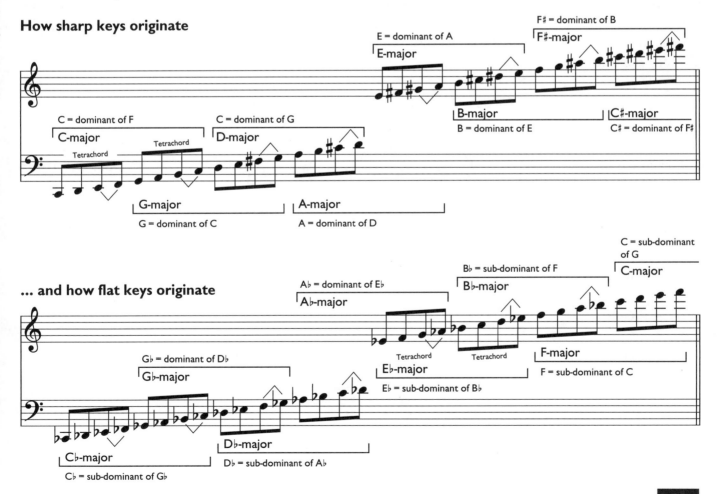

... and how flat keys originate

The Circles of Fifths and Fourths

The Circle of Fourths comes into being ...

... if you form further sharp keys using tetrachords beyond F-major up to B♯ major (enharmonically interpreted = C) and then bend them into a circle.

The Circle of Fifths comes into being ...

... if you form further flat keys using tetrachords beyond C♭-major up to D double flat (enharmonically interpreted as C) and then bend them into a circle.

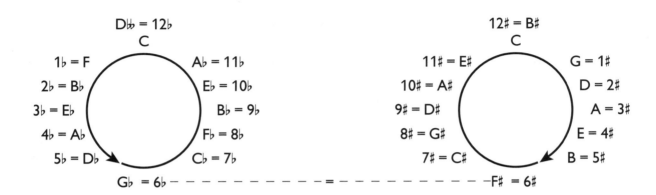

So that you don't have to handle more than six sharps or flats, you cut the flats at G♭ and the sharps at F♯ and let the circle of fifths run into the circle of fourths (and vice versa). F♯ therefore is enharmonically interpreted as G♭.

The circle tells you in all keys who is whose dominant, sub-dominant or minor-parallel. For example rotating from the right: G is the dominant of C. If G is the tonic, the dominant is D etc. Or rotating from the left: F is the sub-dominant of C. If F is the tonic, the sub-dominant is B♭ etc. In addition to this you can determine the dominant, sub-dominant and minor-parallel at any desired position. For example: If A is the tonic, the dominant E is one station further clockwise. One station further anti-clockwise is the sub-dominant D. Directly opposite are the minor parallels.

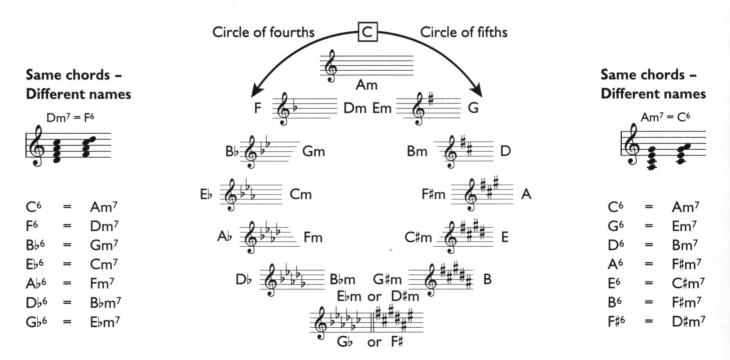

Rule: any Major chord has the same notes as the minor seventh chord a minor third below.

The C-major Family Tree

Now Queen Tonic found the mysterious circle of fifths and rapidly realized that it was more or less her distant relations who were in the circle. She instructed her court scribe to prepare a family-tree – and here it is! Voila!

Everything we have learned up to now concerning the royal relationships is entered in this family-tree. The dominants and sub-dominants from the sidelines are listed, according to their rank as dominants or sub-dominants of 1st, 2nd, 3rd or 4th degree. When you are playing with the C-major household you should try to keep a mental note of the chord family-tree.

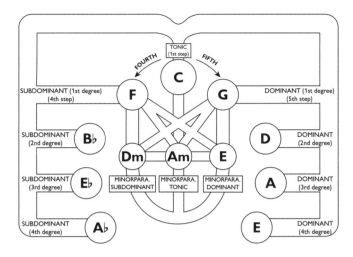

The family-trees for all other keys can be found at the back of the book in the magical keyboard tables. Here you have to imagine that you turn the circles of fifths until the tonic of the desired key is at the top. All relationships between the chords themselves remain the same.

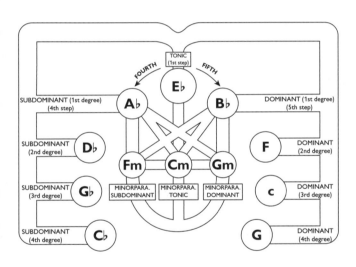

Don't be afraid of Eb-major and other black-keyed chord families

Some keyboard players are horrified by black keys – this isn't necessary. On pages 33 to 35 we have described how to come to grips with them!

Transposing

"Transposing" means transforming a melody or succession of chords from one key to the other. In the process only the key is changed. All other relationships between the chords themselves remain the same. The chord family-tree is well suited to transposing (the circle of fifths is behind this!).
Here is an example:

Assuming that a song is written in the key of Eb-major and you want to play it in C (because it might be easier or you can´t sing that high) – you have to transpose each chord from Eb to C according to their various functions.
Assuming the succession of chords in Eb is

$$Eb – Cm – F – Bb7 – Eb$$

You say: Eb is the tonic in Eb-major, C is the tonic in C – so play C instead of Eb. Cm is the minor parallel of the tonic in Eb-major – so in C-major I should play the minor parallel of C – Am etc. The new succession of chords is then as follows

$$C – Am – D – G^7 – C$$

More on this subject on p. 50/51.

Dominant and Subominant Chains

Keyboard players of the world unite, you have nothing more to loose than your **Dominant Chains!**

Whenever musicians see even the smallest chance, they jump from a chord to the dominant or sub-dominant of some degree or another and then return, mostly to the tonic, step by step via these chains. Here we go ...

Examples of Dominant and Sub-dominant Chains

At the end of the "Swanee River" the chain runs via the dominant of the second degree (also known as dominant of the dominant) to the normal dominant of the first degree.

Here is an example of where the music jumps – with a loud cry of Aaaah – no sorry – Beeee! – to the sub-dominant of the second degree and leads to the tonic via the normal sub-dominant of the first

Swanee River *(Traditional)*

Way down up on the Swa - nee ri - ver,

far   far   a - way.

Bee-jump

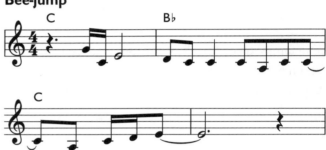

The next number is a real oldie but also filled to the brim with dominants. From the tonic the song jumps to the 5th dominant (see circle of fourths on p. 92 since we haven't listed the fifth dominant in the family-tree because it's so rare). From here it goes downstairs until it reaches the tonic. A prime example of a dominant chain!

Mr. Stoneman

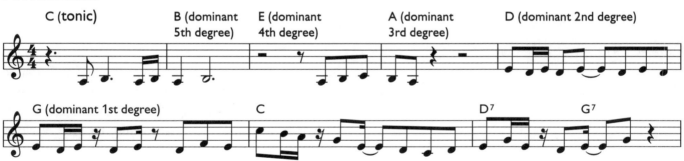

In the small piece which follows we will present a famous succession of chords which you will recognize as being from the song "Hey Joe" by Jimi Hendrix (it also appears in loads of other songs too): Tonic-jump to the sub-dominant of the fourth degree – then step by step (or degree by degree) back to the tonic.

Hey Joe – Succession of Chrods

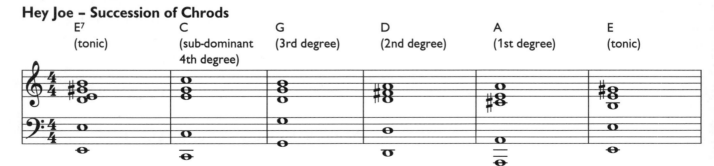

4.10 MINOR

It's all a question of minor differences

Yes, we have to admit these differences. The chapter is coming to an end and we can't keep it a secret any longer. Now that the major part of the section has been dealt with, we must, although we hate trivial, minor points, tell you where these minor differences have their roots. Now in the country of harmonia, there is a second royal castle. Even in this royal household there is a Queen Tonic, a Countess Dominant and a Baroness Sub-dominant, in fact it is **almost** a mirror image of the Major Royal-Household. There are Major Parallels on degrees III, VI and VII and they are a minor third over their basic triads etc. Oh well, have a look at it yourself.

Scalar Chords and their functions in A-minor

Harmonic minor	Am	Bm⁻⁵ (B°)	C⁺⁵	Dm	E	F	Gm⁻⁵ (G°)
Natural minor	Am	Bm⁻⁵ (B°)	C	Dm	Em	F	G

Degree		I	II	III	IV	V	VI	VII
Basic Triad		Tonic		Maj. Par. of tonic	Sub-dominant	Dominant	Maj. Par. of Sub-dom.	Maj. Par. of Dominant
Secondary Triad			Counter Triad of Sub-dominant	Counter Triad of Dominant			Counter Triad of Tonic	

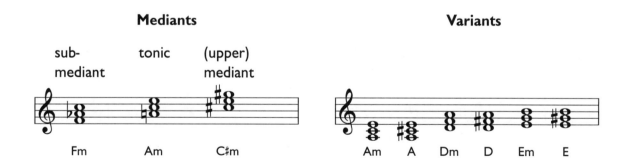

Mediants			Variants					
sub-mediant	tonic	(upper) mediant						
Fm	Am	C♯m	Am	A	Dm	D	Em	E

Songs in Minor Keys

If you look at a list of Rock-, Pop-, Country-, Blues-, Salsa- or Reggae-Hits you will see that many more of them are written in major than in the somewhat sorry-sounding minor key. Why is this so? Well think of the successful Pop-musician - laying the whole day beside his gold-plated swimming-pool with diamonds in the palm trees bordering his Caribbean villa, being served drinks by scantily-clad native girls – it's a hard hard life – and the music he writes is, of course, going to sound hard too – hence the major ... but here are a few songs in the minor key.

1. Message In A Bottle (Police)
2. I Shot The Sheriff (Bob Marley)
3. Hotel California (Eagles)
4. Eleanor Rigby (Beatles)
5. Stayin' Alive (Bee Gees)
6. Killing Me Softly (Roberta Flack)
7. Sound Of Silence (Simon & Garfunkel)
8. You're So Vain (Carly Simon)
9. Play With Fire (Rolling Stones)
10. Dreadlock Holiday (Ten C.C.)

Most Hip-Hop, Techno and Dancefloor-Songs are in minor keys.

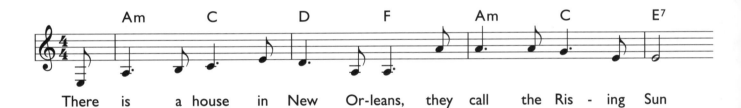

Examples of how you can employ minor chords

4.11 SUBSTITUTION

Temporary jobs in the royal household

We can no longer hold our tongues over certain scandalous conditions in the royal court of Harmonia – to be concrete we mean the laziness of Countess Dominant, which is only ever outdone by her unwillingness to work. While the other ladies of the court worthily and gallantly fulfil their hard, harmonic tasks, Countess Dominant more than willingly allows substitute chords to represent her. There are two poor individuals in particular, who are often called upon by the Countess to relieve her burden.

Substitution of the Vth Degree by the IInd Degree

It is already clear that the minor parallel – the IInd degree – can substitute for the sub-dominant (IV) but what is really amazing is that the dominant (V) now and again also uses the IInd degree as a substitute – anyway, it works in practice and is often used.

As a rule the dominant is not completely substituted. If it should be used to play two bars it usually allows the substitute to deal with the first and then steps in to play the second itself. Here are two simple examples.

He's got the whole world in his hands

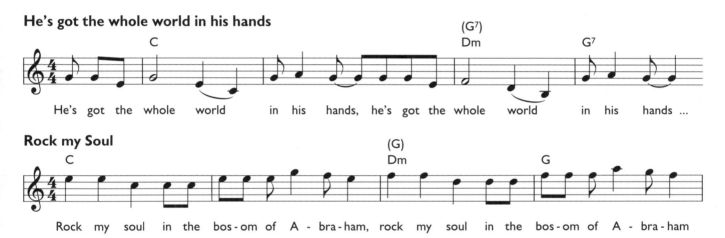

Tritone Substitution

Tritone is another expression for the augmented fourth. Reason: the augmented fourth consists of 3 whole-tone-steps. In certain harmonic situations (try them out!) you can substitute the dominant-**seventh**-chord in a key (here G^7) with the seventh chord, which is based on the augmented fourth of the same scale (here $C\#^7$). This works because the most important intervals for the sound of G^7 (third and seventh) are also chordal notes in C^7. For you, as a connoisseur of triad notes you will be able to remember the rule much better if you make a note of C^7 enharmonically, newly interpreted as $D\flat^7$, since $D\flat$ is the diminished fifth in G-maj. It often sounds better if you don't completely substitute the dominant. Instead you should play the dominant for half the number of usual counts and then switch to the substitute chord – listen for yourself.

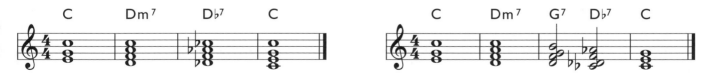

4.12 MODULATION

New robes for the Queen

If Queen Tonic and her court are fed up to the back teeth of always playing the same old-hat pieces in C-major the musical chamber-maids are summoned to "modulate the robes", modulate, of course, being nothing more than a stilted expression for "alter". The chamber-maids then bring in the new robes (= notes), and the Queen, along with everyone else in the court, steps into a new key. The change in key progresses according to a certain ceremony which is known as modulation. As time has gone by, various modulation rituals have become widespread and we want to tell you about them now. In our example we are using the key of C-major as **departure key** or initial key. The new key is known as the **arrival key or final key**. So that you really believe that you have arrived at the new tonic it is reinforced with the dominant or sub-dominant of that new key. Abbreviation: B. And now: Modulate well, kind reader!

Modulation by Shifting (i.–e. C → E♭)

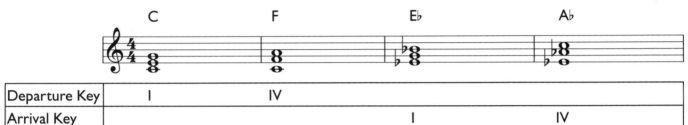

	C	F	E♭	A♭
Departure Key	I	IV		
Arrival Key			I	IV

Modulation through Jump to new Dominant via Circle of Fifths (i.–e. C → E)

	C	B⁷	E	B	E
Departure Key	I	Dominant 5th degree			
Arrival key		V⁷	I	B:V	I

Modulation through Jump to new Dominant with an added IInd Degree (i.–e. C – A)

	C	Bm⁷	E⁷	A	D	A
Departure Key	I	VIIm⁷				
Arrival key		II	V⁷	I	B:IV	I

Modulation through Jump to new Dominant via the Circle of Fifths (i.e. C → D♭)

	C	E♭	A♭⁷	D♭	G♭	D♭
Departure Key	I	Sub-dom. 3rd degree				
Arrival key		Dominant 2nd degree	V⁷	I	B:IV	I

Modulation via the Upper-Mediant of the Departure Key (i.e. C → D)

Departure Key	I	Upper-med.	VI				
Arrival key				IV	V	I	B:V	I

Modulation via the Variant of the VIth Degree (i.e. C → D)

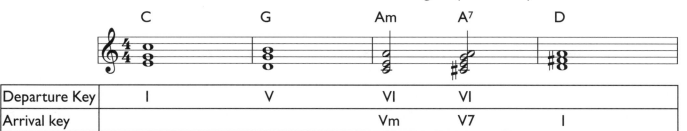

Departure Key	I	V	VI	VI	
Arrival key			Vm	V7	I

Modulation via the VIIth Degree of the Arrival Key (Diminished Chord) (i.e. C → G)

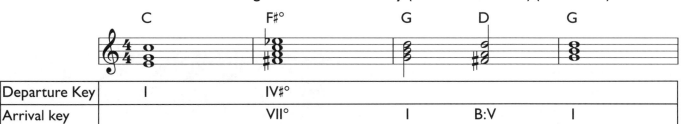

Departure Key	I	IV#°			
Arrival key		VII°	I	B:V	I

Modulation via the Enharmonic (i.e. Cm → C#m)

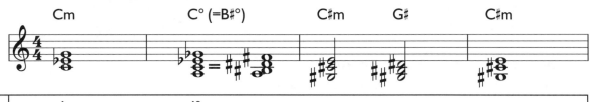

Departure Key	I	I°			
Arrival key		VII°	I	B:V	I

Modulation via the "Neapolitan" (IVth degree in Minor with Minor Sixth = –6 = +5) (e.g. C – Bm)

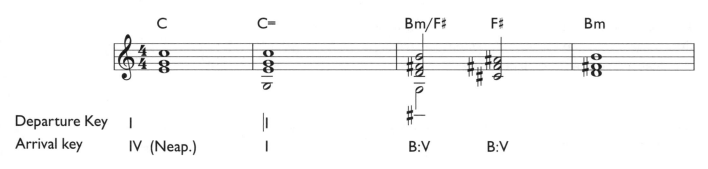

Departure Key	I	II			
Arrival key	IV (Neap.)	I		B:V	B:V	

5 RHYTHMS

From Rock to Pop – Reggae to Alka Salsa

5.1 THE BASS

Fishing for bass in piano bay

In this chapter we are at first going to show you the individual elements of playing rhythms on keyboards and the we are going to piece it all together. It would be better if you had already dealt with sections on chords (without notes from page 12, and with from page 68) and the section on harmonies (from page 46), since we assume you know all about these in this chapter. If you have a synthesizer or an electric organ, it is best to select piano or an Electric Piano sound and – in case you have an automatic rhythm-function – select a Rock-rhythm or an 8- or 16-beat rhythm.

There is one very important element for Rock-Pop-Keyboard-Rhythms and that is the Bass. The starting point for a powerful bass is ...

The Bass-Octave-Chord

Basically what happens here is that the Keynotes are played double in octaves in the bass region; this produces a fuller, more gutty sound. On the right you can see how this is done; we have already talked about this chord in detail on page 24. The advantage of this way of playing: The index finger practically hovers above the fifth of the chord waiting to play it at any time; the fifth having an important function as alternating bass.

Exercises with the Bass Octave Chord:
Here are a few simple variations of the bass octave chord which you need practically all of the time.

Exercise 1 shows you how the octaves are played as chords. It's best if you "freeze" your thumb and index finger in the octave position. A good exercise to prepare with: Play scales in octaves.

Exercise 2 shows that you can sometimes bring a little variety into the rather stiff system by striking the deeper and then the higher note.

Exercise 3 is a rhythmic variation of exercise 2 and almost sounds "funky".

In **Exercise 4** we are showing you a schematic Keynote-fifth-alternating bass.

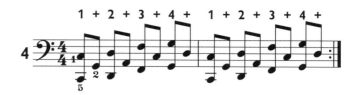

5.2 STRIKE PATTERNS

Strike rules for rhythmic unions

It is not only the bass which functions in a largely schematic form during simple rhythm play: The rhythmic tasks of both hands can be standardised into **Rhythm-Patterns**. The principle is simple. You practise a Rhythm-Pattern using one chord and you then transfer it systematically to all other chords. This works because the strike pattern provides you with all the information you need: Firstly, on which counts you play, and secondly, which fingering you should use. The rest is relatively simple: You just stick to your "Count-fingering Pattern", irrespective of the chord you are playing.

Most of the time the left hand strikes the key note of each chord in the bass octave chord. The right hand normally adheres to its fingering, regardless of wether the chord is played with a closed, a mixed or a broken action (p. 13). If certain notes are sometimes not easy to play using the suggested fingering, you break the rigid rules using the following finger-substitution rule: Instead of finger 2 use finger 3 (or vice-versa), instead of finger 3 use finger 4 (or vice-versa), instead of finger 4 use finger 5 (or vice-versa). The remaining fingers adhere to the fingering patterns provided. if you want to incorporate **additional** notes into a closed action (sixths, sevenths, ninths etc.) so that your chords sound harmonically richer, you have to change the fingering accordingly ... but you must stick to the count-pattern.

Rock-Pop Keyboarders play mostly using so-called lead-sheets – these are sheets upon which information is written using chord symbols as to which harmonies are to be played on certain bars (or parts of bars). It is then up to the keyboarder whether he plays the primary form of a chord or an inversion. Here is an example:

Playing with Rhythm Patterns and Chord Symbols

Using this pattern ...

and these chords on the "Lead Sheet" ...

... you proceed as follows: keep the fingering for the left and right hands and play the notes of the different chords. It is irrelevant if you choose to play the primary form of the chords or one of the inversions. One possible version of the pattern could look like this.

Fingering right ⟶

Counts ⟶

Fingering left ⟶

5.3 SIMPLE RHYTHMS

It's simply really easy

Now we are going to show you how simple rhythms are created; many of which you will hear constantly in hit records. Even though they are easy to learn and simple to play, they sound really good. In the summarizing diagram below are the common note values, both above and below the count bar. The note values above the count bar are for any chord of your choice which you play with the right hand. The values below the bar are for the left hand, which plays the keynote of the right-hand chord in a bass octave chord. You can play the exercises straight away, using a chord or you can practise on the table or on your thigh. The advantage of the knocking-method: You can practise rhythms, whenever and wherever you want.

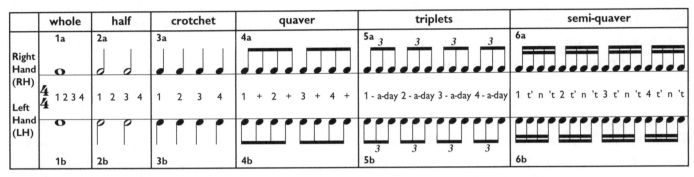

	whole	half	crotchet	quaver	triplets	semi-quaver
Right Hand (RH)	1a	2a	3a	4a	5a	6a
4/4	1 2 3 4	1 2 3 4	1 2 3 4	1 + 2 + 3 + 4 +	1 - a-day 2 - a-day 3 - a-day 4 - a-day	1 t' n 't 2 t' n 't 3 t' n 't 4 t' n 't
Left Hand (LH)	1b	2b	3b	4b	5b	6b

Identical note values left and right

If, for example, you play 3a right, 3b left or 4a right, 4b left, you are left with trite patterns like these:

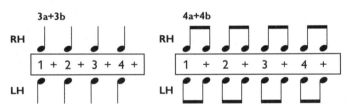

They aren't really overpowering but are useful in some playing situations.

Take a break!

It is often the case that what you don't play counts more than what you do. If we substitute some strikes for pauses in the patterns above they become more interesting. Try it out and play the pattern using a succession of chords.

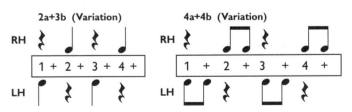

Differing Values left

You can mix the right-hand patterns in the "a-series" with any patterns from the "b-series": (apart from the triplets – you should only mix them with whole, half or crotchet notes!!). In this way you are left with, for example:

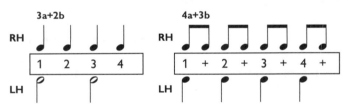

With pauses ...

... you can vary these good-sounding patterns further.

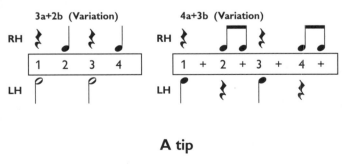

A tip

In the same way you can invent your own accompaniment patterns. More about this on p. 104

You can use these simple rhythms in Rock and Pop in many ways. They do, however, only really begin to sound very interesting through the use of 3 rhythmic style variations which we are now going to introduce to you using a 4/4 bar in quaver feeling.

Accentuation

1. Accentuation of the Main counts 1-2-3-4

You can accentuate the beats in "European Feeling". 1 – very strong, 3 – strong, 2 and 4 weak, or in "Afro-American Feeling": 2 and 4 strong, 1 and 3 weak.

2. Accentuation of the Sub-Counts (+)

This rough structure, which is related to the whole bar can be extended to every quaver group of a quarter. You can accentuate the first quaver (on the beat) or the second quaver (off the beat).

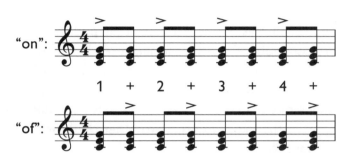

The Syncope

The syncope is a shifting of the accentuation, where a (normally) non-accentuated beat becomes an accentuated beat—not by strengthening or weakening the strike but by shifting the note values. In Pop and Rock it is normally a simple form of syncopation which is chosen – this is usually known as "pushing beat". To do this you play any note from the main count a quaver earlier and bind the note onto the main count note without striking it (a). Particularly popular. the drawn forward first beat (b). This technique produces a driving rhythm, expecially when used often (c). Syncopes are the rolling part of Rock 'n' Roll.

The Shuffle

A relaxed, rocking rhythm which originates from the triplet feeling. When playing triplets you don't play 2 notes to a crotchet but 3 (a). A triplet becomes a shuffle, if the first two notes of the triplet melt into one long note and the third note is shortened (b) or if the second note is replaced by a rest (c). Both shuffle-shades are also called "broad-shuffles". The shuffle is often notated in simplified form as being dotted ♪. ♩ this is wrong – a group which consists of 1 note with a value of 3/16 and one of 1/16 – also called "tight shuffle" (d).

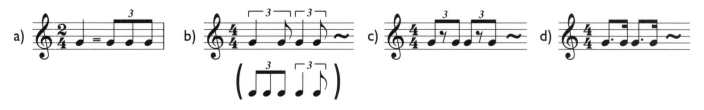

5.4 FEELING

Tootling with sentiments

"Feeling" is one of the many rubber words in the musician's language. Whatever else it might be used to describe, its most important meaning is the most important aspect of music – having the "right" feeling whilst playing and producing the same "right" feeling for the person listening. You can ruin the best Pop song or the hottest Rock number if you don't play with the right feeling. Such records shouldn't be put to one side, they should be thrown out of the window with all might!
Here are a few basic terms to the theme of "feeling" ...

Triplet, quaver and semi-quaver-feeling

First of all, this means that you really play the respective note values, more important, however, is that you are conscious of the basic-feeling, even if you are playing other note values. You have to learn to swing along inside to the "feeling" concerned. You can assist this externally by tapping the note values of the "feeling" with your foot. Do a few tests. Play the following rhythms about four bars long as notated; then you should only strike the crotchets with your left but whilst doing so continue to count and tap the rhythm of the feeling. Do the same with the two other rhythms. You can feel and hear: Crotchets "somehow" sound different in every "feeling".

Quaver-feeling

Triplet-feeling

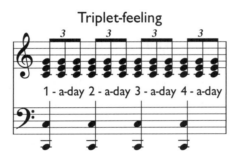

Semi-quaver feeling

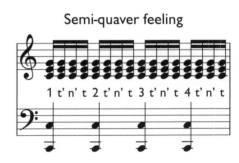

Using the quaver feeling as an example we are now going to show you three steps, how you can get a feeling for feeling. Do the same in triplet and semi-quaver feeling.

1. Left or right equal

At first we divide the eight strikes of a quaver pattern equally between the two hands. Play the pattern for a few bars, using, for example, the succession of chords C-Am-F-G7. Try and find further regular strike patterns like this for yourself.

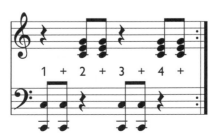

2. Left or right optionally

Strike either left or right. This time however, in any sequence. Try various possibilities out until you find a combination which pleases you. Play your new strike pattern with a succession of chords. That could look like this.

3. Left crotchet, right optional

You should now play a crotchet action with the left hand. You strike with the right on any desired count, even if the left hand strikes too. Try to create a regular strike pattern – that could look like this.

Then another Elton John tear-jerker flows from the radio ...

Candle in the Wind ... Nikita ... Your Song ... Daniel ... Cold as Christmas ... all great music! You are counting along: 1-2-3-4 and you hear how the snare drum "cracks" on every third note. Hmmm ... you think, shouldn't Elton be playing in 4/4 time in "European feeling", accentuating the 1st and 3rd and not in "Afro-American", with accentuation on the 2nd and 4th beats? Is there something wrong with his feeling? No, no – there's nothing wrong with Elton's feeling and in all his ballads he has accentuated the 2nd and the 4th beats – it's just that you have counted wrongly, namely in "normal" 4/4 feeling and not in "Half-Time feeling".

Then there are some Rock numbers whereby, when counting along 1-2-3-4, you seem to think that the snare drum beats, which you expect on 2 and 4, can only be heard on the "and" counts. The studio musicians have even played normal rock in this case – in "double-time feeling", however.

Halftime and Doubletime Feeling

"Halftime" and "doubletime" means the "apparent" halving or doubling of the tempo of a certain "Normal time" without changing the metre (i.e. with a metronome or another form of beat aid).

On the right you can see a practical example:
If you set the metronome on 80 beats per minute, 4 beats = 1 bar last approximately 3 seconds. The two bars therefore last 6 second in normal time. In this same period of time you can play 1 bar in "Halftime-feeling" using the same number of metronome beats or 4 bars in "Double time feeling". Please note that in each case there is a different method of counting and consequently the accentuations are shifted.

The metronome beats in *quaver* time.

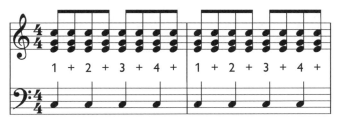

The metronome beats in *crotchet* time.

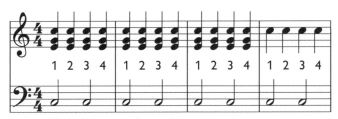

The metronome beats in *semitone* time.

Sit up straight! Bend forwards as if ready to jump! Or lay back and relax!

All seen from a musical point of view of course. The musical "feelings" which we have dealt with up to now are related to the rough structure of a bar; now we want to talk about fine details, about the technique of striking individual notes.

Laid-Back-Feeling and "playing ahead"

You have three possible ways of playing a note: Firstly, exactly as it is notated, exactly on the count, secondly a fraction of a second late – the so-called "laid-back" style; thirdly a fraction of a second too early – then you are "playing ahead" with a somewhat driving, agressive feeling. BE CAREFUL! Before daring to start using professional techniques, you must be able to play exactly to time. And another professional tip: If you play the whole piece "laid back" or if you "play ahead" all of the time, it sounds great. If you play one note so, and another note so, it sounds like beginner's tinkling.

5.5 BASIC RHYTHMS

Something to build on ...

Please shout loudly "COME IN!" If nobody comes in now, you forgot to knock. That is very impolite and we can't accept such a rude attitude. To correct this we have worked out a few tapping exercises for you.
A tip: practise them thoroughly, since they are the basic rhythms for many fields of Pop and Rock music. Most other rhythms can be derived from them.

It's best if you proceed as follows: tap the bass pattern with your left hand and tap the upper pattern with your right, and count out loud while doing this. You can practice this tapping exercise anywhere, anytime (Job, School, Sauna). The tapping exercises are also, at the same time empty schemes for any desired chords or successions of chords (see p. 83). Play any chord you want with the right hand using the given rhythm and play the bass using the bass octave chord!

$\frac{4}{4}$ – **Basic rhythms**

Straight

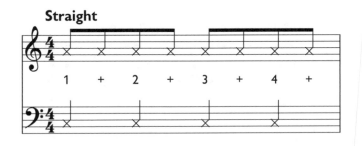

Shuffle (triplet)

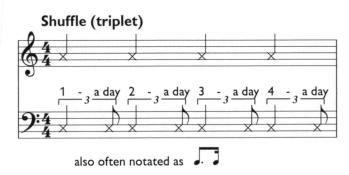

also often notated as

Rock

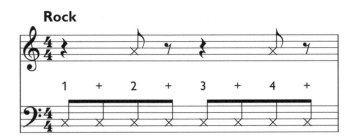

Tight Shuffle

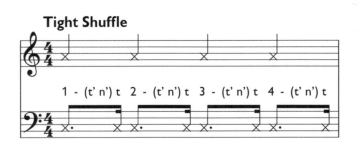

Halftime

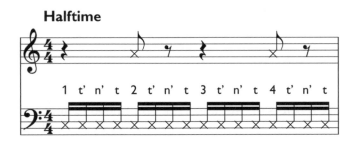

"Halftime" – the basic rhythm for many ballads but also for Disco, Funk. Jazz-Rock and fusion

$\frac{12}{8}$ – Basic rhythms

Rock

1 - a - day 2 - a - day 3 - a - day 4 - a - day

Triplet Feeling

1 - a - day 2 - a - day 3 - a - day 4 - a - day

Shuffle (triplet)

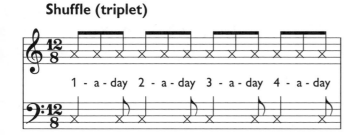

1 - a - day 2 - a - day 3 - a - day 4 - a - day

$\frac{3}{4}$ – Basic rhythms

Straight

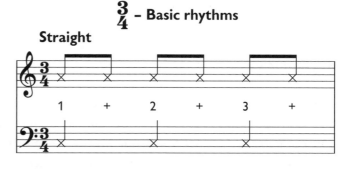

1 + 2 + 3 +

Triplet Feeling

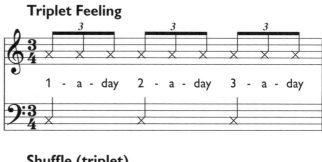

1 - a - day 2 - a - day 3 - a - day

Shuffle (triplet)

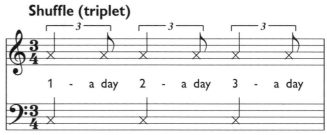

1 - a day 2 - a day 3 - a day

$\frac{6}{4}$ – Basic rhythms

Straight

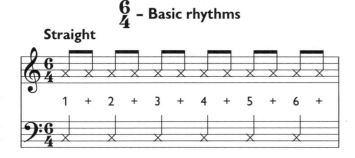

1 + 2 + 3 + 4 + 5 + 6 +

Triplet Feeling

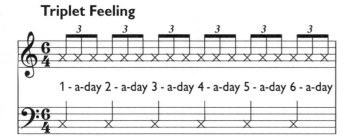

1 - a-day 2 - a-day 3 - a-day 4 - a-day 5 - a-day 6 - a-day

Shuffle (triplet)

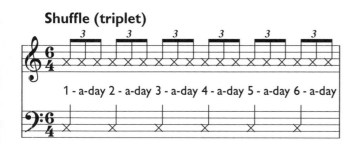

1 - a-day 2 - a-day 3 - a-day 4 - a-day 5 - a-day 6 - a-day

$\frac{6}{8}$ – Basic rhythms

Straight

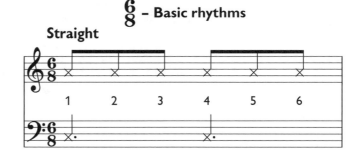

1 2 3 4 5 6

Triplet Feeling

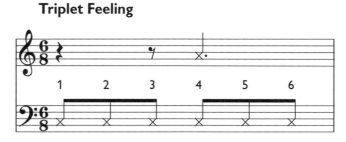

1 2 3 4 5 6

Shuffle (triplet)

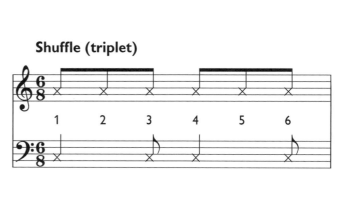

1 2 3 4 5 6

5.6 STANDARD POP RHYTHMS

Rhythm joker

The standard rhythms on both of these pages are rhythmic jokers, which you can find in almost all styles of Pop and Rock music and which you can use at will. Solid craftsmen understand and do their own jobs best; you can't expect specialist work from them. You can emphasize all of these rhythms on the second or the fourth or on the first and third beats. Thus practically giving you double the number of rhythms.

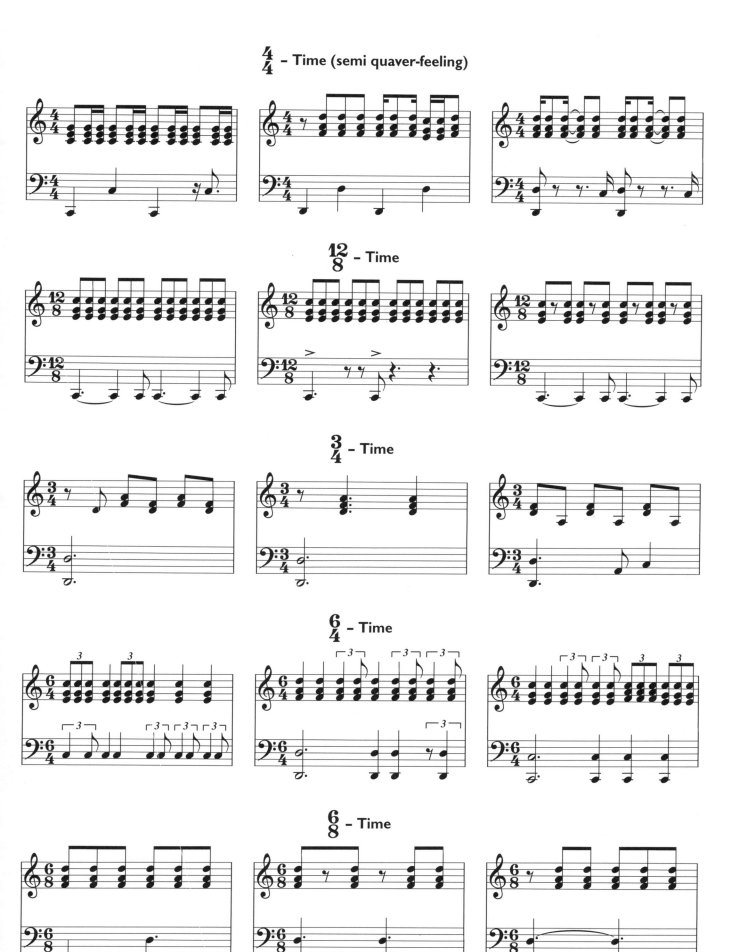

5.7 ARPEGGIOS

One after the other

"Arpeggio" comes from the Italian "arpa" = Harp and means: to play in a broken action as with a harp, one note after the other. The broken action is opposed to the closed action, where all notes of the chord are struck at the same time. A mixture of both actions is the "mixed action" (see also p. 13). Here are some patterns, which can especially be used for ballads in all styles ...

$\frac{4}{4}$ – Strike pattern

$\frac{12}{8}$ – Strike pattern

$\frac{3}{4}$ – Strike pattern

$\frac{6}{8}$ – Strike pattern

5.8 ROCK

People in glasshouses shouldn't throw ROCKS

Rock – Boogie

Halftime – Feeling

Shuffle – Rock

$\frac{6}{8}$ – and $\frac{12}{8}$ – Rock ballads

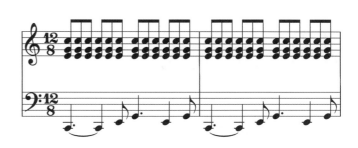

5.9 BALLADS

Musical softies

5.10 COUNTRY-POP

A taste of the beautiful country(side)

Nashville – Feeling

Bluegrass – Feeling

Cajun – Feeling

Memphis – Feeling

5.11 Reggae

Rhythms which put you amongst the palms

Standard

Double – Time

Halftime (semi-quaver feeling and Shuffle)

5.12 FUNK-DISCO

Funky junk

Halftime – Feeling

Quaver-feeling

5.13 LATIN-JAZZ

No dog-Latin here!

5.14 RHYTHMS FOR DRUMSOUNDS

Microchip eardrum punishment

Today Drum- and Percussionsounds are no longer played only by drumcomputers but also by keyboards, computer sound cards and hardware sequenzers. You can produce complete songs with this stuff. Most of these rhythm knights are programable and this means that you can put together your own rhythm patterns. Anything you can do with this little machine is described in the operating instructions. We show you some one and two bar rhythms, which you can program into your rhythm machine.

Tips for best quantization

Quantization means the division of the bar into parts. All rhythm machines allow different quantizations. For the most rhythms we recommend the 1/16 quantization. This means that the bar is divided into 16 small steps, the smallest note duration is a 16th note. In 4/4 bar there would be exactly 16 16th notes.
A 1/12 quantization divides a 4/4 bar in 12 smallest steps, e.g. 4 times 3 eighth which is the same as 4 eight triplets. The 1/12 quantization is suitable for many slow Blues-songs.

Our examples use the 1/16 quantization for 4/4-rhythms and 1/12 quantization for 12/8 rhythms.

How drum sounds are notated

Easy Rock-Pop-drums loos like this:

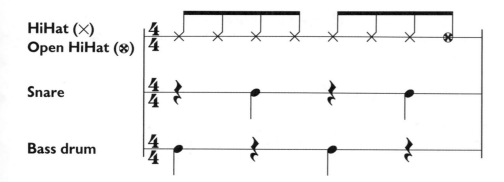

If we use other drum and percussion sounds on the next pages they are indicated through their names.

Rock-Pop-Rhythms $\frac{4}{4}$ – Time

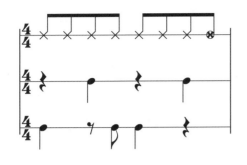
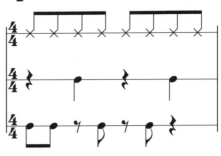

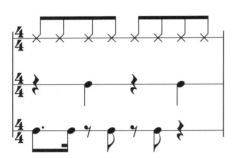
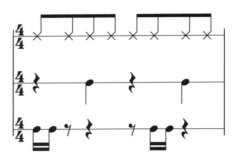

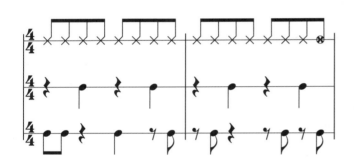
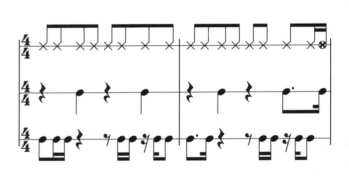

Rock-Pop-Rhythms $\frac{12}{8}$ – Time

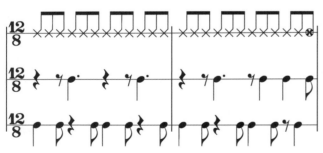

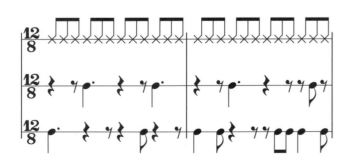
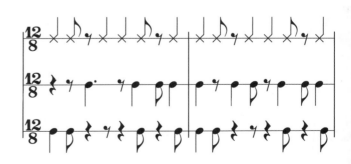

Latin-Rhythms

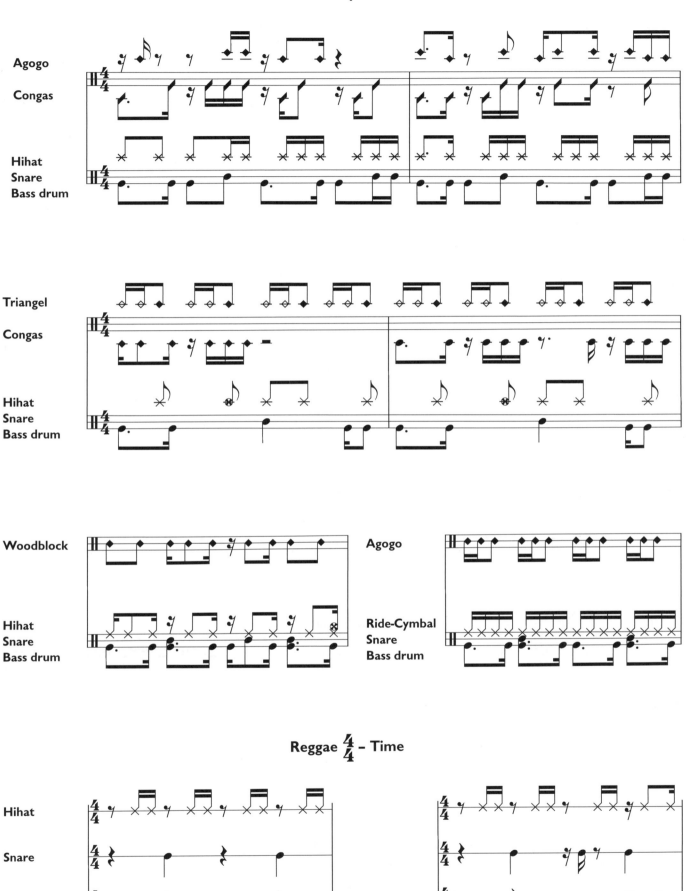

Reggae $\frac{4}{4}$ – Time

Hiphop – Rap

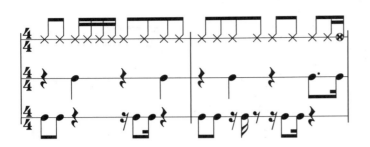
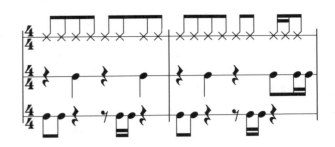

Breakbeats

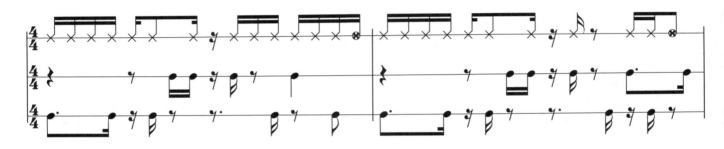

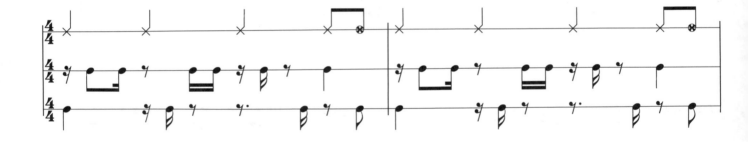

Disco – Dance

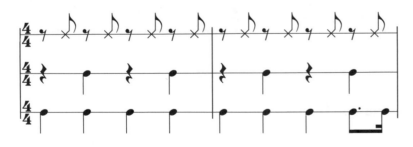
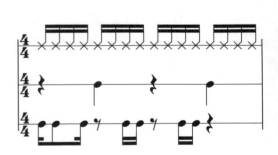

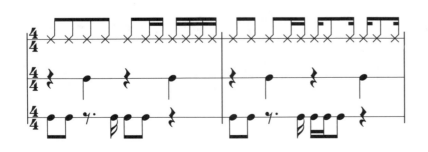
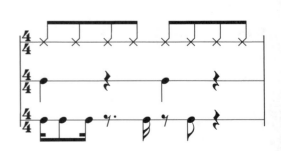

6 IMPROVISATION

About the chances of being hired or fired in Musicland

6.1 IMPROVISATION TECHNIQUES

All about the basic rules in a free democratic society

A path way, trees, a dog on its lead – what happens? The dog walks along the pre-determined pathway from tree to tree, carrying out his daily business; just like musicians who play a pre-determined piece of music from the sheet. If you let the little doggie off the lead, however, it runs about here and there, lingers now and again, does the occasional somersault, runs around in circles ... but it is always certain to find the next tree and continue its business activities; that is Improvisation: By the way, many musicians do business with improvisation.

Improvisation comes from the Italian "improviso" = unexpected and means that you diverge from the prescribed melody or that you artfully play around it. In the following chapter you will find guidance for improvisation in Pop, Rock, Rock-Jazz, Jazz- Rock, Rock-Pop, Funk-Waltzes and Yodel Country-Waltzes. Here are 2 tips ...

1. About the basic rules in a free democratic society

When improvising it's very much like a democracy. You can do what you want, as long as you abide by the laws. When improvising, the laws are dictated by the chords on top of which you want to improvise a melody line. Chords are based on scales (Italian "scala"). Each chord can be placed in **at least one scale** – and often more. These scales contain the notes with which you can relatively freely interpret the chord concerned. A practical example:

We take the succession of chords Cm-F^7-G^7-Cm. The chord Cm is made up of notes from the Cm scale: the keynote C, the third E♭ and the fifth G. We will make a simplified Improvisation scale with the notes C and E♭ and we are going to call it the **"Centigrade Scale"**. Now play the succession of chords with the left hand and improvise freely on top of this using the two notes from our **"Centigrade Scale"**. You can hear that even on F^7 the scale sounds good; Reason: F^7 contains both notes (C as fifth and E♭ as seventh).

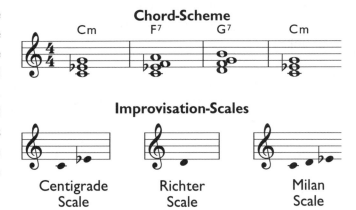

Chord-Scheme

Cm F^7 G^7 Cm

Improvisation-Scales

Centigrade Scale

Richter Scale

Milan Scale

Footnote: When improvising please note that the Richter Scale is open whilst the Milan Scale is closed at the moment.

You will also have heard that the **Centigrade Scale** doesn't sound too hot with G^7. We obviously need a new scale for G^7. We are going to go about this in the easiest way possible and take a D, the fifth of G^7. This single note improvisation scale is called the **"Richter Scale"**.

Now play the chord sequence again and improvise on Cm and F^7 using the Centigrade Scale and on G^7 using the Richter Scale. Result: Sounds good. From this we are able to conclude: Chordal notes can be used as **improvisation notes**. And now we are going to conduct a little experiment: We are going to construct a new improvisation scale using the Centigrade Scale C-Eb and the Richter Scale D, a new scale which contains all three notes C-D-Eb and which is called the **"Milan Scale"**. Now please play the chords again and improvise using the Milan Scale. Now you can hear something very strange: Depending on how you combine the notes the D doesn't sound bad on the Cm and the F^7, although it isn't in either of these chords. On the other hand the C and Eb doesn't sound at all bad on G^7 as long as you play mainly D and you don't linger too long on C's and Eb. And all this even though C and Eb are not chordal notes of G^7! From all this you are able to conclude:

1. Chordal notes always sound good as improvisation notes.

2. Notes from the basic scale from which the chord is derived sometimes sound good, but they have to be introduced with feeling and may only be played for very short periods in some places, as a passing note (p. 189) between two chordal notes or as a suspended note (p. 190).

3. Even non-Chordal and non-scalar notes (such as Eb in G^7) can sometimes sound interesting (you don't always want to eat the same old boring food, you sometimes need a good pizza or a Chinese meal or even truffled Achat-snails aux fines herbes avec pointes d'asperges in a light Beaujolais-Bechemel sauce!).

2. Don't march in uniform step!

If, when improvising, you use rows of notes of the same time value **it tends** to have the effect of a powerful sleeping-tablet on the listener.

Rhythmic variation is normally the order of the day. There are no musical rules of conduct here. How you produce your rhythm is up to you, your taste and your ability.

Here are a few rhythmic phrases using the notes of our Milan Scale. These crop-up in many Rock-Pop improvisations.

6.2 MAJOR AND MINOR SCALES

Will this lead to a major minor catastrophy?

When musicians talk shop about improvisation scales, one hears a lot about pentatonic scales, altered scales, lydian scales or about the advantages of the locrian scale.

It is more than often forgotten that you can improvise extremely well with the normal major and minor scales. We have printed these on the right again for you. There is more about the way they are built up on page 60. All other major and minor scales can be found on page 209-233 in the Magical Keyboard Tables.

Groups such as *Emerson, Lake & Palmer, Procul Harum* or *Focus* spiced up their magnificent Classic Pop using the major scale and natural and melodic minor scales. The harmonic minor scale is often used in Jazz-Rock and Jazz.

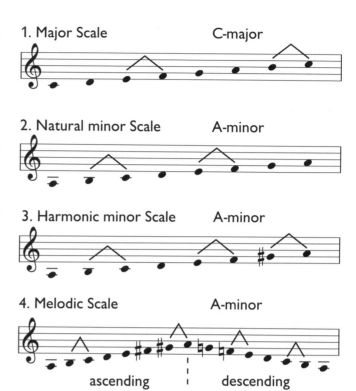

1. Major Scale   C-major

2. Natural minor Scale   A-minor

3. Harmonic minor Scale   A-minor

4. Melodic Scale   A-minor

ascending   descending

The Scales and their Chords

These Scales ...	... suit thes chords
Major Scale	maj, maj^7, maj$^{7/9}$, etc.
Natural-minor	minor, minor^7, minor$^{7/9}$, ^{7}sus^4
Harmonic-minor	minor^{maj7}
Melodic-minor (Seldom used in Rock/Pop)	Ascending: minor^{maj7} Descending: as in natural minor

Here are two harmony-schemes and the suitable major and minor scales. It's best if you start with an improvisation which is centred on chords. Here you play around the basic chords and use the non-chordal scale notes as passing notes (p. 189). After these schemes you will find a few improvisation examples which should encourage you to explore further.

1. **C** C-major Scale   **Am** A-minor Scale (nat.)   **C** C-major Scale   **Am** A-minor Scale (natural)

2.

Improvisation Examples

1. Scheme 1

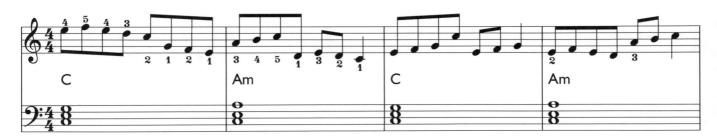

2. Scheme 1

28

3. Scheme 2

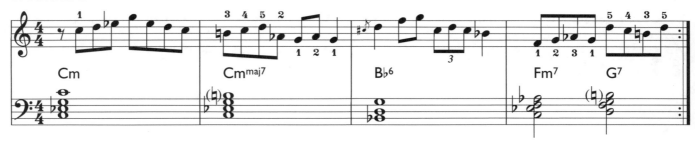

6.3 BLUES SCALES

Exchange of notes with Africa

Probably no one knows how many solos have been played up to now using the Blues-Scale. Uncountable numbers of Pop and Rock songs make use thereof in secret even today. We are now going to show you two most common forms of this scale.

The first form is the minor-pentatonic plus a raised fourth (or a lowered fifth), the famous "Blue-Note". This scale can be used on all three chords within the the Blues-Scheme (almost) without any problems (see p. 139 – Blues-Scheme).

The second form is a considerably extended version of the first. Here there are a large number of passing notes.

Blues-Scale 1

Blues-Scale 2

Tips for improvising

Here we are going to show you the chords with which you can use these scales. They will help you to use these scales correctly, and not only where Blues is concerned.

The scales and their chords

These scales ...	... suit these chords
Scale 1 (minor pentatonic with a tritone as bluenote)	Maj^7, Minor^7 chords Maj^{maj7} on the third.
Scale 1 (extended Blues scale)	all Maj^7 Chords as well as $^{7/9}$, $^{7/-9}$

Here are two chord sequences from Rock and Pop with the relevant scales. Try to improvise by using them on the scheme. If you want, you can strike any rhythm you choose with your left hand (e.g. in crotchet rhythm). The Blues-Scheme is on page 139. It is, by the way, in the same key as the scales which follow this section. Try to improvise using this scheme as well. Blues scales in all keys are contained in the Magical Keyboard Tables from page 209 on.

1.

2.

Improvisation Examples

29

1. Scale 1

30

2. Scale 2

31

3. Scale 2

6.4 Modal Scales

Scaling the church wall

Earlier they were called "ecclesiastical scales", and the monks of the Middle-Ages wrote a few hits with them in their decaying vaults. Today they are called "modal scales" and the scales which were at one time only Dorian to be heard in holy places are now lending Rock and Pop a certain groove!

Modal scales are based on the "natural note series"; it is possible to form a modal scale on every natural note by taking it as the scale-keynote and playing the other notes in scale form from this point – up to the octave of the chosen keynote.

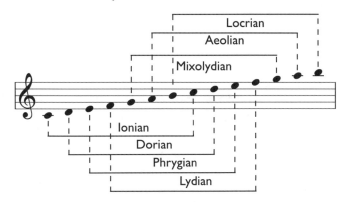

On the right you can see all seven scales for the natural notes upon which the basic and secondary triads (p. 83) of the key C-major are formed (including the diminished chord on B). All modal scales for the other keys are in the Magical Keyboard Tables from page 209 onwards.

Modal Scales

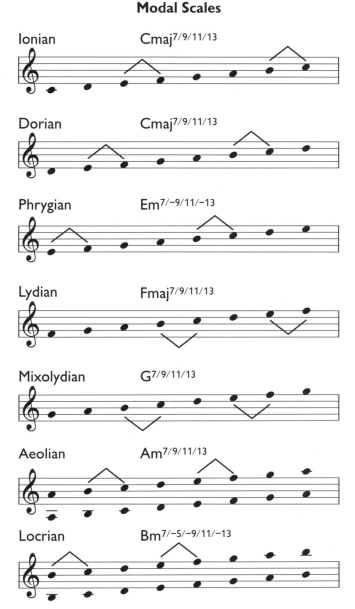

Please note the sequence of the whole and semitone steps in the scales. They remain if you transpose the scale. For example from C-Ionian to C#-Ionian.

The scales and their chords

These scales ...	... suit these chords
Ionian	Maj, Maj^{maj7}, Maj$^{maj7/9}$, Maj$^{maj7/9/11}$ etc.
Dorian	Minor, Minor^7, Minor$^{7/6}$, Minor$^{7/9}$, $^{7/4}$-Hords
Phrygian	Minor$^{7/-9}$
Lydian	Maj^{maj7}, Maj$^{maj7/9}$, Maj$^{maj-7/13}$
Mixolydian	Maj, Maj^7, Maj$^{7/9}$, Maj$^{7/13}$, Maj^{11}
Aeolian = natural minor	Minor, Minor^7, Minor$^{7/10}$, ^{7}sus^4-Chords
Locrian	Minor$^{7/-5}$

A complete collection of the modal scales in all keys can be found on pages 209-233. Here are a few modal scales with two connections of chords which you can try out. Now and again you should try to use some passing notes (p. 189).

1. **Dm** D-aeolian   **C** C-mixolydian   **B♭** B♭-lydian

2. **Dm⁷** D-dorian   **G⁷** G-mixolydian   **Em⁷** E-phrygian   **Am⁷** A-aeolian

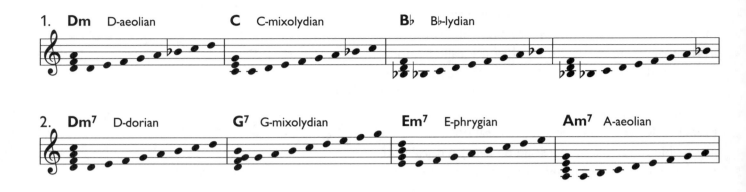

Improvisation Examples

1. Scale 1

32

2. Scale 2

33

3. Scale 2

130

6.5 PENTATONIC SCALES

This five wise men from the Orient

The pentatonic scale is one of the oldest of all scales. The ancient Chinese, the Indians and Celts whistled, twanged and hummed around with them.

There are only five notes within one octave in a pentatonic scale Greek "penta" = five). The normal pentatonic scale assumes the notes 1, 2, 3, 5 and 6 from the diatonian major scale (plus the 8 – the octave of the keynote). Fourth (4) and seventh (7) are therefore left out.

The minor pentatonic scale is derived from the minor scale of the diatonian major scale. It assumes the notes 1, 3, 4, 5 and 7 (again with the 8) of the diatonian (natural) minor scale (which has the same notes as the diatonian major scale, but which begins a third lower).

This minor pentatonic is the basis for the Blues scale (p. 127) and consequently the scale used in most Rock and Pop solos. We have illustrated this on the right using C-major A-minor as examples.

Diatonian Major Scale

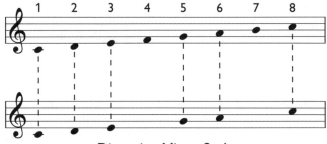

Diatonian Minor Scale

Diatonian Minor Scale

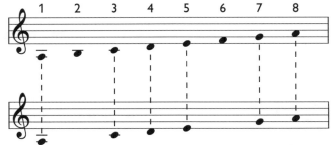

Diatonian Minor Scale

Why can you improvise ...

The scales and their chords

These scales ...	... suit these chords
Major-pentatonic on the keynote	Major-chords (including all major⁶, ⁷, ⁷/⁹ etc., excepting Maj^maj7 chords and all major chords with a fourth
Minor-pentatonic on the keynote	Minor-Chords (the tears tend to run where some complicated exaples are concerned)
Major-pentatonic on the fifth	Maj^maj7-Chords (even maj⁷/⁹ etc.)
Minor-pentatonic on the fifth	Major-Chords with fourth (⁷/⁴, ¹¹ etc.)

The most important pentatonic scales for all other keys can be found in the Magical Keyboard Tables from page 209 to 233.
Here are some pentatonic scales for typical chord progressions in C-major. Have fun!

Example 1

Example 2

Improvisation Examples

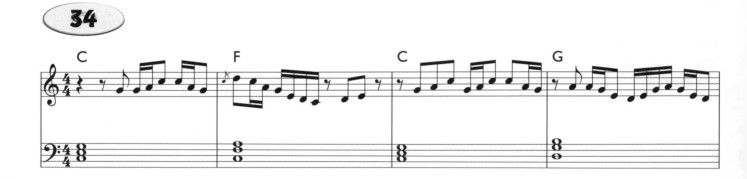

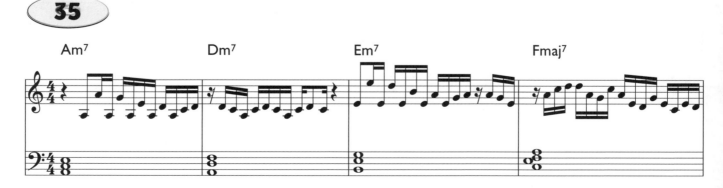

6.6 ALTERED SCALES

How to employ foreign workers

Question: Altered Scales? What are they?

Answer: You need them to improvise on altered chords.

Question: Oh Yer! And what are altered chords?

Answer: Altered chords are chords with non-scalar-notes. For example C^{+5} or $Cm^{7/-5}$.

Question: GULP! When you say non-scalar-notes – what scales do you mean? The diatonian? Major, Minor? The Pentatonic scales?

Answer: As with all normal chords, we mean the diatonian scales. The chord C^{+5} is based on the diatonian C-major scale, $Cm^{7/-5}$ is based on the diatonian C-minor scale.

Question: Do I understand that correctly: With C^{+5}, the +5, the fifth, G♭ which is raised by a semitone is therefore non-scalar? And in $Cm^{7/-5}$, the -5, the G♭???

Answer: Correct!

Question: Hang on a ‚mo! The C^{5+7} chord is therefore an altered chord with the non-scalar notes B♭ (minor 7) and G♯ (+5)?

Answer: Well, hmm you're right in principle, since the B♭ is not a part of the C-major scale, but the B (the maj⁷) is. The minor 7 gets an extra prize. In the major scale it is theoretically an altered note, but when improvising it is treated as a scalar note.

Question: And what about the other intervals? The 9,11 and 13?

Answer: In C-major the 9 is the D, the 11 the F, the 13 the A – all of which are notes in the C-major scale.

There is a simple rule: All chords with + or - are altered chords and need an altered improvisation scale.

How to form altered scales:

You take the basic major and minor scale of an altered chord. If the altered chord contains a diminished fifth (-5) or an augmented fifth (+5) you throw the normal (perfect) fifth out of the scale and replace it with the altered note. This works in the same way with altered sixth (-6, +6), ninths (-9, +9), elevenths (+11) and thirteenth (-13, + 13). Here are three examples.

Formation of Altered Scales

With the help of these rules you can form the scales which correspond to most altered chords. In practise, however, one often uses altered scales, which look a little different. Here we are going to show you the most important scales and where you can use them.

1. The Whole-tone Scale

This consists of purely wholetone steps. There are only two of these, e.g. beginning on C and beginning on C♯. The scale on the keynote D again has the same notes as the one which begins on C.

1. Whole-tone Scale

2. Diminished Scales

We are going to show you the two most important diminished scales.

a) The **Semi-diminshed Scale**. (possibilities for use on the next page)

b) The **Diminished Scale**. This consists of alternating semi-tones and whole-tones. There are two types: **Semi-tone/whole-tone, Whole-tone/semi-tone.**

2a) Semi-diminished Scale

2b) Semi-tone/whole-tone (diminished scale)

2c) Whole-tone/semi-tone (diminished scale)

3. Diminished Minor-Pentatonic

With some chords you can use the respective diminished minor-pentatonic instead of the diminished scale. That is the minor pentatonic with diminished fifth.

3. Diminished Minor-Pentatonic

4. Altered modal Scales

There are altered relations of some modal scales, but we are only going to mention two here. Please look at the modal scales again (p. 129).

a) Lydian ♭7 Scale
This style means that the seventh is lowered in the lydian scale. This scale is used in modern Jazz solos.

4a) Lydian ♭7

b) Lydian Augmented Scale
This is a lydian scale in which the fifth has been raised by a semitone. This is employed with augmented chords.

4b) Lydian augmented

5. Chromatic Scale

This consists purely of semitones. Within one octave there are 12 semitones plus the octaved keynote as 13th note. You produce this scale when you play all keys, one after the other from one note up to the same note in the next octave. If you want you can look at your keyboard as one great, big chromatic scale.

5. Chromatic Scale

The scales and their chords

Here we are going to show you the possibilities of using the different scales. In the right hand column are the Chords and in the left-hand column the scales which suit them.

These scales ...	... suit these chords
Whole-tone scale Lydian Augmented (on the third of the chord)	Major $^{7/+5}$
Lydian b7 scale Whole-tone scale (not for Maj.⁷!)	Major ^{7}, Major $^{7/-5}$
Semitone/whole-tone scale	Major $^{7/+9}$, Major $^{7/-9}$
Semi-diminished scale Diminished minor pentatonic	Minor $^{7/-5}$
Semi-tone/whole-tone scale Whole-tone/semi-tone scale	Minor-dim (= Minor°)
Chromatic scale	All chords

Here are two chord sequences with altered scales. So that they sound good, non-altered scales are of course also contained. The scales in all other keys can be found in the Magical Keyboard Tables.

1.

| **Dm**$^{7/-5}$ D-semi-dim. scale | **G**$^{7/-9}$ G-semitone/
whole-tone | **Cmaj**^{7} Ionian
(C-major-scale) | **Am**$^{7/9}$ Aeolian
(A-minor-scale) |

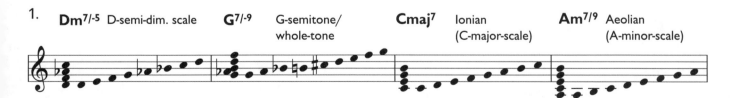

2.

Dm^{7/-5} D-min.
Minor-pentatonic   **D♭⁷**   D♭-lydian-♭7   **G♭^{7/+5}** B♭-lydian-augmented   **F^{7/+5}** whole-tone scale

B♭maj⁷   B♭-lydian

Improvisation Examples

1. Scheme 1

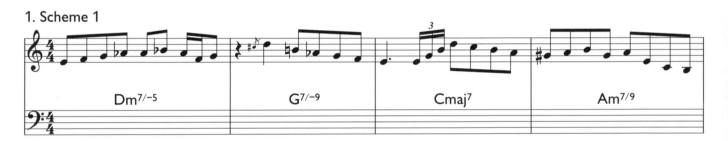

Dm^{7/-5}   G^{7/-9}   Cmaj⁷   Am^{7/9}

2. Scheme 1

Dm^{7/-5}   G^{7/-9}   Cmaj⁷   Am^{7/9}

3. Scheme 2

Dm^{7/-5}   D♭⁷   G♭^{7/+5}   F^{7/+5}   B♭maj⁷

6.7 IMPROVISATION TABLE

Let's spend the knight together (at the Round Table)

The Chord	Major Minor Scales	Modal Scales	Pentatonic Scales	Blues Scales	Altered Scales
Major Triad	Major-scale	Ionian	Major-Pentatonic on keynote	Scale1 on the sixth	
Major-maj7, maj 7/9	Major-scale	Ionian Lydian	Major-Pentatonic on second or fifth	Scale1 on the third	
a) Major +5 b) Major 7/+5	a) Harmonic minor on sixth b) -----				a) Whole-tone scale Lydian augmented b) Whole-tone scale, Lydian augmented on the third of the chord
Major 7, 7/9, 7/13	Major scale on the fourth	Mixolydian	Major-Pentatonic on keynote or seventh	Scale 2	Semi-tone/whole-tone for Major 7 also: Lydian-b7 scale
Major 7/11	Major scale on the fourth	Mixolydian	Major-Pentatonic on seventh	Scale 1 on the fifth	
Major 7/-5					Lydian-b7
a) Major 7/-9 b) Major 7/+9	a) ------ b) Major-scale on the fourth	a) b) Mixolydian	 b) Maj-Pentatonic Minor Pentat.	a) Scale on the fifth b) Scale 1 and 2 on the keynote	a) Semi-tone/ whole tone b) Semi-tone/ whole tone
Minor triad Minor 7, Minor 7/9	Minor-scale (natural)	Aeolian Dorian	Minor-Pentatonic on keynote or fifth	Scale 1	
Minor-maj7	Harmonic minor		Minor-Pentatonic on the fifth		
Minor 7/9/77	Major-scale on the seventh	Dorian		Scale 1 on the fifth	
Minor 7/-5	Minor-scale on the seventh	Locrian		Scale 1	Diminished Minor Pentatonic, semi-diminished scale
Minor 7/-9 Minor 7/-6/-9	Major-scale on the minor sixth Minor-scale on the seventh	Phrygian Locrian	Minor-Pentatonic on the keynote Minor-Pentatonic on the third	Scale 1 on the fifth Scale 1 on the keynote	Semi-tone/ whole-tone scale Semi-tone/ whole-tone scale
Minor diminished					Semitone/whole-tone Whole-tone/semi-tone scales, chromatic
Sus2-chords	Major-Scale Minor-scale	Ionian, Lydian, Mixolydian, Aeolian	Major-Pentatonic on the fourth Minor-Pentatonic on the fifth	Scale 1 on the sixth	
Sus4, 7sus4	Major-Scale Minor-scale	Dorian, Mixolydian Aeolian	Minor Pentatonic on the keynote or the fifth	Scale 1 on the keynote	

7 KEYBOARD – STYLES

The most important styles in current pop music

7.1 THE BUILDING – BRICK SYSTEM

D.I.Y. Keyboard Style

In this chapter we would like to show you some of the basic styles in pop and rock music circles. To make things easier for you at the beginning we have, in the first instance, dealt with each style systematically. On the first page you will find a basic scheme of 8 or 12 bars with harmonies and a very very simple basic rhythm for the style concerned. You should play this piece of music in this raw form and when you have learned it off-by-heart you can add the intro at the beginning and replace the end bars with a new "ending" or make certain other bars a little more interesting by adding "Licks" in their place. Then you should try playing the piece of music using a complicated rhythm pattern. At the end of each section there is a "polished" but still relatively simple number in the style concerned.

And this is how the scheme works: Musical styles in a building brick system!

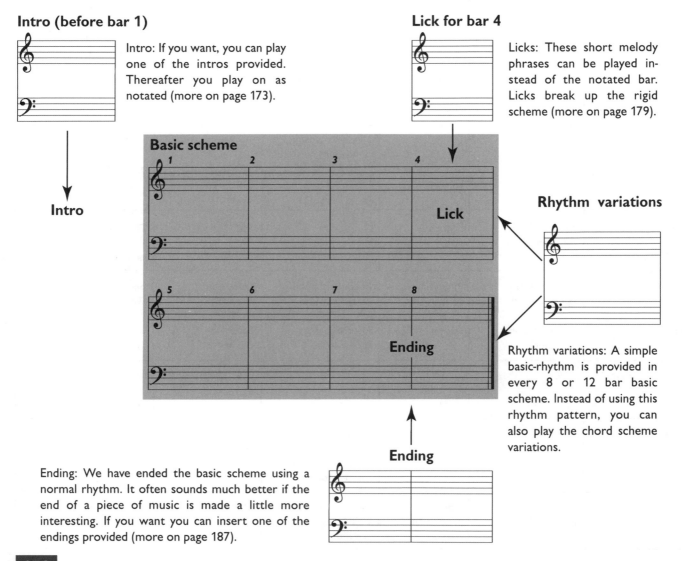

Intro (before bar 1)

Intro: If you want, you can play one of the intros provided. Thereafter you play on as notated (more on page 173).

Lick for bar 4

Licks: These short melody phrases can be played instead of the notated bar. Licks break up the rigid scheme (more on page 179).

Rhythm variations

Rhythm variations: A simple basic-rhythm is provided in every 8 or 12 bar basic scheme. Instead of using this rhythm pattern, you can also play the chord scheme variations.

Ending: We have ended the basic scheme using a normal rhythm. It often sounds much better if the end of a piece of music is made a little more interesting. If you want you can insert one of the endings provided (more on page 187).

7.2 BLUES

In the style of John Mayall, Eric Clapton and ZZ Top

The Blues originated at the end of the last century, derived from the working songs of the Afro-Americans. Rock 'n' Roll subsequently originated from Blues and has since become an important part of modern Pop music. If you like this style of music, you should try to obtain records by Billy Holiday, Muddy Waters, John Lee Hooker, John Mayall and the first releases of the Rolling Stones. Blues consists of a succession of 12 bars with a strongly defined chord scheme – the so-called Blues scheme.

Blues-basic-scheme

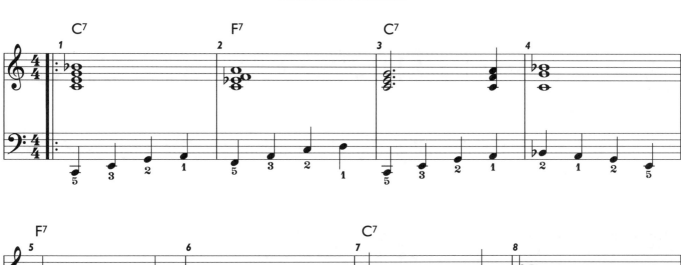

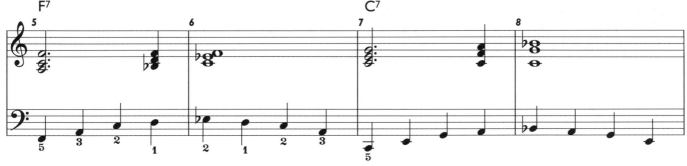

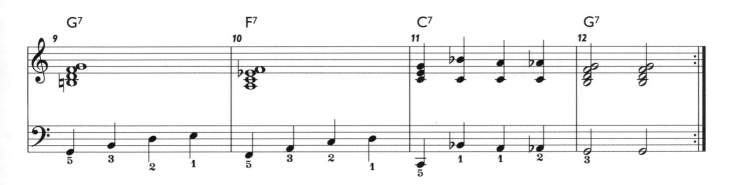

Rhythm Variations

1. You can also play this as a triplet rhythm. the rhythm for one bar:

2. Please play this accompanying rhythm in triplet feeling

Licks for Bars 2 and 6

This is the extended Blues scale

Licks for Bars 4 and 8

Blues-Endings for bars 11 and 12

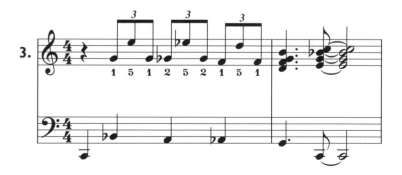

140

39

Blues For Louis

Dreksler/Härle
© 2002 Voggenreiter Publishers

7.3 Rock 'n' Roll

In the style of Jerry Lee Lewis and Fats Domino

Rock 'n' Roll developed in the 50's from Blues and Boogie. This style itself has had influence on many other musical styles such as, for example, a large part of Rock-music, Rockabilly and Hard-Rock etc. For keyboard players it meant the opening of the doors to many new worlds: Rock 'n' Roll contains aggressive ways of playing with small acrobatic additions such as the finger glissandos à la Jerry Lee Lewis and chord hammerings with the speed of a swing machine.

Rock 'n' Roll is almost always built up according to the Blues-scheme – i.e. 12 bar.

Rock 'n' Roll Basic – Scheme

Rock 'n' Roll – Intros

3.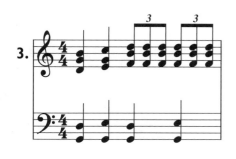

Ending for bar 11 and 12

Licks for Bar 4

1.  **2.**  **3.**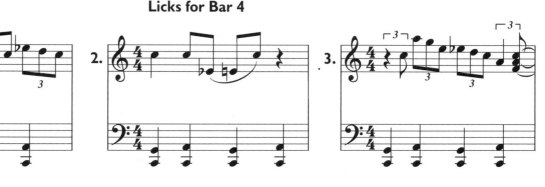

Licks for Bar 8

1.  **2.**  **3.**

Rhythm Variations

1.  **2.**

Rock 'n' Roll – Boogie – Bass-Runs

$\frac{12}{8}$ – Rock (Slow Rock)

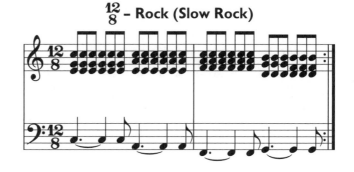

143

40

Jerry's Roll

Dreksler/Härle
© 2002 Voggenreiter Publishers

160 bpm

at half the tempo

*Glissando
white keys*

7.4 ROCK

In the style of Bruce Springsteen, Huey Lewis and Chicago

Many musical directions are gathered together under the term "Rock": Blues-Rock, West-Coast-Rock etc. Rock developed from Blues, Rock 'n' Roll and Country elements. In the early days there was a heavy emphasis on guitars but in the meantime things have changed completely. Rock without Keyboarders is almost unimaginable – we need them for rocky piano sections or piping organ chords. We need them to deliver those super sounds without which Rockmusic just wouldn't be Rockmusic.

Licks for bar 4 and 8

Licks for bar 12 (and eventually also bar 9)

Intros bar 1 **Intro before bar 9**

Rhythm variations

 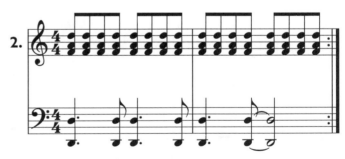

Rock-Shuffle (quavers also played in triplet time)

Someday In April

Dreksler/Härle
© 2002 Voggenreiter Publishers

41

100 bpm

7.5 ROCK BALLAD

In the style of Elton John, Billy Joel and Phil Collins

Ballads tell tales. Ballads are therefore, as a part of Rockmusic, peaceful pieces with an understanding air about them, which are played at slow speeds. The ballad texts, which are sometimes very deep and meaningful, demand an appropriate keyboard accompaniment: you shouldn't hit the keys too hard and you should make the chord accompaniment as interesting as possible. Try a few different voicings (page 197), hammerings (page 175) or arpeggios (page 184). Have fun!

Ballads – Intros

1.
2.

Licks for bars 4, 8 and 11

1.
2.

3.
4.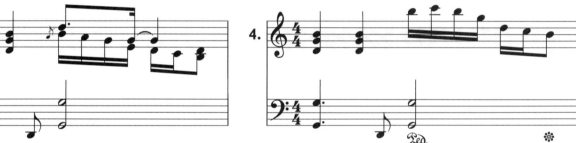

Rhythm variations

1.
2.

3.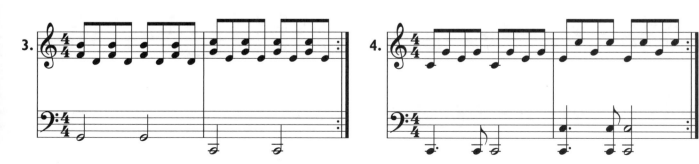
4.

12/8 Rock-Ballads

The 12/8 Rock-ballad experienced its first high-point in 1957 with Fats Domino's "Blueberry Hill" and subsequently with the number "Bring It On Home To Me" (1965 by the Animals, 1974 by Rod Stewart). Since then many years have passed and many 12/8 Rock-ballads have been here and gone; and they will most surely be played again once you and the rest of us manage to move our old and gouty fingers to play the quick and tricky notes needed for Rock-ballads. So get to work before it's too late! To start off with here's a simple basic pattern and to follow a few variations.

42

Ballad Of Talaso

Dreksler/Härle
© 2002 Voggenreiter Publishers

70 bpm

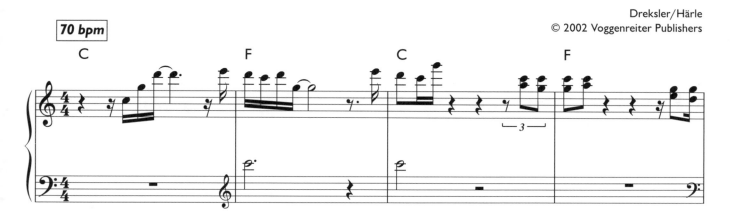

7.6 REGGAE

In the style of Bob Marley, Peter Tosh and UB 40

Reggae developed at the end of the Fifties in Jamaica. This music contains elements of Rhythm and Blues and of Rock-music. Of course, what is characteristic about Reggae is the rhythm: Strong off-beat emphasis, mostly played by guitars and keyboards. Many Reggae songs are played in a half-time feeling (page 105) so as to produce a relaxed sound.
One can hardly imagine Pop-music without the Reggae element. Musicians such as Joe Cocker, Eric Clapton and Sting have written many of their hits using this style.

Reggae – Intros

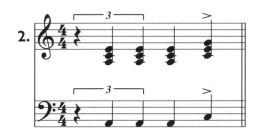

Licks for bars 3 and 4

The scale for the licks

(D-aeolian with +4 = tritone)

Rhythm variations

Jah May Come

Dreksler/Härle
© 2002 Voggenreiter Publishers

65 bpm

7.7 COUNTRY-POP

In the style of Floyd Kramer and Kenny Rogers

Country music is to a certain extent an American home-grown product. The big break-through for Country-Rock came at the end of the sixties. Many songs by the Rolling Stones, Elvis Presley and the Beatles are written using this style.

In Country-Rock music the typical guitar or banjo picking techniques are transfered onto the piano. Further special characteristics are "hammerings", "walk-ups" and "walk-downs" and a few more as well.

Country-Pop – Basic scheme

Country Walk-up (Intro)

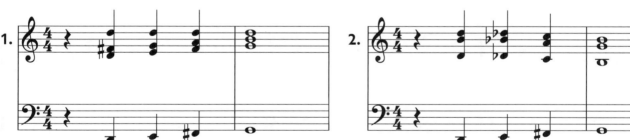

Country Walk-down (Ending)

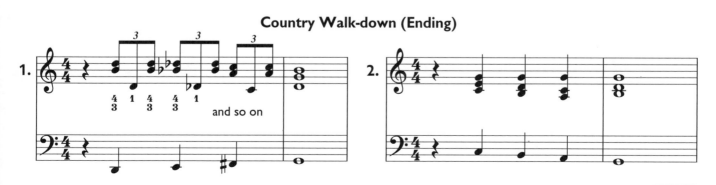

Country-Hammering (*)

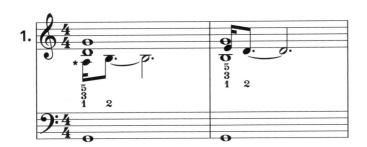

Licks for bar 4

Rhythm variations

Country Shuffle (triplet)

Bluegrass-Rhythm

44

No Ducks On My Trucks

Dreksler/Härle
© 2002 Voggenreiter Publishers

115 bpm

7.8 LATIN-POP

In the style of Ricky Martin and Herbie Hancock

Now and again a Jazz-musician strays into the pop-scene. The end-product of this is a music branch called Jazz-Pop. What of course is meant are the influences of Jazz (Swing, Latin etc.) on Pop-music. In this branch you will also find complicated chords, rhythm patterns and typical Jazz scales.

Licks for bars 4, 8 and 12

1.

2.

3.

4.

Rhythm variations

Swing feeling

1.

2.

Latin

3.

4.

Intros and Endings

1.

2.

A Little Bit Of Latin

Dreksler/Härle
© 2002 Voggenreiter Publishers

45

110 bpm

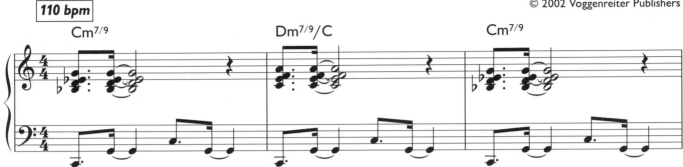

7.9 FUNK

Original Funk was developed in America by Afro-Americans. The following is typical of funk: The remaining rhythm section, which can sometimes be very complicated, add off-beat rhythms to a very forceful and relatively easy drum beat. A groovy wind-section is generally added to this.

Intro

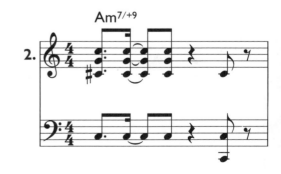

The scale for the licks

1.

Licks for bar 3 and 4

2.

Licks for bar 12

1.  **2.** 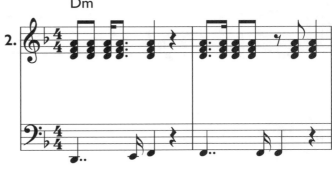 **3.**

Rhythm variations

Dm

1.

Dm

2.

Dm

3.

Dm

4.

46

Windy Earth

Dreksler/Härle
© 2002 Voggenreiter Publishers

Fine

171

8 PROFESSIONAL TRICKS
Intros, Hammerings, Licks - Riffs, Runs Tricks

8.1 INTRODUCTION

Champagne or Soda water?

You've heard it before: The D.J. on the radio has said his piece, the next piece of music begins and after the first or second note you already know which song it is. Play this ...

Of course, you recognized it immediately, the classic intro and chord-riff in the style of the grandfather of all rock songs: Jailhouse Rock!

Most Pop and Rock songs are made up of the same raw-material – rhythms, sounds and melodies, which can be swapped around like jokers in a card game and which cannot be easily recognized. Apart from new sounds it is often very small things which make Rock and Pop songs typical and unmistakeable: Riffs (additions, which fill holes in the melody), Hooks and Turn-arounds (which introduce the beginning of a new harmony or a new section), Intros and Endings – these and similar music structures are the things which stick in our brains and which so often make relatively insignificant numbers a hit.

Stiwi's Hands

In this chapter we would like to present you with a selection of such professional keyboard techniques. These decide whether your keyboard play is like beer and baked beans or Champagne and Caviar.

Kim's Eyes

8.2 Intros

Musical beginnings

Intro is an abbreviation of introduction. Intros are generally short instrumental passages, which open a piece of music. Intros should arouse interest and/or put the listener in the right mood for the music which follows. On the other hand they can be used to grind a basic rhythm into the listener so that the rhythmycally contrasting solo voice has a better effect.

Country-Rock

Rock and Pop

Boogie – Rock

8.3 SUSPENSIONS

Hey big suspender!

Suspensions are non-chordal notes, which are released on a chordal note in an emphasized or relatively emphasized part of a bar (more about that on p. 190). Suspensions, especially if they are used often, have a similar effect to a good detective novel in which the suspense is built up and then released ...

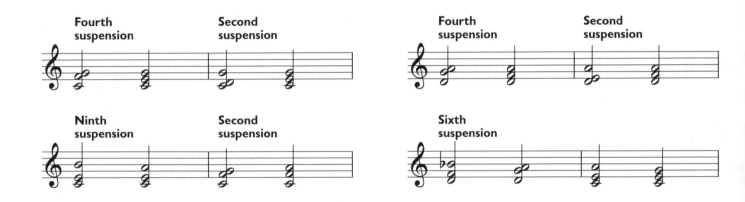

Rock-Pop-chords with suspensions

Ballad-accompaniment with suspensions

Quaver-accompaniment with suspensions

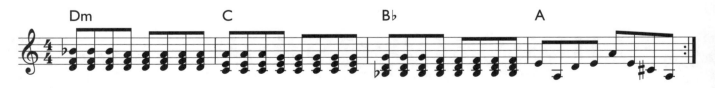

8.4 HAMMERINGS

Go on ... have a bash!

Hammering is a technique of decorating chords and intervals with appoggiatura. This technique was first used by Blues and Country guitarists. In the late Fifties hammering on the piano was made popular by the Country-pianist Floyd Cramer. Hammerings make chord playing more relaxed and make things more melodic and playful ...

Hammering – Basic Forms

Examples from Country and Rock

Double Hammering   **Melodic without Hammering ...**   **... and with Hammering**

8.5 PLAYING WITH INTERVALS

Parrot play

Single voice melodies sound somewhat thin. You can make them more interesting by playing the correct intervals parallel to the melody. Octave parallels and parallel fifths usually make melodies a lot fuller and more powerful. Parallel thirds and sixths sound a little on the "sweet" side ...

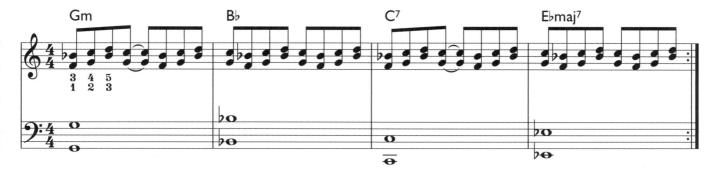

8.6 ROLLS

The Rolls-Royce amongst the trills

"Rolls" are ornamental trills (p. 67) of two or three chordal notes. The technique is mainly used in Blues, Rock and Country. A well-known expression for "Roll" is "Tremolo" …

8.7 HOOKS

Fishing tricks

"Hooks" are short melody phrases, which are often repeated in a piece of music. Hooks give a certain structure to a piece; their main function is to shortly, precisely and recognizably announce a certain chord or a certain section of music (verse begin, chorus begin); by using hooks you can make it clear to the listener what is about to come. Hooks are not normally improvised, but are determined during composing or in the recording studio.

Country-Rock and Pop

Blues – Rock

8.8 LICKS

But not with your tongue, stupid!

"Licks" are short melodic insertions, the main task of which is to fill gaps in the main melody (e.g. Vocals). As opposed to their brothers, the hooks (p. 178), most licks have a clear improvisational nature. Licks are often the building-bricks for a longer instrumental solo ...

Rock – Pop

8.9 BASS-RIFFS

Play it again ... and again ...

"Riffs" are (normally) short melodic phrases or figures which are always repeated in a piece of music at a certain characteristic point. "Grooves" have a similar function. We normally refer to "Riffs" when the melodic side of the phrases is more important, and to "Grooves" if the rhythmic side is more important. Many of the bass-riffs on the following page sound really good if you play your keyboards with a synthi-bass setting ...

Rock-Boogie Bass

Rock

Funk – Disco

Rock – Pop

Latin and Salsa-Bass

8.10 LINEAR GROOVES

Groovy, groovy, groovy lines

"Grooves" are riffs in which the rhythmic rather than the melodic side of the phrase is more important. One tends to refer to the rhythmic basic feeling of a song or a piece of music as the "groove". The word has its origins in the jargon of Swing musicians and originally referred to the production of the "correct" feeling when listening or playing Swing-music. Since the mid-Sixties the word has been used in the adjectival form "groovy" and we all know what groovy means, don't we?

Stiwi's Hands

8.11 SCALAR RUNS

But where are they running to?

Scalar runs are runs with the scale from which the chord originates (Major, Minor, Pentatonic etc). They serve either to combine two chords or to decorate a single chord. You can either play the runs in linear form (up and down the scale) or vary them in a regular pattern e.g. saw-tooth pattern (examples 5 to 8) or in slides (example 4) etc.

Examples

8.12 Arpeggio-Riffs

Stop harping on, of course we'll return!

An Arpeggio is a chord in which the notes are struck one after the other, as with a harp (Italian "arpa" = harp). Arpeggio-riffs (see "Riff" p. 180) are mostly one or two bar patterns which divide up a chord and which are continuously repeated in the whole piece or in parts thereof. You can often hear such arpeggio-riffs on records by Phil Collins, Cindy Lauper, Christopher Cross and many others. The basic chords are usually arpeggiated with additional non-chordal notes.

8.13 ARPEGGIO-RUNS

Chord marathons

Chords, where the notes are struck one after the other – as with a harp – are referred to as "arpeggio" (from Italian "arpa" = harp). Arpeggio-runs are rows of chordal notes which are joined together. With a little practice with the sustain pedal they sound really great and are often used by keyboard players to show off with and to dazzle ...

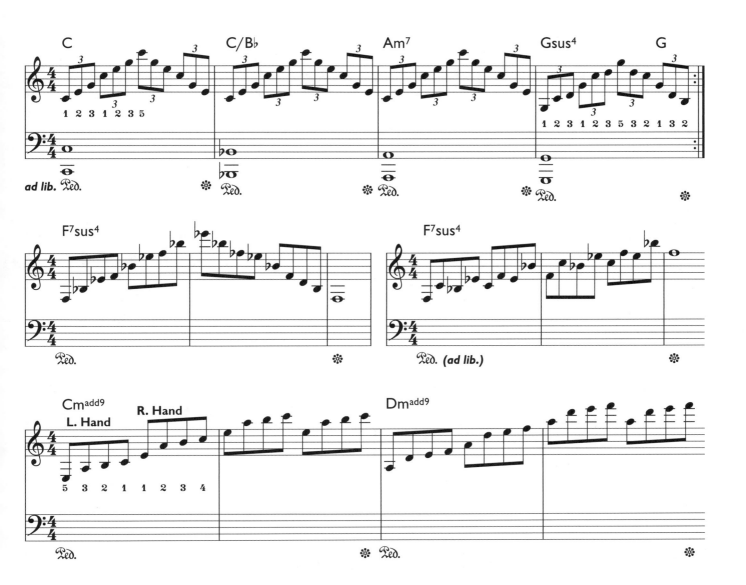

8.14 Chord-Riffs

Not suitable for Omar Shariffs

Chord-riffs are short, rhythmical accentuated phrases which remain in a mostly regular pattern throughout the whole piece or throughout certain passages. A typical chord riff is the one on page 172 from the song in the style of "Jailhouse Rock". Also songs such as "Nikita" (Elton John), "Ride like the Wind" (Christopher Cross) or "While you see a Chance" (Steve Winwood) contain interesting chord-riffs.

Rock and Pop

8.15 ENDING

Musical finals

For many, many years now it has been a naughty habit in Rock and Pop to softly fade out songs at the end, rather than giving them a properly composed ending. The reason: All producers want "airplay" – they want their songs to be played as often as possible on the radio and they want to give the D.J.'s an opportunity to talk over the fade or to be able to leave the song at any point because an interview or a traffic announcement has to go on the air. This is a shame, because a song without an end is like a sentence which ...

9 ARRANGING AND COMPOSING

From Fuzzy to the first Million

9.1 MELODY NOTES

Milady, it's got nothing to do with money

The "invention" of a piece of music is known as "composing", whereas the "processing" of a piece of music or a melody (e.g. with chords) is known as arranging.

We will not be able to make a professional arranger out of you with these few pages; we do however, want to give you a few tips as to how you can analyse relatively simple Pop and Rock songs or self-composed melodies yourself and how you can find suitable harmonies for them. We are going to reduce the whole field to a few clear furrows, provide you with a few basic rules and push the thousands of "Yes – buts" to one side with nonchalent grandeur.

Main rule: Which chords suit a melody depends on the melody notes and the melodic process ...

1. Chordal notes as melody

In the simplest cases, melodies consist only of notes from one triad. In such cases you should choose this triad for the harmony or you add a minor-parallel or the counter triad ...

Dideldumda

It is also often the case that melodies consist of predominantly one note. Usually you can proceed exactly as above. Use your ear to ascertain which scalar chord suits the melody notated and simply vary it, if it sounds okay, using its minor parallel or the counter triad ...

Is there anybody?

2. The Melody consists of scalar notes and passing notes

Imagine a football team with three top players: These tend to be on the ball all the time and largely dictate the game; the other players are normally only brought into the game occasionally or they prepare the forward pass to the top players. This is exactly the way it is with the melody notes: The chordal triad notes are the top players, the passing notes are useful "helpers", which have nothing to say harmonically.

Passing notes are therefore non-harmonic notes, for which you don't need harmonies of their own if they, as is mostly the case, are played on weakly emphasized counts. The whistle blows. Top player C plays the melody ball via D to the triad top player E, who lays the leather on to star G via the passing note F.

When the Saints

Traditional

Oh   when   the   Saints   go   march - ing   in ...

Joshua fits the battle of Jericho

Traditional

Jo-shua fit the bat - tle of   Je - ri - cho,   Je - ri - cho,   Je - ri - cho ...

3. Auxiliary notes
(also known as returning notes, neighbouring notes, alternating notes and changing notes)

Let's stick to football: If the note D, which is a non-harmonic note in the C-major triad, receives a pass from C but doesn't play on to the triad top player E as a proper passing note should but passes back to C instead, you know that it's a "returning" or "auxiliary" note!

These are non-chordal notes, which are a semitone or a whole tone below or above the triad note and which can be reached during melody play and from which it is possible to turn back to the triad note soon after. Such notes can also generally be neglected, left out in the cold since they are generally on non-emphasized counts.

Greensleeves

A - las,   my   love   you   do   me wrong

The most famous auxiliary note of the world is from Beethovens' "Für Elise"

Harmonically the 4 notes belong to the A-minor chord (A-C-E). The two auxiliary notes D♯ do not belong to the chord because they are not part of the A-minor scale.

Für Elise

E   D♯   E   D♯   E   B   D   C   A

4. Suspended notes

The suspension is a non-chordal note, which produces a sound which is full of suspense in the chord. It normally appears in an emphasized or relatively emphasized part of the bar and screams "I can't take this suspense any longer! – cancel me with a triad note!" – "Your wish is our command" shout the triad gang and usually solve the problem in the next non-emphasized part of the bar. Cheers! Oh sorry: In the interest of the good health of our readers, we have simply decided to show the difference between 5 types of suspension (take a good long look at the little devils!) – and to show you a few practical examples with songs.

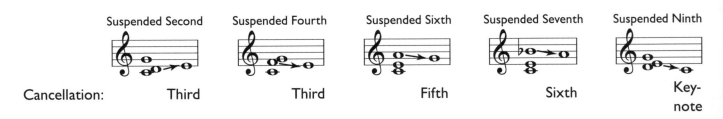

The day before yesterday

Just To Be

5. Anticipation

We use the word "Anticipation" to refer to a non-chordal note which has a chordal note in the subsequent chord. Through this anticipation, a sound is created which is full of suspense and which is eventually cancelled. The anticipation is to be found on non- or little-emphasized counts.

Fire In The Air

9.2 HARMONIES

Plain sailing, arranging!

When you arrange a song, you try to find suitable chords for a melody which already exists. You have already had the most important types of melody notes; now we are going to show you the simple technique of finding the right chords for a melody yourself.

For this you will need two basic rules, which you can simply throw overboard eventually, but which make things much easier to start with when getting into the arranging business.

Rule 1

Choose your chords so that the most important melody notes (on the emphasized counts) are chordal notes.

Rule 2

In the beginning only place your chords on the following counts:

4/4 and 12/8 Time: 1 (and eventually 3)
6/4 and 6/8 Time: 1 (and eventually 4)
3/4 and 3/8 Time: 1 (and eventually 3)

The Practical side

Using a practical example we are now going to show you how you can assign chords to a pre-determined melody in step by step fashion. Let us assume that the melody for the Gospel song "Nobody Knows The Trouble I've Seen!" has just come into your head. "Great – could be my first major world hit if I could find the right chords for it!" – What do you do now? Firstly write your song down in note form – well we've done this for you already – see page 193, where you will find the melody. The next step is to establish the key. Here's another tip: Most songs return to their harmonic resting-place, the tonic, with the last note of the melody (page 80). The last note in most cases is the keynote of the tonic, and less usually the third or the fifth. In our example song, the last note is a C – a strong indication that the song is written in C major.

Step 1: Using the power of your ear you should develop a harmonic skelettone, sorry skeleton – if possible by only using basic triads of the key concerned (here C-major). Compare the melody with the chords in the first horizontal line: Almost all melody notes are chordal notes. The few non-chordal notes which are there (*p-note = Passing note) don't disturb your ear, since they are on weakly emphasized counts – with the exception of the anticipation in Bar 4. It is not always the case that basic triads suffice for the first harmonization. If this is so you have to go on to the second step straight away.

Step 2: We are now going to enrich the harmonic framework with the secondary triads. These can be either minor-parallels or counter triads (pp. 84 and 85 respectively). In each of the bars 2 and 6 there are 5 E's. In the tonic C-major, E is the third, in the minor-parallel Am it is the fifth and in the Dominant of the minor parallel it is the keynote. This arouses our suspicion that we would perhaps be able to play Em and/or Am instead of C-major here. Try them; they are both okay. The same is true for Bar 6. We have also juggled around a little with the minor-parallel of C-major, Am and with the counter triad Em in Bars 10, 11 and 14 (and you always have to juggle a little irrespective of the rules). So if you want to play the song with basic and secondary triads, you should begin at the first level and follow the diagonal arrows onto the second level (and then return to the first line) where possible.

Step 3: Now you check to see whether you can accompany the song in an even more artful way if you bring in the rest of the harmonic tittle-tattle: Variants (p. 90), Mediants (p. 90), Dominants (p. 91), Sub-dominants of higher degrees (p. 92), and Substitutions (p. 97). You will find our suggestions for this on the third level. In Bar 1 we shortly diverge from F to the variant Fm (on the third count as well! – but what do we care about that stupid second rule anyway! It sounds good and really leads back well to the tonic C in Bar 2 (p. 92!)). In Bar 4 we have substituted the first two G-major strikes with the 2nd degree (p. 97!); this delays the use of the real dominant G-major and creates suspense. In Bar 6 we don't play C, not even it's counter triad Em, but we elegantly slip into the dominant of the fourth degree (E) and slide over the dominant of the 3rd degree (A) back to the tonic-counter-triad Em to begin Bar 7 (see circle of Fifths, p. 92). We have also allowed ourselves a little dash into the sub-mediant of the tonic C by playing Ab on the first count of the last bar. On the second count we play F (not because we want to play the variant of the minor parallel on the sub-mediant of the tonic – although we could use that as a pompous excuse. But simply because we find the plagal ending (p. 82) really good). You can see: Rules may be good, but courage is better!

Step 4: We can polish the somewhat flat-sounding triads up by using additional notes. The tetrad Cb in Bar 1 nicely integrates the passing note A, but if you don't want to take any notice of such refinements you can simply choose your chord colourings by ear. A few tips in this direction can be found on page 194.

Melody – Harmony-Table

This table tells you which chords and types of chords suit a certain melody note, since the note concerned is a chordal note.

Melody note	Basic Triad	Minor Parallel	Variant	Mediant	Dominant upper Degree	Sub-dominant upper Degree
C	C	Am	Cm, Fm	Ab	–	Ab
D	G	Dm	D, Gm		D	Bb
E	C	Am, Em	A, E	E, A	A, E	–
F	F	Dm	Fm	Db	–	Bb
G	G, C	Em	Gm	Eb	–	Eb
A	F	Dm, Am	A, Fm, D	A	D, A	–
B	G	Em		E	B	–
Db (C#)	–	–	–	A, Db	A	–
Eb (D#)	–	–	Cm	Ab	B	Ab, Eb
F# (Gb)	–	–	–	B	D, B	–Ł
Ab (G#)	–	–	Fm	Ab	E	Ab
Bb (A#)	–	–	Gm	Eb	–	Eb, Bb

Nobody Knows The Trouble I've Seen

Arranged in 4 steps: 1. Only basic triads, 2. Basic, secondary and counter triads, 3. Dominants and sub-dominants of upper degree, variants, mediant-substitution, 4. Chord colourings through additional notes.

9.3 CHORD COLOURINGS

How to colour notes without using paint

We have harmonized "Nobody Knows" in 4 steps using chords which are really on the Blues/Jazz side because we wanted to show what can be done. Whether these complicated chords are really suited to a straight Gospel song is another question. The additional notes in chord colourings can be viewed as the jewels which a beautiful woman puts on to have even more effect ...

1. Just one diamond choker can't turn a simple village maiden into a lady; in the same way it is not possible that additional notes such as the maj7, the 9th, the 11th or the 13th will be able to turn the tonic into a minor parallel. To put it another way: The functions of a chord in a chordal system do not change: The tonic remains tonic, irrespective of whether it's called C, C^7, $C^{7/9}$ or $maj^{7/9/+11/+13}$ etc.

2. You are just not allowed to decorate your triad with any old jewel of an additional note. A lady of the world is almost certain not to wear a diamond-collar to breakfast but would probably choose an amber brooch which contains the colours of the rising sun; whilst jogging after breakfast in the park she will, of course, wear a sporty head-band with inlaid tourmalines and a few saphires (not too dark ones though!); for Five-o'clock-tea she may wear a powerful ruby or an emerald.
Music is very similar to this: For an easy going Pop or Country number one does not use a showy $^{7/-9}$ chord; a Rock-Jazz number with simple triads would also be met with a loud "YUCK!"
Every Rock and Pop-style has its own typical sound to which the chord extensions often contribute greatly. Of course the rhythm also plays a major role. We have notated a normal run-of-the-mill succession of chords and on the next page we will show you with which additional notes you can brighten them up to create certain styles. We have, of course, changed the basic rhythm to suit the various styles.

Succession of chords

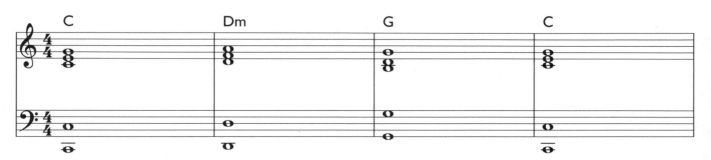

Country Pop

Predominant types of chords: Pure triads, major 7, major 6, sus⁴ – more unusual m⁷ and m⁶. All chords mostly with keynote in the bass-region and fifth as alternating bass, occasionally also the third.

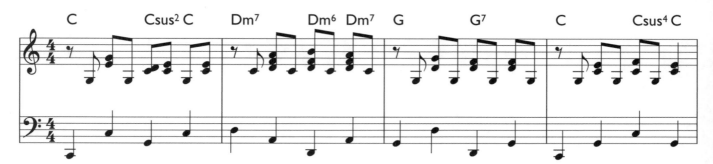

Rock

Predominant types of chords: Major 7, major $^{7/9}$, major $^{7/+9}$, major ^{13}, m^7, m^{11}, m$^{7/9}$. All chords occasionally with other bass-notes. If, then with mostly chordal notes, more seldomly non-chordal notes.

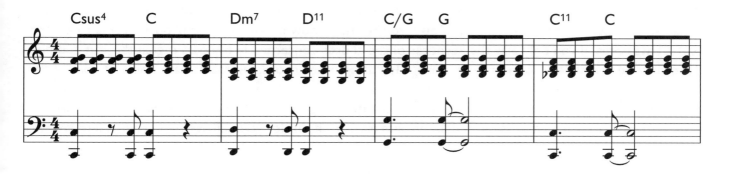

Middle Of The Road Pop

Music with thousands of influences on style. Mostly played with low intensity. Typical exponents: Elton John, Billy Joel. **Predominant types of chords:** Major, major 6, major 7, sus2, sus4, major $^{7/4}$, major ^{9}sus4, major ^{11}, major ^{13}, maj^7, maj$^{7/9}$, minor, m^6, m^7, m^{maj7}, m$^{7/9}$, m^{11}. Often different bass notes to the keynote, often bass notes in semitone steps.

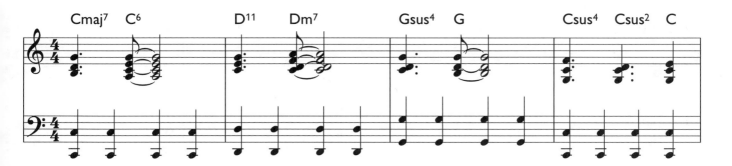

Pop-Jazz

Types of chords: All. Seldomly pure triads; many altered chords (-/+). Mostly keynotes in the bass region.

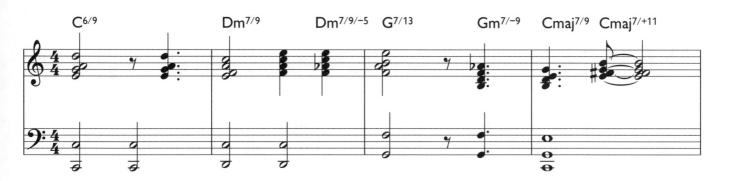

9.4 Bass Notes

Deep C bass fishing

When you have found the suitable chords for your melody it doesn't mean that your work is done. It is not a matter of **which** chords you play but of **how** you set them down. One interesting possibility is to alternate the bass notes. If you only play the keynotes of the chords concerned in the bass region this can in time – depending on the style – sound pretty boring. Try using other chordal notes as bass notes. It sounds particularly good and professional if you arrange the bass notes of the succession in semitone and/or whole-tone steps so that over longer distances for example, an ascending or descending scale is played in the bass region, or so that even a melody is formed in the bass play. Try it out for yourself, it isn't difficult. Here are two examples ...

Downstream

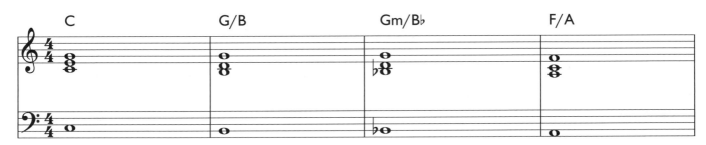

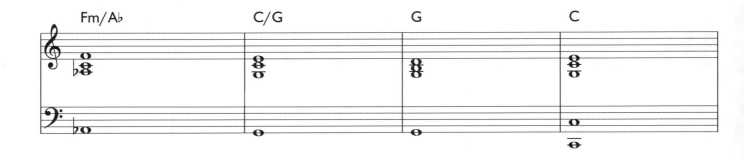

Dreaming

9.5 VOICING

His master's voicing

"Voicing" primarily refers to the selection and order of the intervals in a chord or in a structure similar to a chord, and secondly it refers to the way in which the voices (intervals) are carried in a succession of chords. If you're only playing for yourself, the voicing will depend on your own taste, on the style of the song and on the sound which you would like to produce. If you are playing with other musicians in a band you will also have to take into account which intervals your colleague on the electric guitar is playing, what the bassist is slapping on his strings and of course which complete sound is desired.

If a chord change is notated on the lead-sheet or in the music going from C to F you can emphasize the change in a Happy-sound Pop number (A); in a peaceful, almost solemn number like Phil Collins' "One More Night" you can create peace by neglecting the upper part (B) or in a Heavy Metal number you can create a vigorous sound by only playing a fragment of C-major (C).

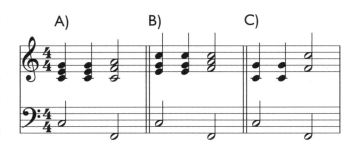

Voicing, of course, plays a major role in the arranging of a song. Basically we can differentiate between 3 main types of voicing. **1. Broad Voicing**, where the chordal notes have a distance of at least one third between each other. **2. Narrow Voicing** where notes occur at an interval of a musical second – which produces a narrow sound. **3. Voicing with Chord Fragments** where intervals from the basic triad are either thrown out completely or sent to the bass region. Here are some examples ...

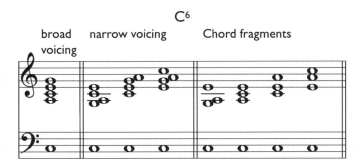

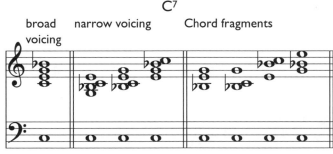

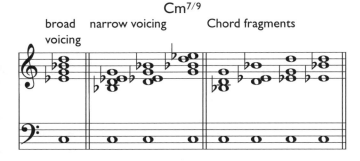

There now follows a succession of chords which is typical of Pop-ballads such as Billy Joel's "Just the Way You Are". We are going to show it to you in all voicing types and then in a combination.

1. Basic forms

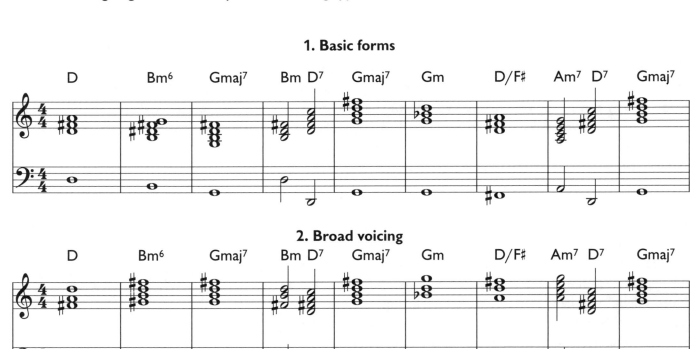

2. Broad voicing

3. Narrow voicing

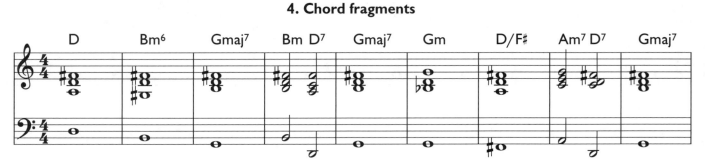

4. Chord fragments

Combination of all 4 voicing forms

9.6 COMPOSING

... or how to boil water

We've trodden on thin ice the whole time in this chapter; and now it's slowly beginning to crack. So, before we sink, let's scurry over the cold zone with a few motivating tips.

We are, of course, unable to show you in just a few lines how to write a global hit. Because, first of all, it doesn't work like that, and second, we'd have written it ourselves years ago.

But what we do want to show you is that, like the rest of us, even the writers of the world's biggest hits only cooked with water. And the biggest hits of all time are folk songs. They survive the decades and centuries and still stay fresh and lively. They're the basic material for most Blues, Country, Rock, Rhythm & Blues, etc.

Here are the three most simple recipes from the song kitchen ....

1. Take notes from a simple triad ...

... and you already have the start of one of the world's most frequently played songs: the starting notes of the American national hymn, "The Starspangled Banner". Many Pop and Rock songs are based on the same concept of thoroughly mixing the three notes of the C major chord (C, E, G) ... and voila!

The Starspangled Banner

2. Take three triad notes and a passing note ...

This method is a slight variation on the first recipe. A passing note is basically a poor sucker: if he were with three others in a group, the other three would be pals and he would just be like a spare tire. Passing notes are usually found on the unemphasized beats and are therefore only played very lightly. In the next example, we'll again take as our basis C, E and G (the notes of the C major triad) and add a pinch of the passing note D – bon appetit!

Home on the Range

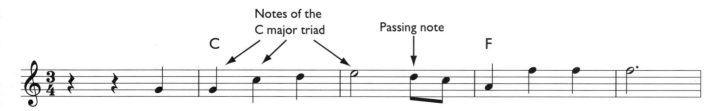

3. Take three triad notes and two passing notes ...

In C major we would take the triads C, E and G, the extra note D that we just picked up and also an additional one - in this case, A. It's also possible to simplify this recipe even further; these five notes are the notes of the major pentatonic scale: C - D - E - G - A. It's hard to keep count of the number of Folk, Pop, Rock, Blues and Country songs that are based on these five notes. And the best of it all: many instrumental solos in Rock, Pop and Country music comprise these five notes.

Here's a song that's only made up of these five notes.

Oh Susanna

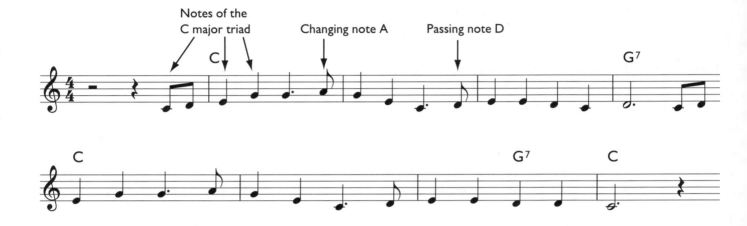

9.7 IMPROVISED MELODY PLAN

Lightning strikes by the Unorganized Musicians' Union

If you want to compose in a professional way according to the chord method, you will also require a professional playing technique (just like those boasted by the musicians you have admired so often). Well, here it is: we call it "improvised chordal melody play". It's not easy, but it can be learnt. Off you go ... During improvised chordal melody play the left hand plays in the bass region and the right hand plays the chords together with the melody. The main rule is: You have to play all melody notes so that they are the highest sounding notes in the chord concerned. There are several ways of doing this.

1. In the simplest of all cases, the melody (or parts of it) consists of notes belonging to the notated chord = chordal notes. Assuming that the melody consists of the notes C-E-G-E-C and the chord is C major, you can produce the melody by a) building Chord inversions and dismantling the primary form of the triad or by b) choosing chord inversions where the desired notes are at the top.

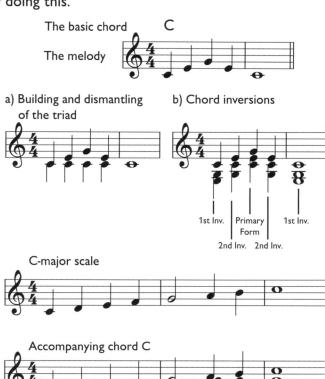

2. Theoretically it is possible to play the melodies by choosing the correct inversions of the chord concerned. Let's take a very peaceful, flowing melody without great leaps in the notation – the C-major scale – and as an accompanying chord the C-major triad in our example. Now you have to play the following:

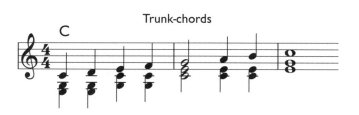

3. Hmm ... for some people that will sound interesting and jazzy, others will find the sound a "bit strange". Reason: D, F, A and B are non-chordal notes in C-major, which are very close to the upper chordal notes and therefore create dissonance. If you like the sound, okay; if not, simply leave the chordal notes which are closest to the melody notes out as is shown in the example – and form C-major.

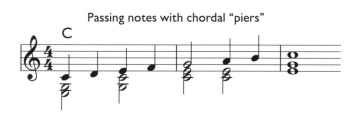

4. If you want to reduce the number of chords you play you can treat the non-chordal notes as passing notes (see p. 189). The chordal notes of C-E-G-C form a sort of chordal-pier in the melody stream over which you span the bridge of non-chordal notes.

5. Let us now take a somewhat more realistic example: The C-major scale goes to make up the melody but this time you should accompany it with the three basic triads in the Key of C-major (C, F, G). You would then have (amongst others) these two possibilities.

In Example a) every scalar melody note is treated as a chordal note from one of the basic triads (or their inversions). This is possible since each melody note is a component of one of the chords C (C-E-G), F (F-A-C) or G (G-B-D). You can also continue to use the "pier-principle" (as in example b). In this case you treat the individual notes as non-chordal notes of the chord played at first. This principle is recommended for use in melody parts which are played quickly as well as in other situations.

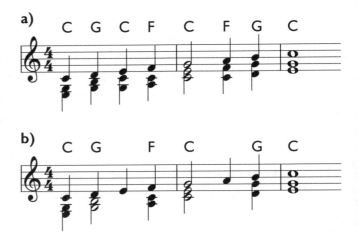

6. In the interest of presenting a complete picture we would now like to show you how pretty method a) sounds if the secondary triads are used in addition to the basic triads as harmonic polish.

7. In many Pop and Rock songs, parts of the melody consist of only one single note. If you want to spice up such passages a little you will have to choose chords which contain these individual notes or which have them in their extensions, for example as sixth, minor or major seventh, etc.

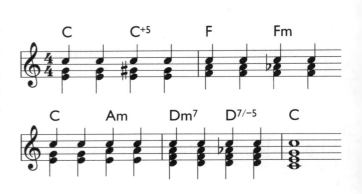

8. When you have polished up your improvised chordal melody play using these tips, you can add the last coat of varnish by adding ornaments, flourishes and all manner of strange things. A simple method of doing this is with the so-called ascents and descents between chords. Here is one example, more on page 176.

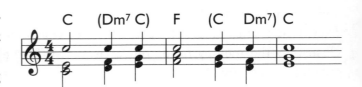

We close up with a little test for you. Here is the beginning of our Song "Some Days Ago"

Some Days Ago

10 MIDI AND COMPUTERS

All about MIDIotic Masters and Slaves

MIDI stands for "Musical Instrument Digital Interface". Using MIDI you can combine instruments and additional equipment of the most varied nature with a computer system. Depending on the extent of the system, the settings and functions of the connected equipment can be controlled from a central point (e.g. keyboard or computer). MIDI is used to convey musical and non-musical information between the individual pieces of equipment.

MIDI operates using 16 Channels

1. Channel-voice Messages

This is information concerning the number of keys struck, their key, their velocity and information concerning modulation possibilities via Joystick Modulation Wheel, After-Touch, Soft Pedal etc.

2. System Common Events

These relate to all channels simultaneously and transfer information such as the current key or song number; or by using a Tune-Command they can tune all linked equipment to a uniform key.

3. System Realtime Messages

These are needed to synchronize several pieces of MIDI equipment such as Rhythm-Machines Sequencers, Computers etc.

4. System Exclusive Messages

This is manufacturer and product specific information such as parameters for synthesizers or the sampling values for samplers.

5. System Reset
This places a MIDI-linked system in a predefined initial state.

6. Channel-Mode Messages

OmniMode: All 16 MIDI channels are used to transmit and receive information. It is not possible to select Individual channels. Poly-Mode: Each piece of receiving equipment is allocated a certain channel this only functions if a transmission is sent on the same channel. Mono-Sound: Equipment using this mode can produce different sounds on different channels simultaneously.

MIDI compatible Instruments and Equipment

- Synthesizers with acoustic capability and keyboard
- Expanders Sound-Modules (= Synthesizers without Keyboards).
- Master-Keyboards (Keyboards without acoustic capability, but with good keys and many MIDI control facilities for the instruments attached). Availaible as standing or table-top equipment and on straps for the stage.
- Organs with built-in MIDI or with MIDI adapter kits.
- Grand Pianos with built-in MIDI or with MIDI adapter kits.
- Sampler (digital recording equipment for acoustic sounds) with and without Keyboards.
- Rhythm-Machines
- Drum-Kits (with MIDI adapter kits)
- Drum-Pads (non-resonating percussion pads)
- Wind instruments with breath controllers.
- Guitars and other stringed instruments
- Effect units (Echo, Chorus, etc.)
- Digital Multi-track recording equipment:
  - Sequencers (Computers without monitors, but with function-keys)
  - Computers with sequencer software (set using Mouse on the monitor or directly with the computer keyboard)
- Digital Music processing equipment (Computers with software for notation, playback and printout)
- Mixing-Desk:
  - Stage mixing desks
  - Mixing desks for multi-track tape machines
  - MIDI-mixer (mixes using only MIDI information, not acoustic)
- MIDI-Matrix (links MIDI-units together at the push of a button)
- MIDI-Thru-Box (Distributor, turns one MIDI-Out into several, functions as does a multiple different chanels simultaneously.
- MIDI-Interface (makes the Computer MIDI compatible) – and many other pieces of equipment, too!

MIDI cables and plugs

MIDI information is sent via two-pole twisted cable with paired screening. The screening has to be soldered at both ends of the cable with the connecting plugs. MIDI cables should not be longer than about 45 feet (signal distortion!). The 5-pole MIDI-DIN-sockets and the corresponding cables are easily mistaken for normal HIFI-cables. Many manufacturers actually market HIFI-cable as MIDI-cable. The HIFI-cables can, however, lead to problems with long cable connections and complex MIDI-systems. Reason: They are not connected in two-pole, but in four-pole format, the 4 wires are not twisted and are not screened together, each cable being individually screened So: Only buy the best material!

MIDI-DIN-CONNECTION/JACK

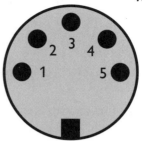

Forward view of the male jack: Pins 1 and 3 are not occupied. Pin 2 carries the earth. Pins 4 and 5 carry signals. The relationships are mirror-inversed for the female connector.

MIDI-connections and Line-connections

Digital musical information is transmitted via MIDI – binary number codes, the number components of which, 1 and 0, are represented by strong and weak electrical impulses. Analogous musical information is transmitted via Line – electro-magnetic waves which form a copy of the music. The working-instructions for the keyboard are transmitted via MIDI (e.g. play the note C at mid-volume); but when the keyboard has carried out these instructions, the result still has to be converted into an analogue signal by means of a digital-analogue converter, transmitted to an amplifier and made audible by means of loudspeakers. The further conveyance of the result of the instruction occurs by means of Line-connections. When working with a MIDI-system therefore, you do not only require MIDI-cable, but also Line-cable (Cinch or Jack-connections).

Master and slave

The simplest MIDI-system consists of two keyboards. The keyboard upon which you play is known as the "Master-Keyboard" and the keyboard which is controlled by the Master is known as the "Slave". In the "Set-up" shown below the Master produces, for example, an organ sound which is to be heard over the built-in loudspeakers. At the same time the Master controls the "Slave" and instructs it to produce a stringed instrument sound, directs it back to the Master via a line connection and plays the sound simultaneous to the organ sound over the Master-loudspeaker. The mixture-ratio is set using the volume controls on both keyboards. Both keyboards should be set in the Omni-mode as is shown in the keyboard instructions.

1 Master + 1 Slave (Master loudspeaker provides sound)

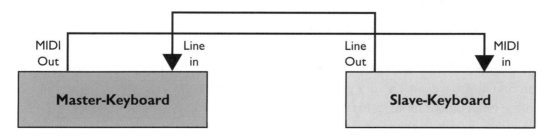

Now look at two very similar MIDI-set-ups with two keyboards. You should, above all, pay particular attention to the nature of the Line-connections – if you do this you should grasp the essentials of the effect of transmitting musical data using MIDI ...

1 Master + 1 Slave
(Slave loudspeakers provide sound)

The master plays, for example, organ, the Slave strings – as before. The difference here is that the Mastersound is conveyed via line-connections to the Slave's loudspeakers. This would be done if the Master has a better keyboard, but the Slave better loudspeakers.

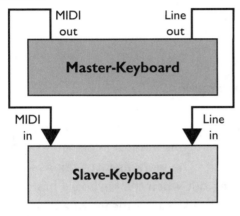

Set both in Omni-mode!

1 Master + 1 Master
(Both sets of Speakers under steam)

With this set-up you can hear the sound from both keyboards on both loudspeaker systems and you can produce the sounds on both keyboards. This is a most democratic system – there are no masters and no slaves.

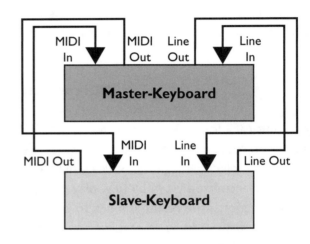

Set both in Omni-mode!

Even more slaves

You already know that synthesizers are small computers upon which sounds are produced by striking a conventional piano keyboard.

You have however also seen that two keyboards can be played simultaneously using only one set of keys – the ones on the Master-Keyboard. What is better than not using the keyboard on the slave to pack the sound-functions and the remaining electronics into a small, handy box.

Such boxes are – depending on the manufacturing company – called Modules or Expanders, etc. You can use and switch them just like a normal Slave-Keyboard. Instead of buying two keyboards with different sound and control characteristics it is better to purchase one keyboard with a very good set of keys and many MIDI-functions as a Master and one expander-module which is then controlled by the Master-Keyboard.

Expander Module as Slave

By not having a keyboard mechanism the expander is much cheaper, or for the same amount of money you can obtain many more sounds and a better sound quality.

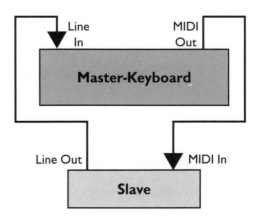

Set all units in Omni-mode!

Series- and Star-Connections

If you want to produce even more sounds of the same or varying kind by only depressing one key on the Master Keyboard – you can do this with MIDI without any problems at all! You buy or borrow several keyboards or expanders and connect them either in a chain system, one after the other (series-connection), or you connect them in a radiating system (star-connection).

Series-connection

If a piece of equipment receives sound information via the MIDI-In-Socket it does not normally convey this information via the MIDI-Out-Socket to the next piece of equipment. All information which is transfered via the MIDI-Out-Socket on the Master is conveyed unchanged to the next piece of equipment via the MIDI-Thru-Socket. It is unwise to connect more than 3 units in series since this could lead to distortion or delays in the information signals. When using so many sound sources it is recommendable to connect the line outputs via a mixing desk to an amplifier.

Star-connection

This functions using a so-called MIDI-Thru-Box – a box filled with electronic gadgetry which works like a distributor. From one MIDI-Out Channel it creates several MIDI-Outs. The same information is conveyed on each channel. This has two advantages: Firstly more than three units can be interconnected; secondly there isn't as much cable spaghetti and the data does not become distorted in the long cables. The amount of outputs on your MIDI-Thru-Box can be determined at purchase – as long as your wallet is willing.

It is also recommendable to relay the signals to an amplifier via the mixing desk as is the case with the series-connection.

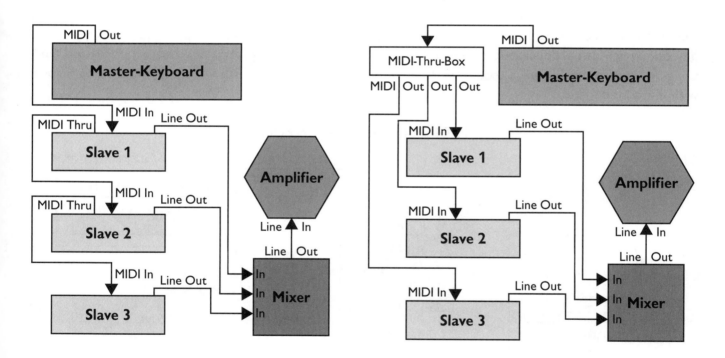

In the set-ups illustrated so far, the Slaves always play parallel to the Master. That means that if you play a C-major chord on the Master, the Slaves will also play C-major with the same or with another sound. The idea of the whole set-up is to make sounds "fatter" and "richer". You should note: If the Slave is in the Omni-Mode, the Master can also be set to the same mode or set in the Poly-Mode on any channel. If the Slave is in Poly-Mode – the transmitting and receiving channels on the Master (Poly!) and the Slave have to correspond.

Key-split

That means that your keyboard is split up into 2 or more sections. Where the split is, can often be chosen freely. Let us assume that the keyboard is to be divided into two, then you could set the left hand part of the keyboard aside for bass sounds and play bass patterns in this section with your left hand, whilst at the same time playing, for example, a Piano Arpeggio on the right. Depending on how your keyboard is fitted out there are two ways of doing this ...

Normal Key-split

It is most sensible to set up the Key-Split with a Master and as many Slaves as there are split sections – each section is allocated a Slave, each Slave is set in Poly-Mode and is allocated its own channel.

Internal Key-split

If your keyboard has this function and its own loudspeakers, you can produce one of the two sounds using the Master and the other using the Slave.

Home-Recording

When you are confronted with the choice of either buying a "reasonable" MIDI-Set-up for at home or one for the stage there nearly always seems to be one enormous problem: Money! Now it is normally the case that nobody has enough dough to buy a complete system straight off. Therefore you should be really clever and plan for additions. Where is the best place to begin? With a good Master-Keyboard (with or without its own sound-module). After that you only really need an expander for keyboard sounds. Those who have the money, should buy one which can receive in the Mono-Mode, i.e. which can produce several different sounds simultaneously. A Mono-Expander is practically one which contains several keyboards in one unit. The next element would be a Rhythm-Computer. If you only have enough money to buy one effect unit, you should buy one which can produce two or several effects simultaneously (e.g. echo and chorus). Now the "only" things which are missing are a sequencer or a computer with sequencer software and a four-track recorder with integrated mixer.

MIDI-Set-up for Home-Recording

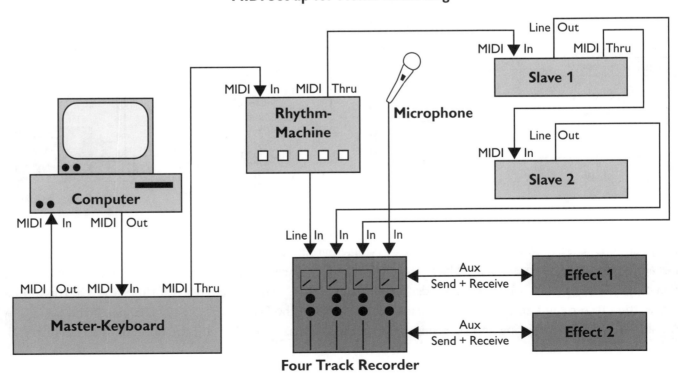

208

11 THE MAGICAL KEYBOARD TABLES

Everything at a glance: Chords, Harmonics, Scales, Improvisation Scales, Intervals – with and without notes

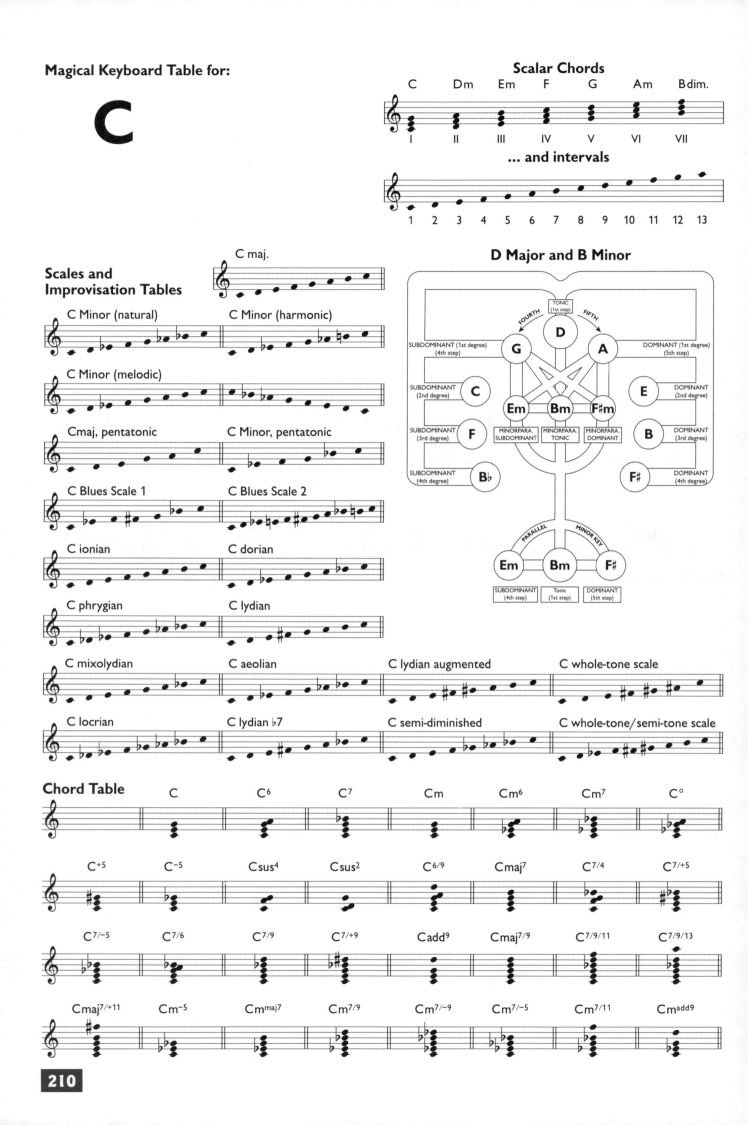

The Intervals

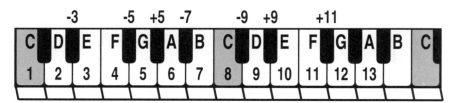

Scales and Improvisation Tables

C major-scale

C major pentatonic
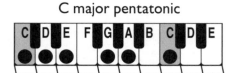

C Blues Scale 1
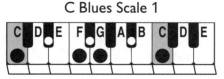

C minor scale (natural)

C minor pentatonic
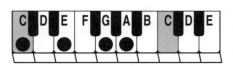

C Blues Scale 2

Chord Table

C

C⁶
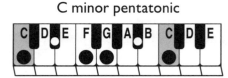

C⁷
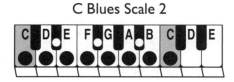

Cmaj⁷

Csus⁴

C⁷ᐟ⁴
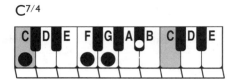

C⁷ᐟ⁺⁵

Cm

Cm⁶
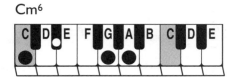

Cm⁷

Cm⁷ᐟ⁻⁵
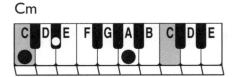

C°
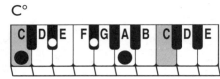

C⁷ᐟ⁹
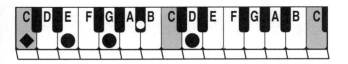

C⁷ᐟ⁺⁹
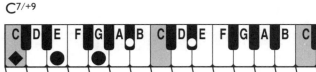

Cm⁷ᐟ⁹
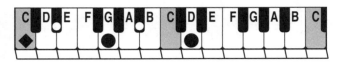

Cm⁷ᐟ⁻⁹
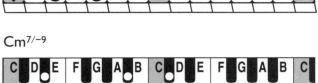

C⁷ᐟ⁹ᐟ¹¹

C⁷ᐟ⁹ᐟ¹³
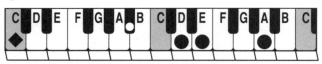

Magical Keyboard Table for:

C♯/D♭

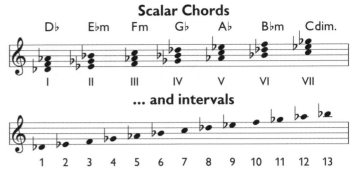

Scalar Chords

Db   Ebm   Fm   Gb   Ab   Bbm   Cdim.

I   II   III   IV   V   VI   VII

... and intervals

1 2 3 4 5 6 7 8 9 10 11 12 13

Scales and Improvisation Tables

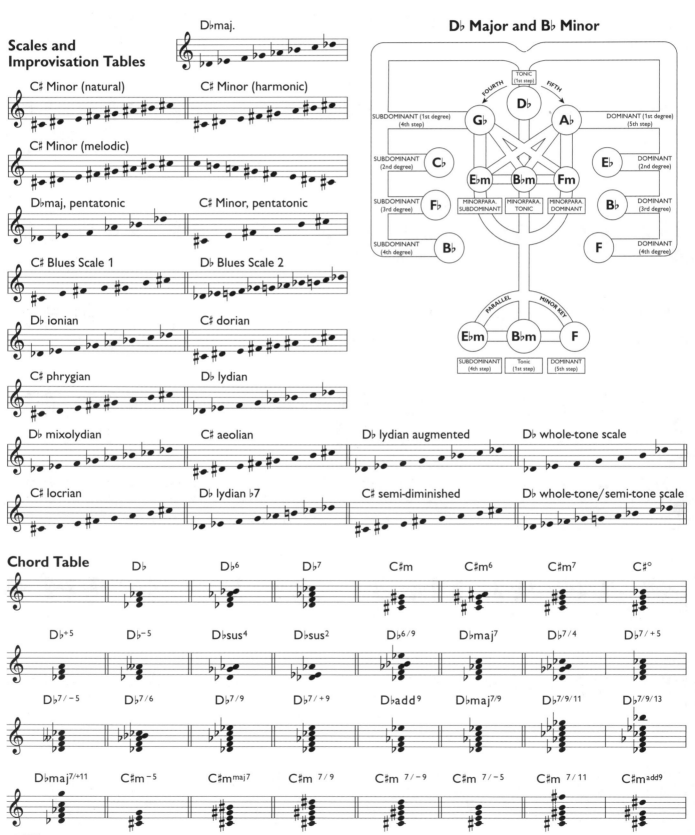

Db Major and Bb Minor

Chord Table

The Intervals

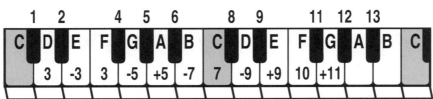

Scales and Improvisation Tables

D♭ major-scale

D♭ major pentatonic

D♭ Blues Scale 1
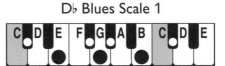

D♭ minor scale (natural)

D♭ minor pentatonic

D♭ Blues Scale 2
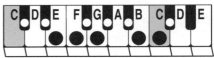

Chord Table

D♭

D♭6

D♭7

D♭maj7

D♭sus4
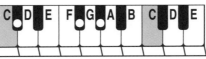

D♭7/4

D♭7/+5

D♭m

D♭m6

D♭m7

D♭m7/−5

D♭°

D♭7/9

D♭7/+9

D♭m7/9

D♭m7/−9
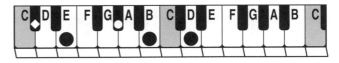

D♭7/9/11
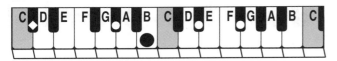

D♭7/9/13

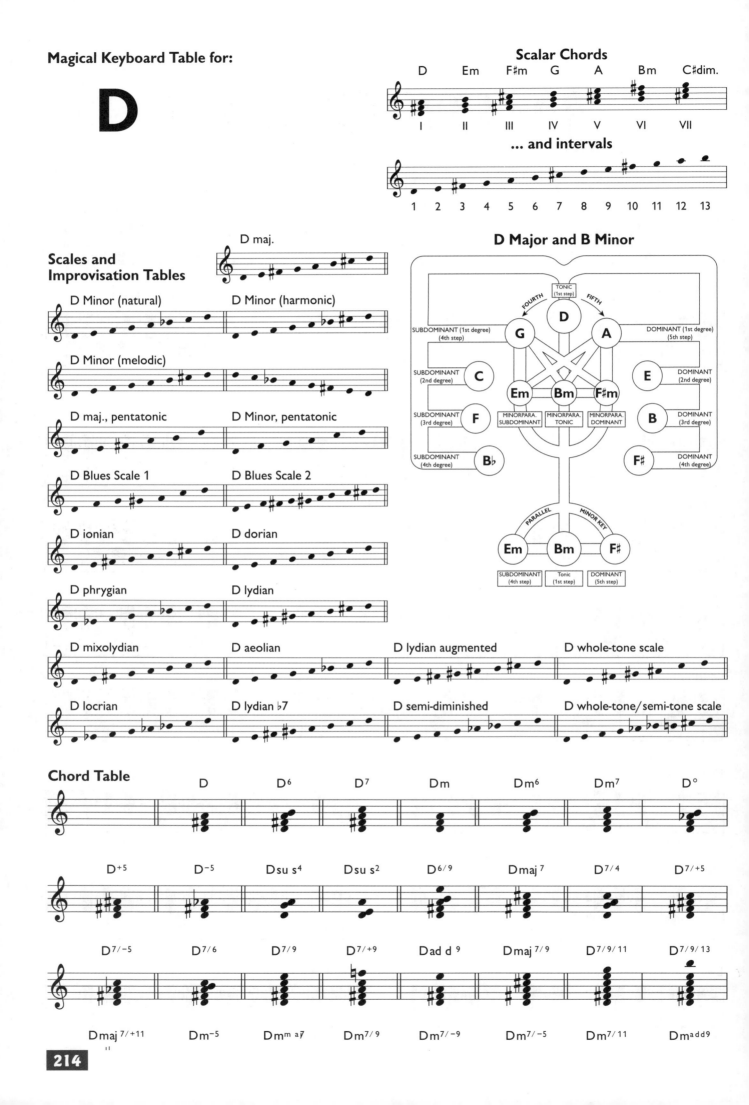

The Intervals

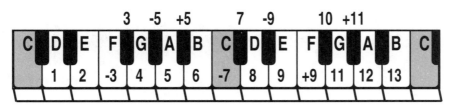

Scales and Improvisation Tables

D major-scale

D major pentatonic
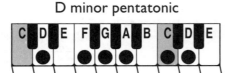

D Blues Scale 1
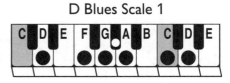

D minor scale (natural)

D minor pentatonic
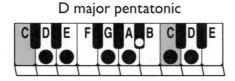

D Blues Scale 2
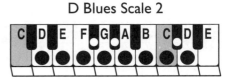

Chord Table

D

D⁶
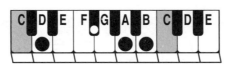

D⁷

Dmaj⁷

Dsus⁴
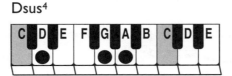

D⁷ᐟ⁴

D⁷ᐟ⁺⁵

Dm

Dm⁶
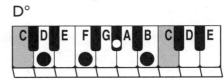

Dm⁷

Dm⁷ᐟ⁻⁵

D°
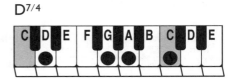

D⁷ᐟ⁹
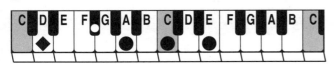

D⁷ᐟ⁺⁹

Dm⁷ᐟ⁹
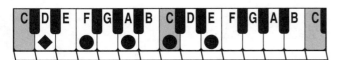

Dm⁷ᐟ⁻⁹
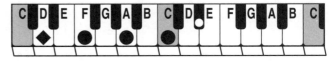

D⁷ᐟ⁹ᐟ¹¹

D⁷ᐟ⁹ᐟ¹³

215

Magical Keyboard Table for:

E♭

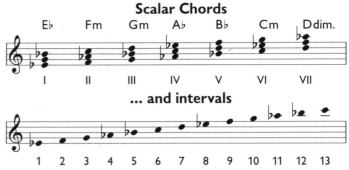

Scalar Chords

... and intervals

Scales and Improvisation Tables

E♭ maj.

E♭ Minor (natural)   E♭ Minor (harmonic)

E♭ Minor (melodic)

E♭ maj. pentatonic   E♭ Minor, pentatonic

E♭ Blues Scale 1   E♭ Blues Scale 2

E♭ ionian   C dorian

E♭ phrygian   C lydian

E♭ mixolydian   E♭ aeolian   E♭ lydian augmented   E♭ whole-tone scale

E♭ locrian   E♭ lydian ♭7   E♭ semi-diminished   E♭ whole-tone/semi-tone scale

E♭ Major and C Minor

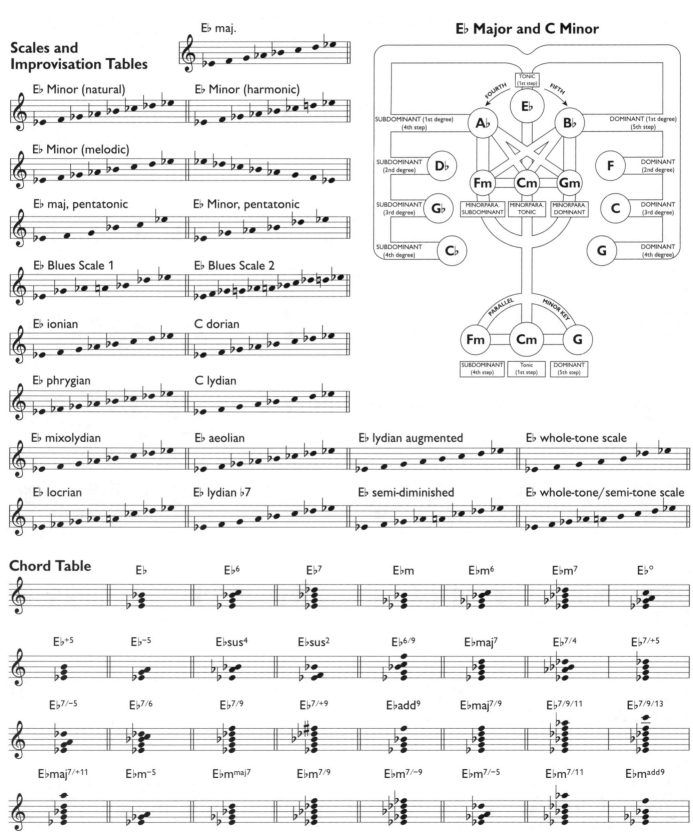

Chord Table

E♭   E♭6   E♭7   E♭m   E♭m6   E♭m7   E♭°

E♭+5   E♭−5   E♭sus4   E♭sus2   E♭6/9   E♭maj7   E♭7/4   E♭7/+5

E♭7/−5   E♭7/6   E♭7/9   E♭7/+9   E♭add9   E♭maj7/9   E♭7/9/11   E♭7/9/13

E♭maj7/+11   E♭m−5   E♭mmaj7   E♭m7/9   E♭m7/−9   E♭m7/−5   E♭m7/11   E♭madd9

The Intervals

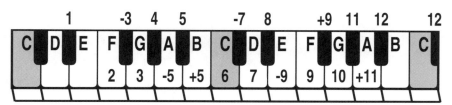

Scales and Improvisation Tables

E♭ major-scale

E♭ major pentatonic

E♭ Blues Scale 1

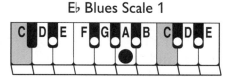

E♭ minor scale (natural)

E♭ minor pentatonic

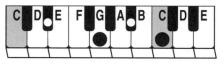

E♭ Blues Scale 2

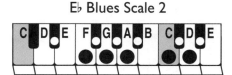

Chord Table

E♭

E♭⁶

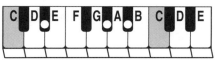

E♭⁷

E♭maj⁷

E♭sus⁴

E♭⁷/⁴

E♭⁷/⁺⁵

E♭m

E♭m⁶

E♭m⁷

E♭m⁷/⁻⁵

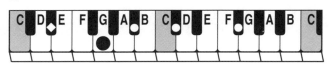

E♭°

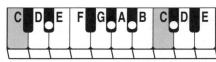

E♭⁷/⁹

E♭⁷/⁺⁹

E♭m⁷/⁹

E♭m⁷/⁻⁹

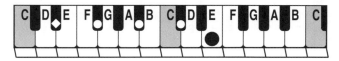

E♭⁷/⁹/¹¹

E♭⁷/⁹/¹³

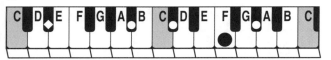
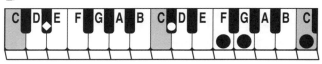

217

Magical Keyboard Table for:

E

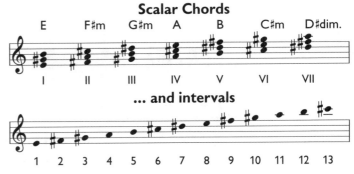

Scalar Chords

E   F#m   G#m   A   B   C#m   D#dim.

I   II   III   IV   V   VI   VII

... and intervals

1 2 3 4 5 6 7 8 9 10 11 12 13

Scales and Improvisation Tables

E maj.

E Minor (natural)   E Minor (harmonic)

E Minor (melodic)

E maj, pentatonic   E Minor, pentatonic

E Blues Scale 1   E Blues Scale 2

E ionian   C dorian

E phrygian   C lydian

E mixolydian   E aeolian   E lydian augmented   E whole-tone scale

E locrian   E lydian ♭7   E semi-diminished   E whole-tone/semi-tone scale

E Major and C# Minor

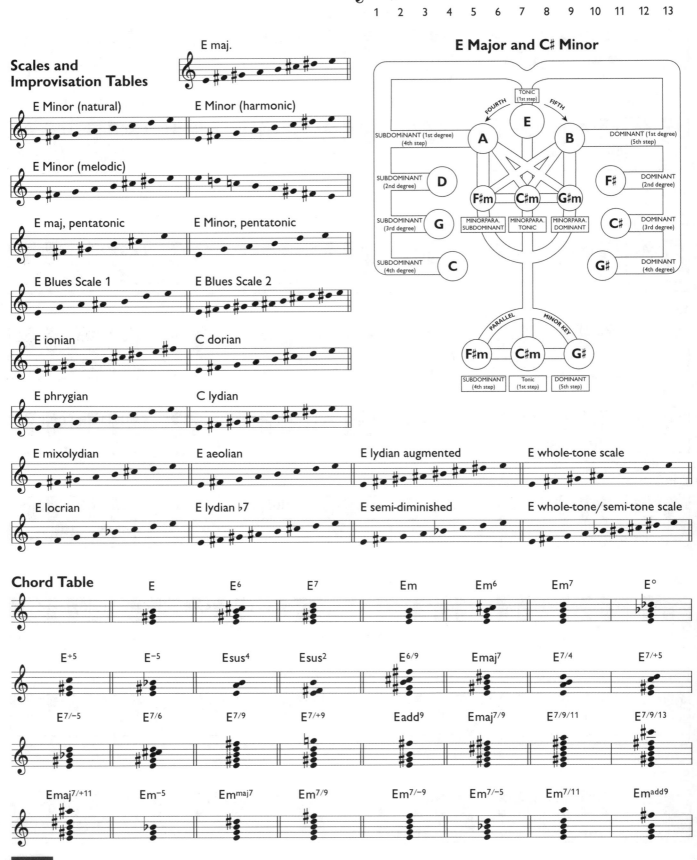

Chord Table

E   E⁶   E⁷   Em   Em⁶   Em⁷   E°

E⁺⁵   E⁻⁵   Esus⁴   Esus²   E⁶/⁹   Emaj⁷   E⁷/⁴   E⁷/⁺⁵

E⁷/⁻⁵   E⁷/⁶   E⁷/⁹   E⁷/⁺⁹   Eadd⁹   Emaj⁷/⁹   E⁷/⁹/¹¹   E⁷/⁹/¹³

Emaj⁷/⁺¹¹   Em⁻⁵   Em^maj7   Em⁷/⁹   Em⁷/⁻⁹   Em⁷/⁻⁵   Em⁷/¹¹   Em^add9

The Intervals

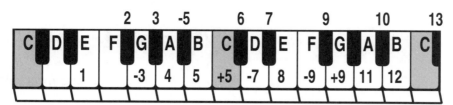

Scales and Improvisation Tables

E major-scale
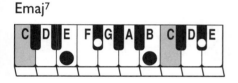

E major pentatonic

E Blues Scale 1
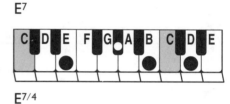

E minor scale (natural)

E minor pentatonic

E Blues Scale 2
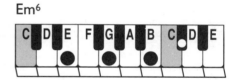

Chord Table

E
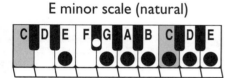

E⁶

E^6
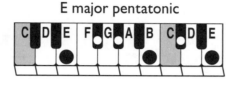

E^7
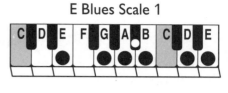

Emaj⁷

$E\text{maj}^7$
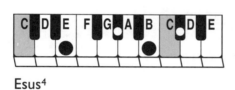

Esus⁴

$E\text{sus}^4$
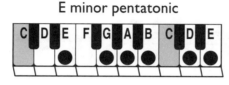

$E^{7/4}$
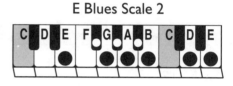

$E^{7/+5}$

Em

Em^6
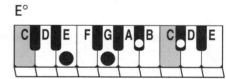

Em^7
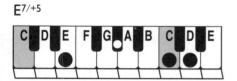

$Em^{7/-5}$
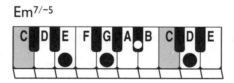

E°
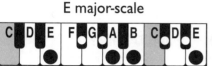

$E^{7/9}$
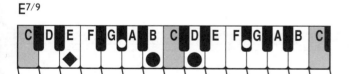

$E^{7/+9}$
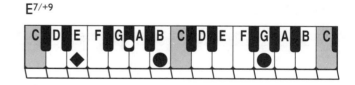

$Em^{7/9}$
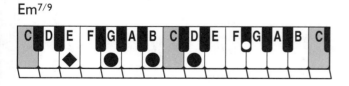

$Em^{7/-9}$
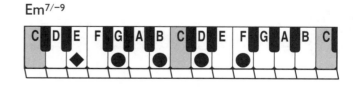

$E^{7/9/11}$
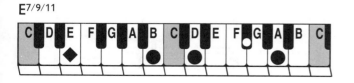

$E^{7/9/13}$
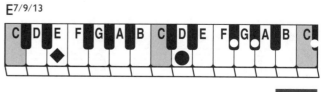

219

Magical Keyboard Table for:

F

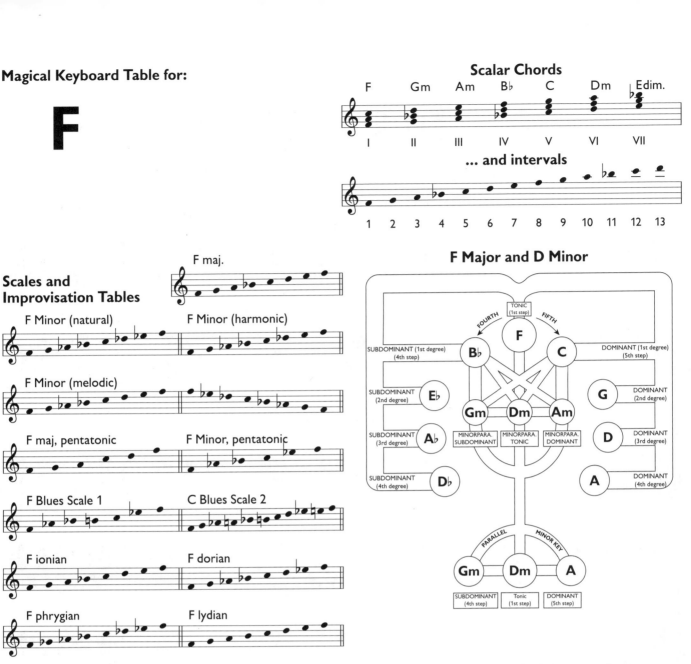

Scalar Chords

F   Gm   Am   B♭   C   Dm   Edim.

I   II   III   IV   V   VI   VII

... and intervals

1 2 3 4 5 6 7 8 9 10 11 12 13

Scales and Improvisation Tables

F maj.

F Minor (natural)   F Minor (harmonic)

F Minor (melodic)

F maj, pentatonic   F Minor, pentatonic

F Blues Scale 1   C Blues Scale 2

F ionian   F dorian

F phrygian   F lydian

F mixolydian   F aeolian   F lydian augmented   F whole-tone scale

F locrian   F lydian ♭7   F semi-diminished   F whole-tone/semi-tone scale

F Major and D Minor

Chord Table

F   F⁶   F⁷   Fm   Fm⁶   Fm⁷   F°

F⁺⁵   F⁻⁵   Fsus⁴   Fsus²   F⁶ᐟ⁹   Fmaj⁷   F⁷ᐟ⁴   F⁷ᐟ⁺⁵

F⁷ᐟ⁻⁵   F⁷ᐟ⁶   F⁷ᐟ⁹   F⁷ᐟ⁺⁹   Fadd⁹   Fmaj⁷ᐟ⁹   F⁷ᐟ⁹ᐟ¹¹   F⁷ᐟ⁹ᐟ¹³

Fmaj⁷ᐟ⁺¹¹   Fm⁻⁵   Fmᵐᵃʲ⁷   Fm⁷ᐟ⁹   Fm⁷ᐟ⁻⁹   Fm⁷ᐟ⁻⁵   Fm⁷ᐟ¹¹   Fmᵃᵈᵈ⁹

The Intervals

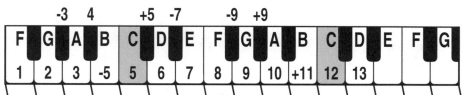

Scales and Improvisation Tables

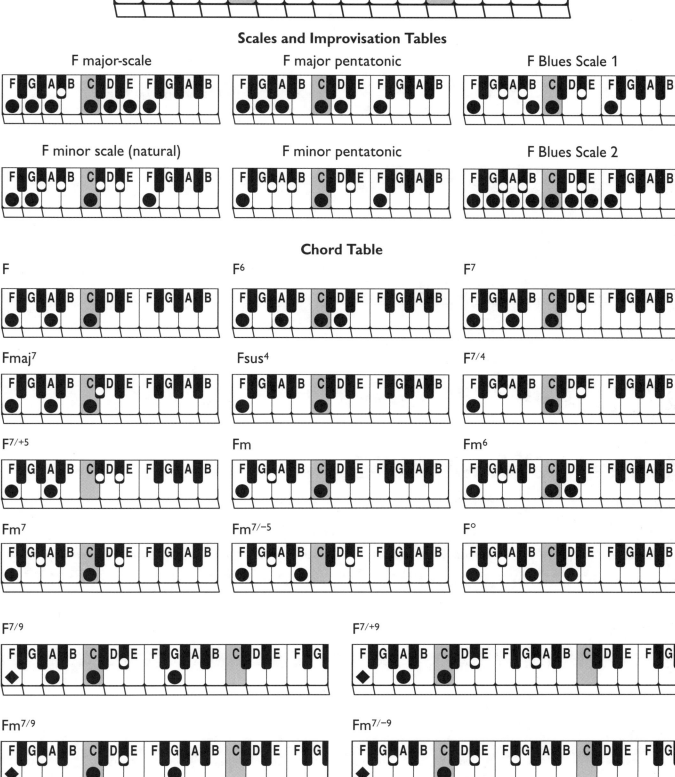

F major-scale

F major pentatonic

F Blues Scale 1

F minor scale (natural)

F minor pentatonic

F Blues Scale 2

Chord Table

F

F^6

F^7

$Fmaj^7$

$Fsus^4$

$F^{7/4}$

$F^{7/+5}$

Fm

Fm^6

Fm^7

$Fm^{7/-5}$

F°

$F^{7/9}$

$F^{7/+9}$

$Fm^{7/9}$

$Fm^{7/-9}$

$F^{7/9/11}$

$F^{7/9/13}$

Magical Keyboard Table for:

F♯/G♭

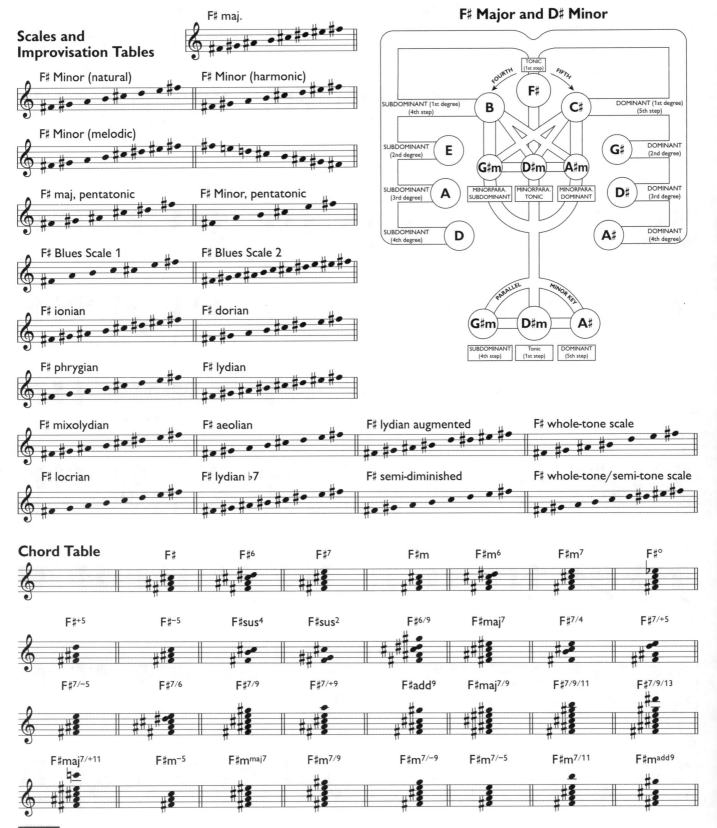
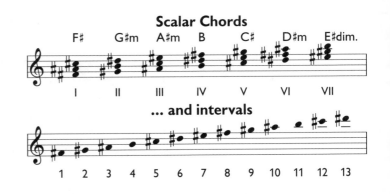

Scalar Chords

F♯	G♯m	A♯m	B	C♯	D♯m	E♯dim.
I	II	III	IV	V	VI	VII

... and intervals

1 2 3 4 5 6 7 8 9 10 11 12 13

Scales and Improvisation Tables

F♯ maj.

F♯ Minor (natural)   F♯ Minor (harmonic)

F♯ Minor (melodic)

F♯ maj, pentatonic   F♯ Minor, pentatonic

F♯ Blues Scale 1   F♯ Blues Scale 2

F♯ ionian   F♯ dorian

F♯ phrygian   F♯ lydian

F♯ mixolydian   F♯ aeolian   F♯ lydian augmented   F♯ whole-tone scale

F♯ locrian   F♯ lydian ♭7   F♯ semi-diminished   F♯ whole-tone/semi-tone scale

F♯ Major and D♯ Minor

Chord Table

F♯   F♯6   F♯7   F♯m   F♯m6   F♯m7   F♯°

F♯+5   F♯−5   F♯sus4   F♯sus2   F♯6/9   F♯maj7   F♯7/4   F♯7/+5

F♯7/−5   F♯7/6   F♯7/9   F♯7/+9   F♯add9   F♯maj7/9   F♯7/9/11   F♯7/9/13

F♯maj7/+11   F♯m−5   F♯mmaj7   F♯m7/9   F♯m7/−9   F♯m7/−5   F♯m7/11   F♯madd9

The Intervals

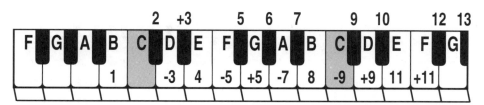

Scales and Improvisation Tables

F# major-scale
F# major pentatonic
F# Blues Scale 1

F# minor scale (natural)
F# minor pentatonic
F# Blues Scale 2

Chord Table

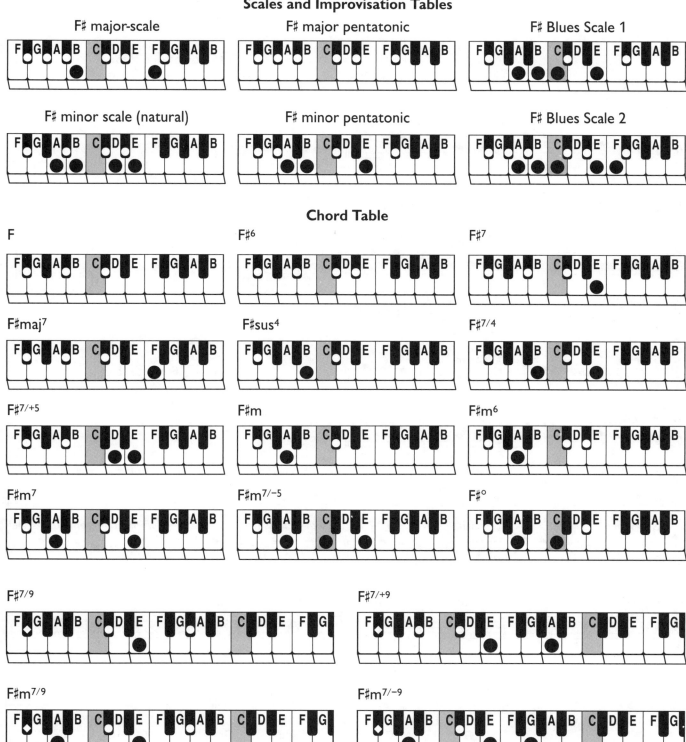

F

F#6

F#7

F#maj7

F#sus4

F#7/4

F#7/+5

F#m

F#m6

F#m7

F#m7/−5

F#°

F#7/9

F#7/+9

F#m7/9

F#m7/−9

F#7/9/11

F#7/9/13

Magical Keyboard Table for:

G

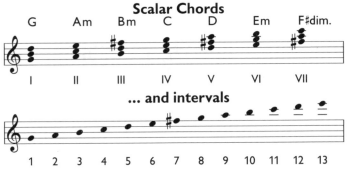

Scalar Chords

G   Am   Bm   C   D   Em   F#dim.

I   II   III   IV   V   VI   VII

... and intervals

1   2   3   4   5   6   7   8   9   10   11   12   13

Scales and Improvisation Tables

G maj.

G Minor (natural)   G Minor (harmonic)

G Minor (melodic)

G maj, pentatonic   G Minor, pentatonic

G Blues Scale 1   G Blues Scale 2

G ionian   G dorian

G phrygian   G lydian

G mixolydian   G aeolian   G lydian augmented   G whole-tone scale

G locrian   G lydian ♭7   G semi-diminished   G whole-tone/semi-tone scale

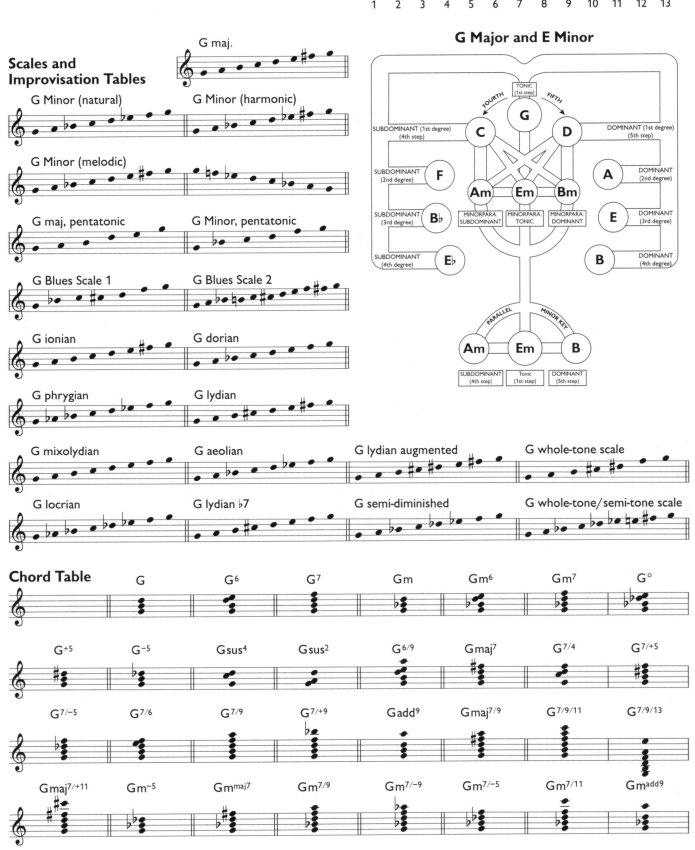

G Major and E Minor

Chord Table

G   G⁶   G⁷   Gm   Gm⁶   Gm⁷   G°

G⁺⁵   G⁻⁵   Gsus⁴   Gsus²   G⁶ᐟ⁹   Gmaj⁷   G⁷ᐟ⁴   G⁷ᐟ⁺⁵

G⁷ᐟ⁻⁵   G⁷ᐟ⁶   G⁷ᐟ⁹   G⁷ᐟ⁺⁹   Gadd⁹   Gmaj⁷ᐟ⁹   G⁷ᐟ⁹ᐟ¹¹   G⁷ᐟ⁹ᐟ¹³

Gmaj⁷ᐟ⁺¹¹   Gm⁻⁵   Gmᵐᵃʲ⁷   Gm⁷ᐟ⁹   Gm⁷ᐟ⁻⁹   Gm⁷ᐟ⁻⁵   Gm⁷ᐟ¹¹   Gmᵃᵈᵈ⁹

224

The Intervals

Scales and Improvisation Tables

G major-scale

G major pentatonic

G Blues Scale 1

G minor scale (natural)

G minor pentatonic

G Blues Scale 2

Chord Table

G

G⁶

G⁷

Gmaj⁷

Gsus⁴

G⁷/⁴

G⁷/⁺⁵

Gm

Gm⁶

Gm⁷

Gm⁷/⁻⁵

G°

G⁷/⁹

G⁷/⁺⁹

Gm⁷/⁹

Gm⁷/⁻⁹

G⁷/⁹/¹¹

G⁷/⁹/¹³

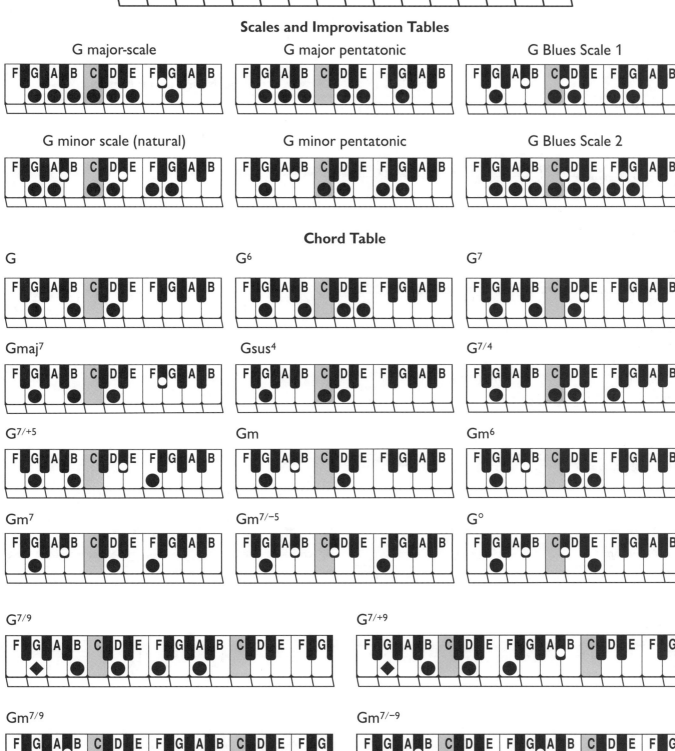

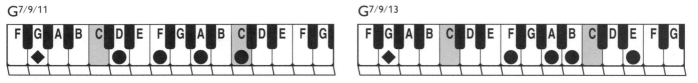

Magical Keyboard Table for:

A♭/G♯

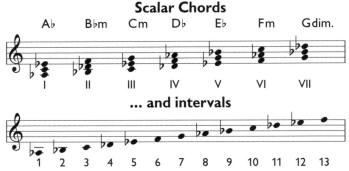

A♭	B♭m	Cm	D♭	E♭	Fm	Gdim.
I	II	III	IV	V	VI	VII

... and intervals

1 2 3 4 5 6 7 8 9 10 11 12 13

Scales and Improvisation Tables

A♭ maj.

A♭ Minor (natural) A♭ Minor (harmonic)

C Minor (melodic)

A♭ maj, pentatonic A♭ Minor, pentatonic

A♭ Blues Scale 1 A♭ Blues Scale 2

A♭ ionian A♭ dorian

A♭ phrygian A♭ lydian

A♭ mixolydian A♭ aeolian A♭ lydian augmented A♭ whole-tone scale

A♭ locrian A♭ lydian ♭7 A♭ semi-diminished A♭ whole-tone/semi-tone scale

A♭ Major and F Minor

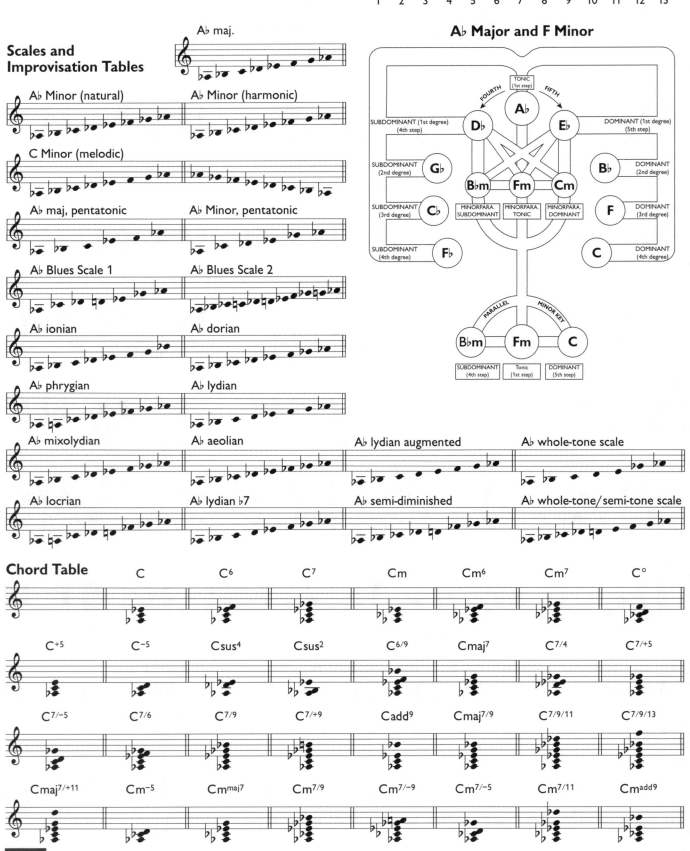

Chord Table

| C | C⁶ | C⁷ | Cm | Cm⁶ | Cm⁷ | C° |

| C⁺⁵ | C⁻⁵ | Csus⁴ | Csus² | C⁶ᐟ⁹ | Cmaj⁷ | C⁷ᐟ⁴ | C⁷ᐟ⁺⁵ |

| C⁷ᐟ⁻⁵ | C⁷ᐟ⁶ | C⁷ᐟ⁹ | C⁷ᐟ⁺⁹ | Cadd⁹ | Cmaj⁷ᐟ⁹ | C⁷ᐟ⁹ᐟ¹¹ | C⁷ᐟ⁹ᐟ¹³ |

| Cmaj⁷ᐟ⁺¹¹ | Cm⁻⁵ | Cmᵐᵃʲ⁷ | Cm⁷ᐟ⁹ | Cm⁷ᐟ⁻⁹ | Cm⁷ᐟ⁻⁵ | Cm⁷ᐟ¹¹ | Cmᵃᵈᵈ⁹ |

The Intervals

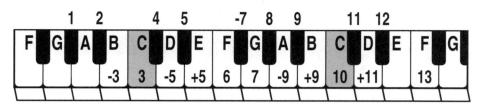

Scales and Improvisation Tables

A♭ major-scale

A♭ major pentatonic

A♭ Blues Scale 1
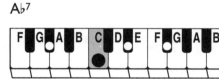

A♭ minor scale (natural)
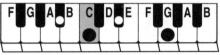

A♭ minor pentatonic
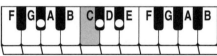

A♭ Blues Scale 2
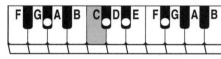

Chord Table

A♭
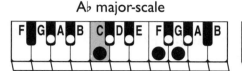

A♭⁶

A♭⁷
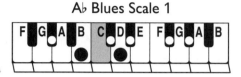

A♭maj⁷

A♭sus⁴

A♭⁷/⁴

A♭⁷/⁺⁵

A♭m
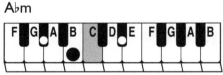

A♭m⁶
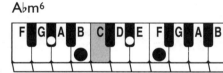

A♭m⁷

A♭m⁷/⁻⁵

A♭°
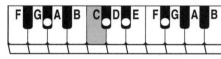

A♭⁷/⁹
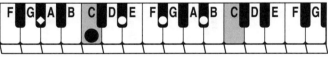

A♭⁷/⁺⁹

A♭m⁷/⁹

A♭m⁷/⁻⁹
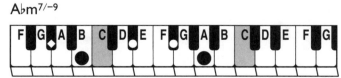

A♭⁷/⁹/¹¹
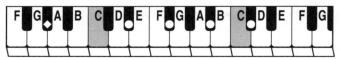

A♭⁷/⁹/¹³

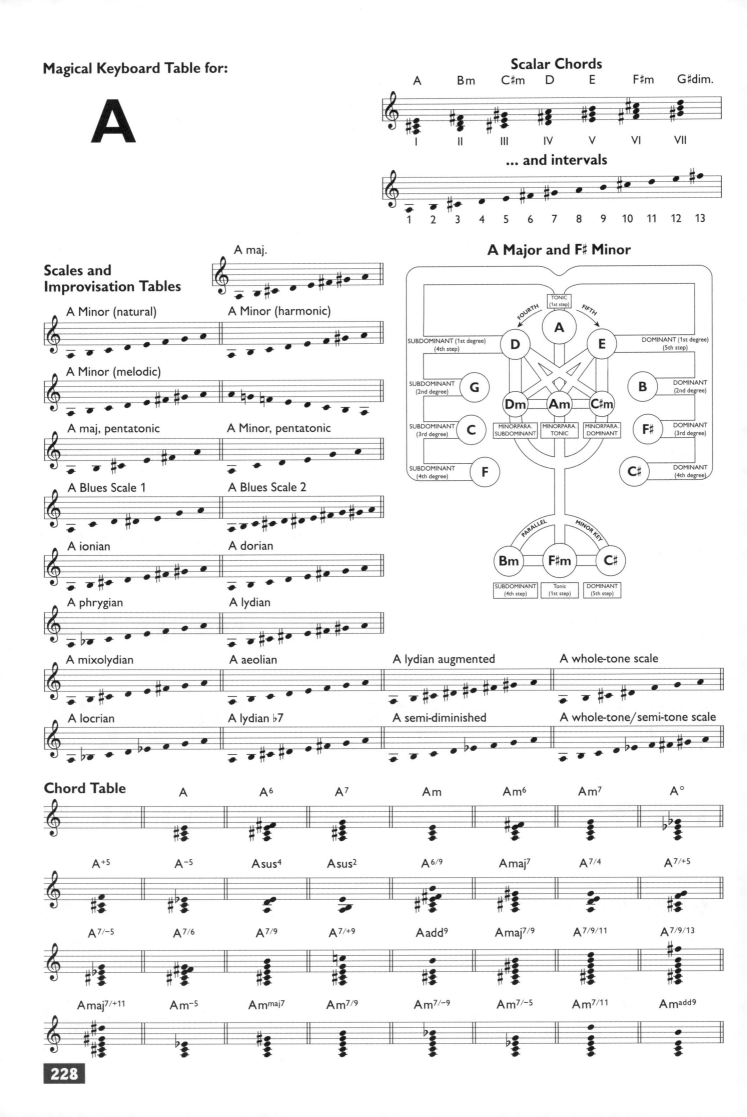

The Intervals

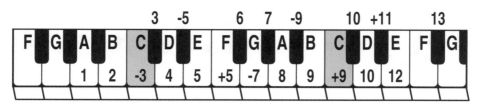

Scales and Improvisation Tables

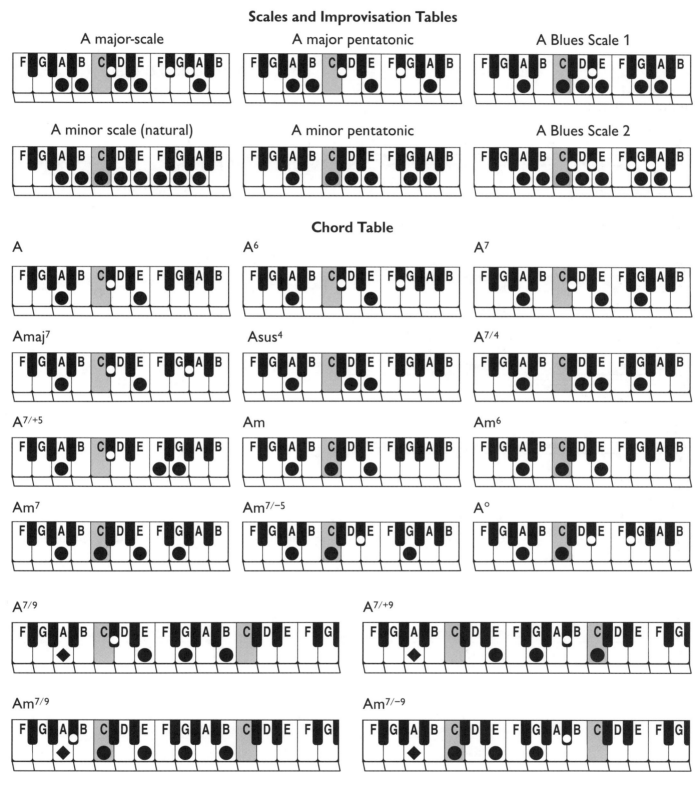

A major-scale   A major pentatonic   A Blues Scale 1

A minor scale (natural)   A minor pentatonic   A Blues Scale 2

Chord Table

A   A⁶   A⁷

Amaj⁷   Asus⁴   A⁷ᐟ⁴

A⁷ᐟ⁺⁵   Am   Am⁶

Am⁷   Am⁷ᐟ⁻⁵   A°

A⁷ᐟ⁹   A⁷ᐟ⁺⁹

Am⁷ᐟ⁹   Am⁷ᐟ⁻⁹

A⁷ᐟ⁹ᐟ¹¹   A⁷ᐟ⁹ᐟ¹³

229

Magical Keyboard Table for:

B♭/A♯

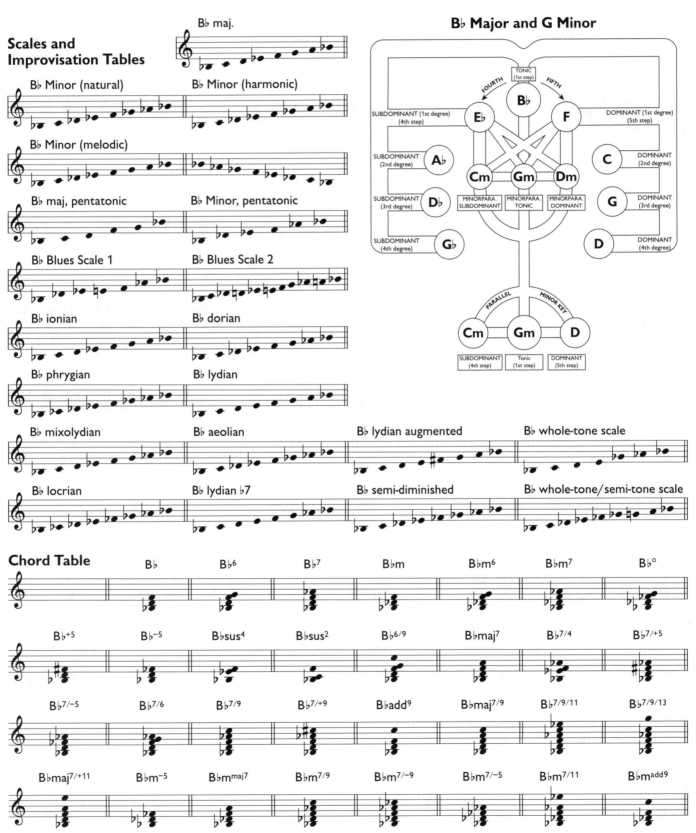

Scales and Improvisation Tables

Bb maj.

Bb Minor (natural)   Bb Minor (harmonic)

Bb Minor (melodic)

Bb maj, pentatonic   Bb Minor, pentatonic

Bb Blues Scale 1   Bb Blues Scale 2

Bb ionian   Bb dorian

Bb phrygian   Bb lydian

Bb mixolydian   Bb aeolian   Bb lydian augmented   Bb whole-tone scale

Bb locrian   Bb lydian b7   Bb semi-diminished   Bb whole-tone/semi-tone scale

Bb Major and G Minor

Chord Table

Bb   Bb⁶   Bb⁷   Bbm   Bbm⁶   Bbm⁷   Bb°

Bb⁺⁵   Bb⁻⁵   Bbsus⁴   Bbsus²   Bb⁶/⁹   Bbmaj⁷   Bb⁷/⁴   Bb⁷/⁺⁵

Bb⁷⁻⁵   Bb⁷/⁶   Bb⁷/⁹   Bb⁷/⁺⁹   Bbadd⁹   Bbmaj⁷/⁹   Bb⁷/⁹/¹¹   Bb⁷/⁹/¹³

Bbmaj⁷/⁺¹¹   Bbm⁻⁵   Bbmᵐᵃʲ⁷   Bbm⁷/⁹   Bbm⁷/⁻⁹   Bbm⁷/⁻⁵   Bbm⁷/¹¹   Bbmadd⁹

230

The Intervals

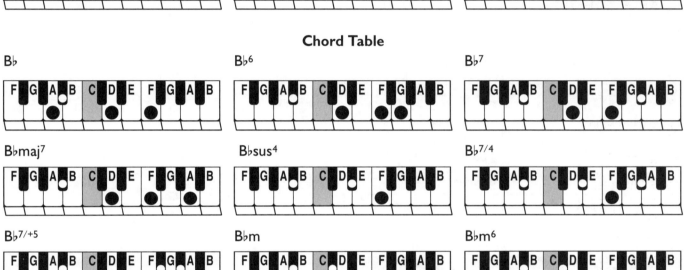

Scales and Improvisation Tables

B♭ major-scale

B♭ major pentatonic

B♭ Blues Scale 1

B♭ minor scale (natural)

B♭ minor pentatonic

B♭ Blues Scale 2

Chord Table

B♭

B♭⁶

B♭⁷

B♭maj⁷

B♭sus⁴

B♭⁷/⁴

B♭⁷/⁺⁵

B♭m

B♭m⁶

B♭m⁷

B♭m⁷/⁻⁵

B♭°

B♭⁷/⁹

B♭⁷/⁺⁹

B♭m⁷/⁹

B♭m⁷/⁻⁹

B♭⁷/⁹/¹¹

B♭⁷/⁹/¹³

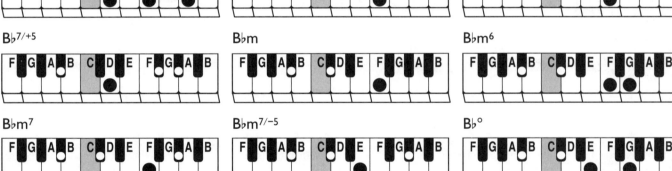
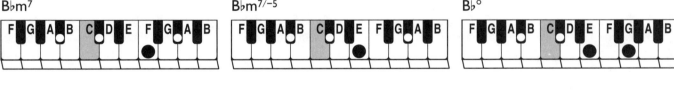
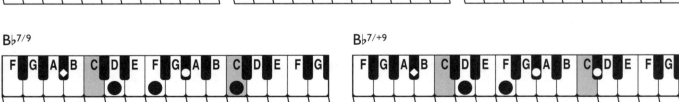
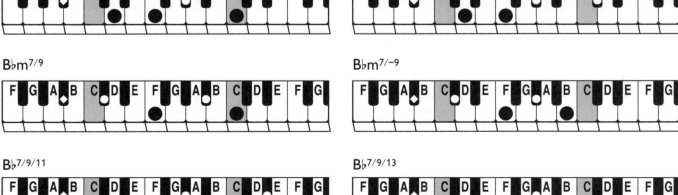

Magical Keyboard Table for:

B

Scalar Chords

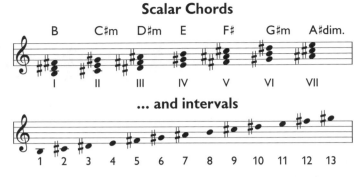

... and intervals

Scales and Improvisation Tables

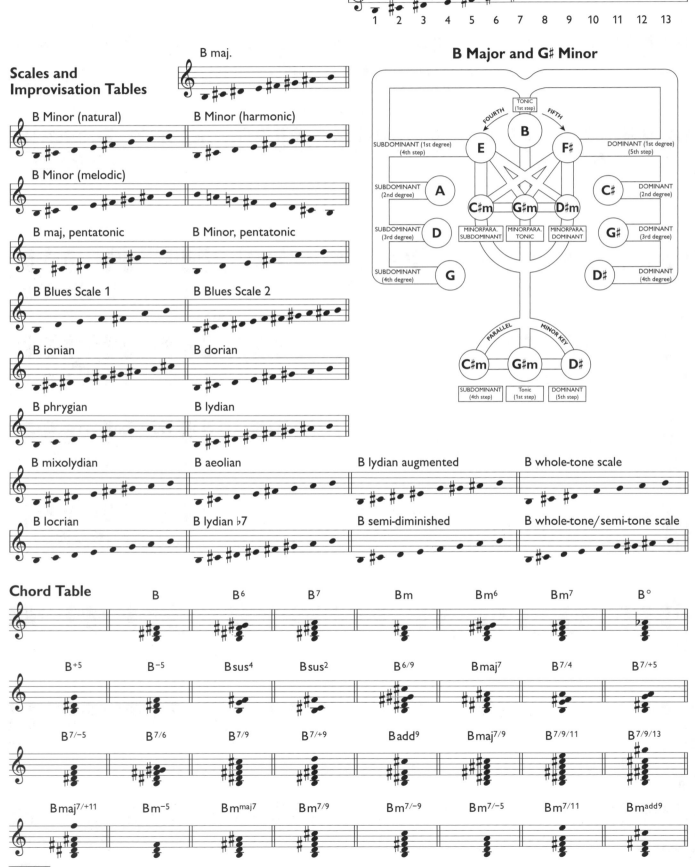

B Major and G♯ Minor

Chord Table

The Intervals

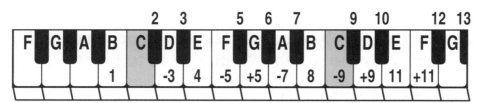

Scales and Improvisation Tables

B major-scale

B major pentatonic
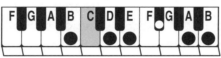

B Blues Scale 1
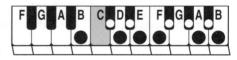

B minor scale (natural)
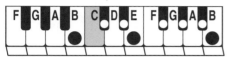

B minor pentatonic
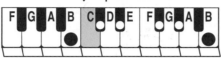

B Blues Scale 2
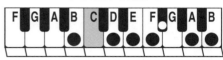

Chord Table

B
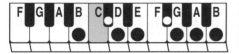

B⁶

B⁷
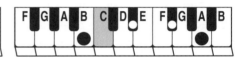

Bmaj⁷
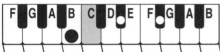

Bsus⁴

B⁷/⁴
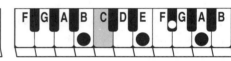

B⁷/⁺⁵

Bm
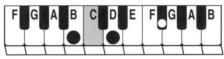

Bm⁶

Bm⁷

Bm⁷/⁻⁵

B°

B⁷/⁹

B⁷/⁺⁹

Bm⁷/⁹

Bm⁷/⁻⁹

B⁷/⁹/¹¹

B⁷/⁹/¹³

12 KEYBOARD DICTIONARY

From Analogue–Synthesizer, Attack Time and Adagio via MIDI, Master-Keyboard and Mixing Desk to Xylophone

A

Abbreviation: abbreviate: to shorten

Absolute hearing: The seldom ability to exactly determine pitch without aids or comparison tones

AC: Abbreviation for Alternating Current

a capella: choral vocals without instrumental accompaniment

Accelerando: Musical direction = gradually increasing speed

Accent: the emphasis of a sound or noise, e.g. the snare drum on a rhythm machine. →Dynamics

Access: ability to reach, e.g. a place in the memory

Accidentals: Whereas the symbol (♯) raises a tone by one-half, the symbol (♭) diminishes it by one-half. A ♯ makes, for example, C become C sharp; a ♭ makes C become C flat

Accidentals: Every major chord (except C major) has to have a certain number of notes with →accidentals (sharp, flat or natural), in order to maintain the structure of the whole and half steps. These accidentals often make the note picture very difficult to decipher, which is why the characteristic accidentals that belong to each type of note are bundled together at the start of a piece of music i.e. in the key signature. They are then known as accidentals.

AC/DC: Means "can be used for either alternating current or direct current". Musician's jargon for "gay" or "bisexual". Also a cool Hardrock band that was successful during the last three decades of the last millennium.

AC-Hum: interference occuring in electric transmission units which has the frequency of 50 Hz. (60 Hz in the USA). Occurs normally because of the false earthing of the unit.

Acoustics: the science of sound

Act: 1. musicians on a record label 2. musical or show presentation

Action: 1. refers to the number of occurences in a musical show. 2. mechanism of a piano, for example

A/D-Converter: →Sampling

Adagio: →Tempo

Adaptation: the modification of parts of already existing music in another musical style
(e.g. Classical music to Rock music).

Adapter: used to connect plugs and sockets of differing standards

Additive Sound Synthesis: →Synthesizer

Ad libitum (ad lib): at pleasure, to any extent

Aeolian: eccelesiastical mode

AF: abbr. for Audio Frequency (30 to 20.000 Hz)

Afro-American Music: American music which is strongly influenced by elements of African music. Afro-American elements can be found in Jazz, Blues, Reggae and others

Afro-Rock: music from Rock-musicians from (West) Africa, which combines American-European Rock music with African music.

After-Touch: function with which the sound produced by striking a key can be changed by depressing the key strongly

Agogics: everything which refers to variations in tempo: Rallentando (rall) = gradually becoming slower; ritardando (rit) = slower; rubato = time varied for expression; accelerando (acc) = gradually increasing the speed.

Al Fine: play up to (the word) Fine = End.

Algorithm: 1. prescribed calculating process, sequence of instructions and rules to solve a problem 2. permanently wired chain of units.

Algorithmic Synthesizer: →Synthesizer

Alla breve: →Half time

Allegro: →Tempo

Alternating current: electrical current which at a certain frequency constantly changes polarity at its poles.

Alteration: the raising or lowering of a scalar note

Alto: →Voice modes

Amount: value, strength, size

Amplifier (amp): unit or circuit with which a current, a voltage or an output can be increased. For the stage there are amplifiers with built-in loudspeakers and effects, so-called combo-amplifiers

Amplitude: →Sound, -extent of vibration or oscillation: The greater the amplitude, the louder the note.

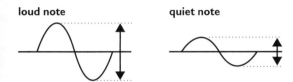

loud note   quiet note

Amplitude modulation: →Synthesizer; Tremolo

analogue: continual, uniform, constant; something which can assume any intermediate value (opposite: digital)

Analogue Recording: recording made with tape recorders or cassette recorders. (Opposite: →Digital Recording)

Analogue Synthesizer: →Synthesizer

Analyzer: unit used to inform of and set the frequency

Andante: →Tempo

Aria: extended song in three sections/opera – also song-like instrumental section

Arpeggiator: effect unit (often built into keyboards), which produces an automatic or freely programmable Arpeggio

Arpeggio: striking of notes in a chord in succession (usually ascending) often in a certain pattern which is continuously repeated.

Arranger: automatic accompaniment function

Arrangement: the processing of a piece of music

Articulation: the way in which individual notes are joined together: 1. Legato – smoothly without breaks; 2. Staccato – in abrupt sharply detached manner; 3. Portato – notes are carried, struck softly but without being connected. 4. Tenuto – sustained giving it's full value.

legato   staccato   portato   tenuto

Artist: refers to the singer or instrumentalist irrespective of whether it has anything to do with art

assemble: gather together - collect, fit together

assignment: allotment, attribution, task allotted, use

asymmetrical: wiring, consisting of only one lead; the shielding functions as the second lead which is necessary to complete the circuit

A tempo: return to the old tempo

Atonal/ity: not conforming by any system of key or mode

Attack-Time: build-up time of an oscillation (note), →Contour Curve

Attenuator: unit which reduces the force of a signal →Damper

Audio: from the Latin "I hear"; collective name for all pieces of equipment which can record or reproduce audible sounds

Audio Frequency Oscillator: →Oscillator which produces oscillations in the audio range/frequency

Augmented chord: triad where the fifth has been raised by a semitone; e.g. C^{+5}

Aural Exiter: →Exiter

Authentic ending: if a piece of music of song (or a section thereof) ends with the succession of chords Dominant – Tonic (V-I)

Auto-Chord: auto accompaniment function

Auto-accompaniment: playing aid →Electric organ →Synthesizer: enables chord and melody storage in memory, usually combined with rhythm unit.

Autodidact: self-taught person

Autolocator: automatic function which locates a certain place on a tape

Auto Repeat: the automatic switching of an envelope generator

Aux: abbreviation for Auxiliary: what is meant is the additional assisting input on a mixing desk or amplifier into which additional equipment can be connected e.g. Effects etc.

B

Back beats: the emphasized beats 2 and 4 in a straight bar

Background: musical support for vocal or instrumental soloists

Backing group: vocal or instrumental group, which provides support for one or more soloists at concerts or in the studio

Balance: the setting for the volume between the two stereo channels

Balanced: method of switching and transmitting without distortion, where the interference is cancelled using its own opposite phase. →(Phase)

Ballad: slow, reflective or romantic song, in which a story is usually told

Banana plug: Long, old-fashioned single pin connector for studio and entertainment electronics. Can still be found in ancient valve radios as outputs or inputs

Band: a small group of musicians

Band width: the scope of the →Frequency range which is let through, amplified or dampened by a →Filter or an →Amplifier

Bandoneon: square built instrument, similar to an accordion with buttons in the treble and bass region, often used for tango

Bank: a group of individual memory stores which belong together

Bar: vertical line across stave dividing piece into sections of equal time value; the section itself

Baritone: →Voice modes

Barrelhouse Piano style: earlier from the "Boogie-Woogie-Style" from New Orleans

Basic: programming language: Beginners All purpose Symbolic Information Code

Basic Track: primary track in musical recordings (usually Rhythm section)

Bass: Voice Modes

Bass Drum: Large drum, played with foot mechanism

Bass Line: the bass or bass-figures in chord accompaniment

Basso ostinato: a continually repeated bass-figure on a continually changing melody

Beat: 1. stroke on drum; signal so given: measured sequence of strokes or sounds; 2. style of music, late 50's on (Beatles etc.)

Beats per minute: A new name for the classic tempo description on Maelzel's Metronome (MM)

Bebop: Jazz-style, developed in 1940 – New York

Bi-directional polar pattern: →Microphone

Big-Band: large group of instrumentalists with at least 10 musicians, large wind section (trumpets, saxophones and trombones), rhythm section (bassist, drums, piano and/or guitar)

Binary: mathematical system with the values 0 and 1. All numbers can be expressed using these two figures: O=O, 1=1, 2=10, 3=11, 4=100, 5=101 etc. Digital computers accept binary codes well because the codes can be translated into currents very easily 1 = large current, 0 = small or no current

Binary rhythm: Division of a basic beat into two equal parts. If the basic beat is a quarter, it would be divided into two eighths. Instead of counting 1, 2, 3, 4 in four-four time, you count 1 and 2 and 3 and 4 and. If the basic beat is an eighth, it would be divided into two sixteenths. In ternary rhythm, the beats would be divided into three equal parts. Instead of counting 1, 2, 3, 4 in 4/4 time, you would count 1-a-day, 2-a-day, 3-a-day, 4-a-day

Bit: abbreviation for Binary Digit: One bit is the smallest unit in a binary system with which information can be conveyed. 1 bit can have the value 0 or 1

Block Chording: playing chords one after the other so that the intervals (mostly) remain the same. This means the hand moves from chord to chord without considerable change in fingering

Bluegrass: Country and Western style

Blue note: typical blues interval: minor third, seventh, diminished fifth

Blues: the melancholy, sentimental music of black Americans. Original form of Jazz and modern Rock and Pop music: mostly 12 bar scheme

Bobbin: tape spool

Bolero: 1. Spanish folk-dance in 3/4 time; 2. Cuban folk-dance (Rumba-Bolero) in 4/4 time

Bongos: two to four drums, mostly struck with the fingers

Boogie-Woogie: rhythmical (Jazz) Piano Style, since 1920's with typical "Walking Bass" and repeating

bass: later also fashionable (Jive), forerunner of Rock and Roll. Contains mostly Blues harmonies

Booster: additional amplifier

Bootleg: illegal copy of record or tape

Bossa Nova: Brazilian music style with Jazz and

Samba-elements

Bounce: tempo and expression mark in swing music

Bourdon: low pitched stop in organ: similar stop in harmonicum drone of for example, bagpipes Indian musical instrument

Bpm: →Beats per minute

Brass: part of the wind section (metallic instruments)

Break: 1. short melodic or rhythmical figure. During the B. most instruments sit out whilst one instrument or voice delivers a solo; 2. obvious pause in the rhythm during drum play

Break-Point: the turning point →Envelope Generator

Breath Controller: mouthpiece which can be connected to a synthesizer. By blowing with varying intensity you can vary the note struck →Modulation

Bridge: middle section of a song

Bright: →Tempo

Bucket brigade: bucket chain memory, analogous memory to delay electric signals, hardly used nowadays due to bad quality

Buffer: intermediate memory, working memory

Bus: distributing bar in mixing desk where different sound signals are brought together

Buzz: humming caused by lack of earth or shielding or an incorrect earth connection, leading to AC-frequency build up in your system which causes the loudspeakers to "buzz" unpleasantly

By-pass: switching on effect units which allows the sound to pass through unchanged

Byte: data unit; 1 Byte = 8-Bits and 1 check bit with one byte

C

Cadence: 1. succession of harmonies; 2. improvisation within a classical instrumental concert

Cajun: Country and Rock-style from Louisiana

Calibrate: calculation of irregularities

Call and Response: play between two soloists. Short melodic phrases which are played by one soloist are repeated or intensified by another

Calypso: South American dance-music style

Cardioid Characteristic: →Directional Characteristic

Capacitor microphone: →Microphone

Capacity: 1. the electronic size of the content capability of a capacitor →measured in Farad (F) and 2. the amount of information which a computer can accomodate

Cardioid polar pattern: →Microphone

Cartridge: plugable memory for computer, Rhythm machine, synthesizer, sequencer

Carrier Frequency: frequence during frequency modulation →Synthesizer

Celesta: Glockenspiel with piano mechanism

Cello: 75 cm long violin, which stands between the legs whilst being played

Cembalo: keyed instrument where the strings are plucked by a spring block

Cent: logarithmic measure concerning intervals; One octave = 1200 cent; a semitone = 100 cent

Chain: in sequencers, parts of the melody, and in rhythm units rhythmical patterns can be connecred to form chains

Changes: successions of chords

Channel messages: →MIDI messages

Chanson: (French) accompan ied song

Chase: quick succession of solo parts by several musicians, mostly lasting only 4 bars

Check: control

Chinch: →Cinch

Chip: 1. minute Silicium lamina upon which a complicated electric circuit is engraved; 2. the component containing such a lamina

Chocallo: (chocalho chocolo) tubular wood, filled with stones: shaker

chop: a single, short, rhythmically accentuated strike

Chord: the simultaneous sounding of at least three notes

Chord memory: →Automatic Accompaniment

Chord scale theory: →Church modes

Chord symbol: The tones of a chord are often described by a combination of letters and numbers. Capital letters describe the → major triad (C thus stands for the C major triad C-E-G); minor chords have a small m appended to the letter of the chord (Cm for example, stands for the C minor triad C-E♭-G). All additional notes, which can also be called →Options/Extensions, are symbolized by appended superscript numbers. A C major chord (C-E-G) with an extra A would then be known as C^6; with an additional B♭, the C major chord would then be known as C^7. If you would like to play an added D to a C^7 chord (the ninth note of the scale), i.e. the notes C-E-G-B♭-D, we would call it $C^{7/9}$. Play also F (the 11th note of the scale) and you have the chord $C^{7/9/11}$. An A instead of the F would result in $C^{7/9/13}$

Chorus: 1. refrain; 2. effect unit, often built into keyboard which produces a hovering, circling effect which multiplies the number of voices

Chromatic scale: A scale that solely comprises of half-note steps (→half note). For example: C, C♯, D, D♯, E, F, F♯, G, G♯, A, A♯, B, C

Church modes: In the major scale, each of the seven steps (every tone) can form the basis of a chord as well as each of them forming the basis of a scale. In the 8th century these scales were named after Greek tribes; later they were developed into the system of church modes. They played a similar function then to major and minor today. In the 17th century they were superseded by the introduction of the major/minor system and →tempered tuning. In the 20th century a few Jazz artists hit on the idea that one can improvise superbly with them, and they developed the old system further to become the chord scale theory. The theory says that you no longer need to decide between chords and their matching scales because they consist of the same notes

Cinch: plug connector for HIFI, tape and effect units

Circle of Fifths: progression through all keys in intervals of fifths

Clap Hands: Hand clap function

Claves: Rumba sticks, two round, wooden sticks

Clavichord: early keyed instrument, the strings of which are played with a metal rod

clean: undistorted

clear: make free, erase

Click Track: metronome track for tempo orienta-tion during sound recording

Clipping: overloading region in →Power Amplifier; can destroy loudspeakers in certain circumstances

Clock: time/beat impulse Rhythm Units

Clock Generator: provides beat

Clock generator: an oscillator which produces a beat impulse to control or →Synchronize different pieces of equipment

Clock Track: beat track; →click track

Clock track: beat track; →Click Track

Close: to shut, i.e. a database

Coarse Tune: basic tuning, basic setting

Coda: appendix to a piece of music

Code: direction for coding data, signals and other information

colour: attribute of a sound, mainly determined by the combination of overtones and by a process of inward and outward oscillation →Envelope curve

Combo: small group of Jazz or Dance-musicians

Combo: →Amp

Combo organ: portable electric organ without loudspeakers or amplifier for stage use

Combo amplifier: →Amplifier

Command: (computer) directive

Common messages: →MIDI messages

Compander: "Compressor and Expander" combined element/unit to influence the dynamics of a sound signal

Composer: sequencer

Compressor: effect unit which compensates the considerable differences in volume of instrument signals

Computer: appliance for the processing of data. Main component is the CPU (Central Processing Unit) which controls the appliance by means of impulse directives/control voltages

Computersynthesizer: digital synthesizer, music computer. Term for a computer-controlled →Sequencer for sound synthesis and/or as a memory for music programmes

Condenser Microphone: →Microphone

Conga: Barrel or ball-shaped wooden drum

Consonance: concord, agreement, harmony, sounding of two notes in harmony

Consonance: Concord, harmonize →intervals. We differentiate between perfect consonance (→prime, →octave, →fifth, and imperfect consonances (minor and major →third, →sixth)

Contour: →Filter contour, →Envelope curve

Control: Button, key or switch to regulate certain functions

Controller: →MIDI messages

Control Voltage: voltage used to control electronic processes. For synthesizers (e.g. →Oscillators and →Filters) mostly -15V and +15V. The Pitch of a synthesizer is determined by a CV usually using the 1V per Octave Characteristic

Converter: (Transducer, Transformer) term for a unit which changes one form of oscillation to another →Loudspeakers and microphones are electromechanical converters. A/D-Converter transforms analogous signals into digital signals. D/A: vice-versa

Copy: instruction to copy a stored word or pattern

Copyright: exclusive right given by law for term of years to author, designer, composer etc. to print, publish or sell copies of his original work

Counter point: →Polyphone music

Country Rock: American style of music which combines Rock music with Country and Western, Hillbilly and Ragtime music

Couplet: song with topical content, music hall song

Cover version: New version of an old song/piece of music by another artist

CPU: Central Processing Unit →Computer

Crescendo (cres.): →Dynamics

Crossfade: The joining of two sounds (such as two songs) by overlapping them in order to create a seamless transition – the end of one tune gradually fades out as a new tune gradually fades in

Cross Modulation: correlative control of the →Oscillators of a →Synthesizer →FM-Modulation

Cross over: put or pass finger or thumb under the other

Crossover Frequency: divisional frequency in a crossover-network

Cross Talk: relationship between wanted signal and unwanted signal (interference) which arises from other channels on a transmission unit, e.g. mixer. Expressed in dB

Crystal-microphone: →Microphone

Cue: audible or visible control on a recorded signal during winding or rewinding

Cursor: marker on a computer monitor controlled by keys or joysticks, indicates the location of the writer

Cut-off-frequency: frequency stop →Filter, →Synthe-sizer

CV: abbreviation for →Control Voltage

Cymbals: one pair of concave bars or bronze plates struck together to produce a ringing sound

Czordas: Hungarian national dance

D

Da capo (al Fine): repeat sign

D/A Converter: →Sampling

Dal segno: repeat sign

Damping: →Attentuator

Data entry: key controlled submission of information, as slide control or with Yes/No keys

Data set/file: grouping of data

Data specification: collective name for information, commands, values, notes etc. in the form of numbers, letters or other symbols

dB: abbreviation for decibel, unit of measure with which the replay strength of a signal is represented

DC: abbreviation for Direct Current

DCO: abbreviation for Digital Controlled Oscillator; →Synthesizer

Decay Time: dying, setting, falling phase of the contour curve of an oscillation process →Synthesizer

Deceptive cadence: or delusive cadence. The succession of chords Dominant – Tonic parallel

Decibel: →dB

Decoder: appliance which converts a coded signal back into its original form

Decrescendo (decrsc.): →Dynamics

Default: Appears on computer screens from time to time. Never look for an explanation in a dictionary. The bigger the book, the more incomprehensible translations you will get. If you click on default, the computer will do exactly what the manufacturer of the program has preprogrammed as a type of standard setting'. In other words, default tells you that, unless you choose other settings, you will have to accept that preprogrammed settings will be selected or run.

defeat: switch off/make ineffective

Delay: 1. time shift difference between the original signal in relation to the reproduced signal; 2. corresponding effect units are called Delay Units or Time Processors. See also →Echo, →Flanger; 3. Musicians jargon for echo unit

delete: erase

Demo: abbreviation for demonstration tape, a recorded tape which is played to a record company or producer to approximately indicate musical talent and wishes of a group

Depth: strength, intensity

detune: to place out of tune

diatonic: order of wholetone and semitone steps in a scale

Diatonic chords: Every note of a →scale can be taken as a step on this scale. The first note is thus the first step, the second note the second step, etc. The chords that are created by this layering of thirds are then called chords of the first degree, chords of the second degree, etc. These degrees are identified by Roman numerals. In C major scale, the following relationships result: C (I), D (II), E (III), F (IV), G (V), A (VI), B (VII). The chords created above this level would be: C (I), Dm (II), Em (III), F (IV), G (V), Am (VI), B-5 (VII). The progression C-Am-F-G⁷ could also be written as: I-V-IV-V

Diatonic scale: →The C major scale is a diatonic scale. It consists primarily of whole steps, but between the third and fourth notes and between the seventh and eighth notes, there is a half step

Diatonic scale: This consists of a certain sequence of whole tone steps and half tone steps (→half note). Every major scale has half tone steps, e.g. between the third and fourth notes and between the seventh and eighth notes.

Digital: graduated: something presented in figures or numbers. Time, for example, is an analogue process – it is a continual process. The shadow on a sundial is an analogous representation of the time, it wanders infinitely. On a digital clock the time is represented in figures in graduated form i.e. without the intermediate values of secondous timing. The smaller the units used for digital representation, the closer the digital representation becomes to the analogue representation. (e.g. Hundredths of a second measurement at sport events, instead of tenths of a second measurement)

Digital Controlled Oscillator: →Synthesizer

Digital ensemble: Instrument combination. Features a synthesizer, high quality sample sounds, piano-like velocity, a drum machine, an amplifier, loudspeakers and nearly always a microphone connection, plus auto-accompaniment that can simulate a whole orchestra or a band with bass and drums

Digital Recording: recording of sound with digital processes: →Sound Sampling

Digital Reverb: →Echo unit

Digital Sound Memory: natural sound store: →Sound Sampling

Digital Synthesizer: →Synthesizer

Diminished Chord: e.g. C⁻⁵ (diminished seventh etc.)

Diminuendo: gradually decrease volume

DIN plug: 5-pin plug connector that is used, for example, with MIDI connections

direct: without influence on timbre

Direct Injection Box (DI-Box): is connected between instrument and →Mixing Desk to reduce →Distortional currents

Directional Characteristic: term for the directionally dependent sensitivity of a microphone. Where an omnidirectional characteristic is concerned, the mike picks up sounds from all directions at the same volume, but where lobe characteristic is concerned only sound which comes from the front is picked up. In addition to this there are bidirectional, cardioid and super-cardioid characteristics

Dirty notes: forced notes from, for example, saxophones and trumpets. Common in Jazz and Blues

Disc: 1. Floppy Disc, magnetisable thin flexible disc used for the storage of computer information; 2. record

Discant: descant/treble, highest voice region, upper half of keyboard

Disc drive: working area of a computer where data is ordered, stored or recalled

Display: monitor etc., where figures, letters or graphics can be presented

Dissonance: Discordant →intervals. They include: all →seconds and →sevenths, as well as all augmented and diminished intervals

Distorter: electronic machine with which signals are overloaded, thus causing the frequency response and the overtone composition to change. The effect can be particularly well achieved using tube amplifiers by turning the →Pre-amp up to its maximum level. The effect units have names such as Overdrive, Fuzz-Box, Tube Screamer etc.

Distortion: collective name for all forms of acoustic falsification originating from the amplification of a signal. In linear distortion the frequency response of the signal is changed, in non-linear distortion new overtone oscillations occur in addition to the signal

Distortion Corrector: electronic component which corrects a distorted sound signal i.e. which corrects the advanced distortion which occurs when playing a record

Distortion Corrector Amplifier: pre-amplifier, which corrects the advanced distortion which occurs when playing a record

Dixieland: originally a Jazz style with which the whites attempted to copy the Jazz style of the blacks in New Orleans from around 1921

Dobro: acoustic guitar with resonance body made of metal

Dolby System: noise reduction system

Dominant: chord on the 5th degree of a scale

Doo-Wop: vocal groups from the 50's

Doppler's Effect: named after the physicist Doppler. A phenomenon where an advancing sound appears higher and a retreating sound appears lower than they actually are (police car). An effect which is used in a →Rotary Loudspeaker

Dorian: ecclesiastical mode

Doubling: duplicating of an instrumental or vocal part during musical recordings, either by double playing the same parts or by using electronic effect methods e.g. delay with a short delay time setting

Downbeat: the 1 in a bar

Drawbar: slider control on an organ to set the volume of the Register

Drive: the rhythmical intensity of a piece of music: is created above all by the tension between beat and off-beat

Drop-out: short sound failure on tapes caused by a fault in the coating or dirty recording heads. On floppy disks a D.O. can cause the data to be lost

Drum computer: →rhythm unit

Dry: recording or replaying of a signal without any effect units in use

Dual system: binary counting system

Dubbing: the duplication of one tape onto another

Duplet: if instead of playing three notes, two of the same value are played this produces a duplet.

Dynamics: everything to do with the strength of the sound. *ppp* = as quiet as possible; *pp* (pianissimo = very quiet; *p* (piano) = quiet; *mp* (mezzopiano) = moderately quiet; *mf* (mezzoforte) = moderately loud; *f* (forte) = loud; *ff* (fortissimo) = very loud; *fff* = as loud as possible; crescendo (cresc.) = gradually becoming louder, symbol: decrescendo (decr.) = gradually becoming quieter, symbol: individual notes are emphasized using an accent (>); 2. Relationship between largest and smallest values of an electronic size

Dynamic microphone: →Microphone

E

Earphone: →Phones

Easy listening music: light music/music category

Echo: delayed repetition of sound by reflection of sound waves. Since the reflection itself is reflected yet again it is usually the case that a multi-echo occurs. Reflections which follow each other in close succession are known as shatter echos. Lots of quick and indefinable reflections are known as reverbs.

Echo units: →Delay unit; produces →Echo. Analogous: the signal is divided by means of delay circuitry. A part of the signal is delayed in time and is eventually mixed together with the original signal in varying intensities. The effect can be produced using a tape recorder with separate record and play-back heads or simulated using a digital echo unit

edit: to process, correct, cut tape(s), data etc.

Edit recall: control facility to resummon the changed or new sounds

Effect: term for changes in the original sound e. 9. using certain effect units →Echo, →Reverb, →Chorus, Wah-Wah, →Vibrato, →Tremolo, →Exiter, →Phaser, Distorter, →Transposer etc.

Effect pedal: foot pedal used to control an effect unit

Effect pedals: Small effect pedals for wah-wah, reverb, compressor, distortion, fuzz, overdrive, tremolo, etc. Most come equipped with a sound controller and various adjustment possibilities. Are switched on and off with your foot. Also available as a footboard for multi-effect pedals

EG: abbreviation for Envelope Generator →Contour generator

EG-Bias: shifting the envelope/ contour curve level

Eighth-note feel: →Microtiming

Electromicrophone: →Microphone

Electric Grand Piano: Grand piano with electromechanic or electric mechanism

Electric organ: organ functioning by means of electricity

Electronic drums: electronically memorized or →Sound sampled drum noises are recalled by the drummer striking small pads.

Electronic music: originated around 1950 as a result of experiments with electrical oscillation generators (e.g. Cologne Studio for Electronic Music – K.H. Stockhausen)

Eleventh: →Interval →(Symbol no. 11). The eleventh corresponds to an octave plus a fourth in terms of sound. A perfect eleventh has an interval distance of 17 half steps - e.g. C-F'; an augmented eleventh has an interval distance of 18 half steps e.g. C-F#'

Emphasis: 1. special distortion in sound-conveyance; 2. term for the overload-effect in the →Filter of a —> →Synthesizer; 3. To make more noticeable

Emulator: system which can copy the qualities of another system, e.g. which can memorize natural sounds and replay them

Ending: the last bar of a piece of music

Ending: final beats of a song; the opposite of →intro

Enhance: sound effect in →Reverb Unit – increase, improve, make more attractive

Enharmonic change: the alternative term for a sound, e.g. C sharp = D flat

Ensemble: 1. term refering to several instruments playing together; 2. term for a setting on an →Electric Organ or →Synthesizer

Ensemble: →Digital ensemble

Envelope Curve: curve produced by the attack and fading of a noise or a sound if volume is graphically represented against time →Envelope Generator

Envelope Filter: a filter unit in synthesizers which is influenced by envelope generators/contour generators

Envelope Generator: component of a synthesizer which controls the attack and fade of a sound; 1. without the volume and 2. the filter, i.e. the timbre. The three most common forms: ADSR, ADBSSR, AD (Level/Rate)

E-Organ: abbreviation term for Electric Organ

E-Piano: abbreviation term for Electric Piano, which generally has a mechanical action and an amplifier to boost the sound.

EPROM: Term for a read-only component, which is programmable. Erasable Programmable Read Only Memory

EQ: abbreviation for →Equalizer

Equalizer: electronic component which controls the frequency range of an amplifier system.

Erase: to wipe out/delete

Erase (delete): term for the demagnetisation of a magnetic tape or of a Floppy disk using an erasure head

Error: comp. mistake, e.g. by handling the computer software

Evergreen: piece of music which remains popular over decades

Exiter: effect unit which causes sounds and voices to sound more brilliant and more transparent, vocal texts become easier to understand, the stereo effect is increased

Expander: 1. amplifier which increases the dynamics of a transmitted signal; has the opposite effect to a compressor; 2. Additional unit for →Synthesizer

F

Fader: slide control on a recording apparatus to slowly kill a signal

Fade-In: Gradual increase in volume at the beginning of a song

Fade-Out: Gradually dying sound, like the autumn wind playfully carrying the notes that pour forth from your Beloved's mouth into the night that is falling until they drop silently like pearls into the fiery red gold of the setting sun ...

Fairly slow: →Tempo

Falsetto: head voice in men, used by male altos

Fandango: Spanish national dance

Feedback: the return of a fraction of the output signal from one stage of a circuit, amplifier etc. Happens, for example, if a microphone is too close to a loudspeaker (also Regeneration, Recovery)

Feeling: that certain "something"

Fermata: hold symbol: you can hold the note as long as you want

FF: short for "fast forward", winding the tape forwards quickly

Fifth (symbol no. 5) Diminished fifth →Interval distance of 6 half steps – e.g. C-G♭; perfect fifth interval distance of 7 half steps – e.g. C-G; augmented fifth: interval distance of 8 half steps – e.g. C-G♯

File: collection of data

Fill-in: short rhythmic or melodic insert by instrumentalists or vocalists

Filter: electronic system which can change the frequency response or timbre of a signal. The most common filter in synthesizers is the Low Pass Filter. Deep frequencies are let through where high frequencies are weakened at a certain level →cut off point

a) Low-Pass-Filter (with cut-off-frequency)

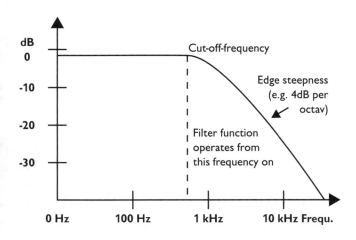

b) Low-Pass-Filter (Resonance area,) Emphasis etc.

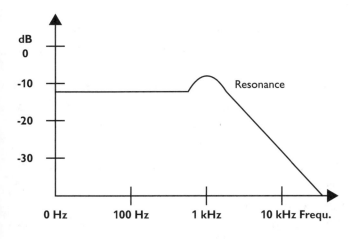

Filter contour: control of the filter using a contour/envelope generator

Filter tracking: also keyboard tracking: influencing of the filter using the keyboard e.g. the higher the note played, the brighter its timbre

Fine: end

Fine Tune: exact tune facility

Fixed: the same key over the whole keyboard

Flanger: effect unit which processes the signal on two different conveyance routes causing a phase modulation. The result is more or less quick beating

flat: 1. linear; 2. term for a lowered note, e.g. B♭; 3. if a singer sings a note below the true pitch required he is flat, or is singing flat

Flip-side: B-side of successful hit-single

Floppy Disk: (Computer) flexible data store

Fluegelhorn: instrument similar to a trumpet

FM: abbr. for →Frequency Modulation

FM-Synthesis: harmonic synthesis according to the principle of →frequency modulation

Foldback: monitor or effect route on a →Mixing Desk

Folkrock: combination of folkmusic with rockmusic

Foot controller: device operated with foot to control a piece of equipment

Footroom: the lower level range in, for example, recording units

Foot switch: on/off device operated with foot

Formant: resonance phenomenon

Forte: →Dynamics

Fortissimo: →Dynamics

Fourier synthesis: harmonic synthesis by combining sinus notes

Fourth: (symbol no. 4) Perfect fourth → Interval distance of five half steps – e.g. C-F; augmented fourth: interval distance of 6 half steps - e.g. C-F♯

Four part harmony: set of four voices or chords

Free Jazz: form of Jazz, originating in about 1960 which is rhythmically and tonally very free

Frequency: number of oscillations per second, unit: Hertz (Hz)

Frequency Modulation: modulation of the frequency of an oscillation. If the modulation occurs with a second, slower oscillation (up to 20Hz), a vibrato becomes audible. At very high modulation frequencies, more complex sounds are created. This is utilized in the FM-Synthesis synthesizer

Frequency Range: the scope of all frequencies from the lowest to the highest, which an instrument can produce or which can be processed by an audio unit

Frequency Response: representation of the →Frequency range as a function of the volumes of the frequency concerned

Frequency to voltage converter: turns frequencies or keys into currents

Fretted Piano Signal: keyboard technique which copies an instrument with frets, i.e. by playing in the typical "fingerpicking" style of a western guitar

Fugue: A form of →Polyphonic music: the theme played wanders through all voice modes, which are normally plaited with each other and Counterpointed

Function: key to determine playing aids

Funk: musical style which is based on Blues scales, rhythm rich in syncopes, mid 1960's

Funky: →Tight

Fuse: circuit interrupter/safety device

Fusion: Jazz-Rock

FX pedal: →Effect pedal

G

Gain: amplification

Gate: control current

Generator: apparatus for producing something, usually Power-G or Sound-G

Ghost notes: The "swinging along" of a musician in →microtiming. Suppose your song is written in sixteenth feel (microtiming) and your hands "swing" over the keys in the same feel, your fingers would then move in the direction of the keys with each of the following main and secondary beats. Naturally, you don't have to play every beat each time, but you could do so. When swinging along, it frequently happens that you play some or all of the possible notes in the microtiming really gently, and that you play the notes in the actual musical text louder – so that "unintentional auxiliary sounds" are heard, so to speak. These beats that are played only lightly, or not at all, are called ghost notes. They make an important contribution to a good rhythmic feel.

Gig: performance, concert

Gimmick: gag, trick, device to attract attention or publicity

Glide: movements between two notes in semitone steps

Glissando: quick, scalar runs where a diagonally positioned fingernail is drawn or pushed across the keys

Glockenspiel: Musical instrument consisting of metal bars which are struck with two light hammers

GND: abbr. for →Ground = earth

Gospel: vocal style of North American Afro-Americans, used in church services

Grammaphone record: Discs, normally of black plastic, on which music was recorded in the last century of the last millenium

Grand Piano: (Grand) large horizontal concert piano

Graphic Equalizer: →Equalizer, frequency range can be increased or reduced using controls

Groove: the rhythmical basic feeling of a piece of music

Ground: earth connection (electronics)

Ground/Earth: →Reference for points in electric circuits rated at 0 Volts

Guiro: wooden pipe with long slit and notches burnt into the surface over which a stick is rubbed to produce sound.

H

Half tones: The distance on a keyboard between one key (irrespective of whether black or white) and the next. These are the half tone distances: C-C♯, F-F♯, B-C. On the guitar, a half tone step is the distance between one fret and the next. A whole tone, a whole tone step thus comprises two half tones – e.g. C-D, F-G, F♯-G♯, G♭-A♭

Hammond Organ: semi-electric organ

Hand Claps: effect sound →Rhythm Unit

Hardcopy: paper printout of data on monitor

Hardware: all technical components pertaining to a computer

Harmonic: overtone, partial tone, flagelot tone

Harmonium: keyboard instrument in which notes are produced by air blown through reeds (metal)

Harmonizer: →Transposer

Harmony: combination of simultaneous notes to form chords

Harpsichord: →Cembalo

HD recording: Hard-disc recording. You record the sound data onto the →hard disc of a computer or onto a stand-alone hard disc recorder

Headphone: phones

Headphone amp: A small, handy amplifier that you can carry on your belt or place in front of you on the keyboard – with a headphone inlet. Features good effects, depending on the price

Headroom: upper range in level control

Hertz: (Hz) unit of measure for the frequency of an oscillation; 1 Hz = 1 oscillation per second

HF: abbr. for High Frequency

High Com: noise reduction system (High Fidelity and Compounder)

High Hat: →Cymbal; operated with a foot pedal or struck with a stick

High Note Priority: →Key priority

High Pass Filter: →Filter

hold: to continue a note or chord or effect (an echo in hold repeats endlessly)

Home Recording: home studio technique using mostly 4 or 8 track recording facilities

Homophone Music: →Polyphone music

Honky Tonk Piano: type of Piano

Hookline: The short melody piece (and corresponding text) that grabs (hooks) the listener and says: Sing me, love me, buy me. In Pop songs, its normally the line that contains the song title

HP: High Pass Filter; →Filter

Human Feeling: term for the rhythmic and dynamic variations or irregularities in human musical play

Humanizer: effect which electronically attempts to create →Human Feeling in Rhythm units

Hypercardioid Characteristics: →Directional Characteristics; Microphone

I

IC: abbr. for Integrated Circuit

Impedance: term for electrical resistance measured in Ohms (Ω)

Improvisation: playing ad hoc/off the cuff

Impulse: short signal, current surge

Indie: abbr. for Independent, small to mid-sized record companies →Labels

Injection Box: Direct Injection Box

Insert: →Loop-in point

Interface: connection point (computer)

Interference: external influence of waves

Interludium: section of play between two main sections

Internal: contained in the unit (as opposed to → Cartridge)

Interpretation: creative reproduction of a piece of music

Interval: The distance between two notes. We differentiate between perfect, major, minor, augmented and diminished intervals

Intro: abbr. for introduction (play up to a piece/song)

Inverter: amplifier which when operating on positive current delivers a negative output signal

Ionian: ecclesiastical mode

Inversions: A →chord can contain any sequence of notes. The sequence of root, third, and fifth is called the "root" position – for example in the C major triad C-E-G. The tone series E-G-C or G-C- E are called "inversions"

J

Jack: form of connector

Jack connector: Mono – 2-pin plug-in connector (also available in a stereo version)

Condenser microphone: →Microphone

Jam Session: musicians playing together just for fun

Jazz: music form – often improvised – which combines European and African music elements. Mostly using complex chords and almost never triads

Jitterbug: form of swing music

Joystick: also known as x-y controller →Synthesizer, →Computer

K

Key: 1. system of notes definitely related to each other and based on a particular note, 2. lever pressed by finger in playing organ, piano etc.

Keyboard: 1. Collective name for a row of levers; 2. collective name for all keyed instruments

Keyboard player: Human-like being that sleeps during the day and is mainly active at night in search of prey and sexual partners. Feeds mainly on fluids with British names (Jim Beam, Johnny Walker, Glen Fiddich); makes loud noises that are similar to music when trying to attract a mate

Keyboard Voltage: the voltage within an electronic keyboard →Synthesizer

Key Dynamics: level control for strikes on keys

Key Priority: on a monophone keyboard generally only three kinds come into question:
1. High Note Priority: The highest key struck sounds.
2. Low Note Priority: opposite to point 1.
3. Last Note Priority: the last note struck sounds, irrespective of whether it is higher or lower.
On polyphone keyboards, Last Note Priority is normally installed

Key Start: an effect switches on automatically if the keyboard is played i.e. Auto-accompaniment

Key Transposer: →Transposer

L

Label: refers to the record company, the characteristic label being stuck onto the record. Some of the larger record companies have several labels under which different musical styles are published

Lag: delay

Laid back: Relaxed method of playing in which you almost unnoticeably let your strokes fall behind the beat – you let yourself be "pulled by the beat", so to speak.

Larghetto: →Tempo

Largo: →Tempo

Last Note Priority: →Key Priority

Latin Rock: combination of American Popmusic with Latin American or Spanish-Portuguese music

Leading note: a note which is a semitone below an arrival note. The most important leading note is the 7th in a major or minor scale. This leads back to the 8th degree (Keynote) of the scale. The playing of the leading note creates a suspense/tension which demands to be released by playing the arrival note

Lead Sheet: note sheet, which normally contains the chord succession in a piece of music (sometimes also melody)

Legato: →Articulation

Leslie-Speaker: →Rotational loudspeaker

Level: term for the relationship (measured in dB) between two electric dimensions (usually currents) in a transmission system. In audio systems, the term for volume relationships

Level Control: Setting of the strength of a sound or voice signal. Levels are read on a VU-Meter (Volume Unit Meter), an indicator found on many tape recorders or mixing desks. Other measuring possibilites: →LED-Display, →LCD

LF: abbr. for Low Frequency

LFO: Low Frequency Oscillator. An oscillator which produces oscillations which are mostly below the range of audibility. The LFO serves as a modulator for oscillations (e.g. Vibrato), filters (e.g. Wah-Wah), envelope generators and VCA's (e.g. Tremolo)

Lick: short melody phrase which fills a hole in a melody

Limiter: →Compressor, which reduces the level of loud signals during singing, speaking or playing from a certain predetermined level

Line: term normally used to refer to the inputs and outputs of an amplifier or for high level signals

Locrian: →One of the church modes

Loop: endless repetition of a process (e.g. →Echo, →Sound Sampling)

Loop-in: this process is used to, for example, connect an effect unit between the sound producer and the amplifier

Loop-in point: connection for Loop-in

Loudness Contour: term for the control of a →VCA with an →Envelope Generator

Loudspeaker: electric acoustic transformer/converter which converts electrical oscillations into air oscillations. They consist of a magnetic core and a membrane

Low Note Priority: →Key Priority

Low Pass Filter: →Filter

M

MagicTouch: Touch Response

Major: greater by chromatic semitone than minor intervals etc.

Major/minor system: →Church mode

Mandoline: small instrument which is plucked, having a pearshaped resonance body and four double-strings

Manual: Keyboard played with the hands

Maracas: two round wooden bodies filled with stones etc. produce Rumba-sound

Marimba(phone): or resonaphone: musical instrument built lika a xylophone, which, however, has resonance tubes under the bars

Master: Sound-recording medium (a recording tape in the old days, nowadays CDs, etc.) onto which the finished product is recorded after a song has been multitracked and mixed. The master is used to make copies

Mastering: Preparation, polishing and re-recording of a song on a →mastertape

Micky Mouse effect: The faster a recording is played (e.g. a song), the higher it sounds, and vice versa

Master Tape: 1/4 inch sound tape, produced subsequent to the final →mixing of a recording, serving as the original sound tape for the production of records

Master Keyboard: in the →Midi System, the Keyboard which controls all other synthesizers or units connected to it

Mastering Machine: usually two channel tape machine which serves to produce a →Master tape subsequent to the final mixing of a multi-track recording

Matching: the setting of an actual value on a desired value. Calibration is a matching process

Measure: beat

Mediant: the third between the keynote and fifth

Medium Tempo: →Tempo

Medley: sequence of songs which run into each other

Mellotrone: electronic keyed instrument upon which sounds are produced by playing back a sound tape. The tapes, one per key, contain recordings of natural instruments (i.e. strings etc.)

Memory: data store

Memory Protect: data store protection

Menu: a list of the choices available in a computer programme. Parts of the computer programme can be called-up using the short menu code words

Mezzoforte: →Dynamics

Mezzo piano: →Dynamics

Mezzosoprano: voice between soprano and contralto

MG: abbr. for Modulation Generator, →LFO, →Oscillator

Mic: abbr. for →Microphone

Microphone: A-ha! Apparatus which converts sound into electrical signals. Microphones differ according to their physical and their acoustic operation principles. 1. Physicall differences: 1.1. Carbon microphone; 1.2. Crystal or Ceramic microphones; 1.3. Moving coil/dynamic microphone; 1.4. Capacitor microphone; 1.5. Electret-microphone; 2. Acoustic diffe-

rences: 2.1. non-directional microphone; 2.2. cardioid pattern microphone; 2.3. super-or hyper-cardioid micro-phone; 2.4. bilateral cardioid microphone and 2.5. low characteristic microphone

Microphone: If you throw a stone into water, waves result that move away from the source (where the stone hit the surface) in all possible directions. These waves consist of wave peaks (i.e. higher than the normal level) and wave troughs (i.e. lower). The same kind of thing happens with sound waves in the air, with the exception that the peaks and troughs consist of thicker and thinner zones of air. In other words: Sound waves consist of periodic air pressure variations that travel through the air. Microphones basically consist of a diaphragm (membrane) that is flexibly suspended in the microphone head. This diaphragm vibrates on account of the variations in air pressure that hit it (via the sound). In order to transmit and record the resulting mechanical waves that have hit the diaphragm, the mechanical vibrations have to be transformed into electromagnetic vibrations. In order to achieve this, two basic principles are employed: the transformation of the vibration via dynamic microphones and via condenser microphones. A transducer connected to the diaphragm in a (cheaper) dynamic microphone is kept mobile in a magnetic field. When the diaphragm vibrates, the transducer in the magnetic field also moves, thus causing a change in voltage, which is then processed further. In a (more expensive) condenser microphone the diaphragm is one of two plates located opposite each other that are able to store charges (electrical energy) – one plate has a positive charge, the other a negative one, thus forming a so-called condenser. If the vibrating diaphragm moves, the distance between both plates changes and thus their ability to store electrical energy. Some of these charges are conducted via cables and the electricity generated can be processed further. In a →symmetrically designed condenser microphone, electric phantom power of around 48 volts is necessary. It is either delivered via the microphone input on the mixing console or via a network adapter. Microphones have different directional characteristics, which refers to their directional sensitivity. An omni-directional microphone reacts equally sensitively to sound sources from all directions; a cardioid pattern microphone reacts to sources in front of the mic more sensitively than those behind it; a mic with a bi-directional polar pattern is equally sensitive to the front and the rear but is less sensitive to sounds that come from the sides

Microprocessor: central unit in a micro-computer accomodated on a Chip

Middle of the Road (MOR): light entertainment music, related to Mainstream Rock

Midi: abbr. for Musical Instrument Digital Interface, standardized connection for electronic instruments or equipment

MIDI: Acronym for Musical Instrument Digital Interface

MIDI-In: 5-pin DIN jack for receiving data

MIDI messages: MIDI data are divided into system messages, i.e. messages that relate to the whole system, and channel messages, i.e. messages that relate to the MIDI channel used. System messages are either real time messages, i.e. messages in real time that relate to the synchronization of several MIDI devices; common messages, i.e. general messages such as, for example, the position in a song; and system exclusive messages that contain information on how to connect several devices from the same manufacturer. Channel messages subdivide into voice messages, i.e. the voices that relate to sound generation, and mode messages that relate to the operating mode. Voice messages include →Note-On and →Note-Off commands, program change commands, volume, (balance, modulation, panorama, portamento, effect-intensity, etc.). Voice messages that contain control commands are called controllers. They have strictly defined tasks on account of the industry standard for MIDIs and are described with a combination of letters and numbers. Controller type SC 64, for example, controls the sustain, i.e. control of the →sustain pedal.

MIDI-Out: 5-pin DIN jack for sending data

MIDI-Thru: 5-pin DIN jack via which data received by the MIDI-In are transmitted to the MIDI-In jack of the next device without undergoing any change.

Midrange: middle frequency range

Mike: yet another abbreviation for →Microphone

Mixdown: →Sound Studio In multitracking (multitracking process), a decision is taken on how loud each track should be, what effects should be added, and what timbre each should have

Mixed: state of sound subsequent to passing through the mixer

Mixer: apparatus for combination, mixing and influencing of several sound sources. It controls volume, timbre and the effect mixed rate of the individual signals. It is used in studio recordings and at concerts to mix the individual instruments and voices

Mixing: →Sound Studio

Mixing Console: →Mixer

Mixing Engineer: person controlling sound on mixer

Mixolydian: ecclesiastical mode

M.M.: abbr. for Maetzel's Metronome. The Viennese engineer Maetzel constructed the metronome following an idea by Beethoven. A beat measure which provides individual clicks. M.M. ♩=80 means: 80 crotchets per minute; ♪=40 means: 40 crotchets per minute, often the letters "M.M." are left out: ♩=80

Mod: abbr. for →Modulation

Mode: way, manner, scale system

Mode messages: → MIDI messages

Mode of motion: oscillation contour. Electrical oscillations can usually be presented on an oscilloscope and may sometimes be classified according to their typical form: sinus, saw-tooth, square etc.

Moderate: →Tempo

Moderately: →Tempo

Moderately bright: →Tempo

Modes: →Church modes

Modifier: →Modulator

Modulation: 1. shift from one key to another and 2. the changing of an electronic signal. One distinguishes between →Frequency, →Amplitude-, →Phase- and Pulse-width Modulation

Modulation Frequency: →FM-Synthesis

Modulation Wheel: handwheel on synthesizers with which synthesizer functions can be influenced, for example the frequency of oscillations; LFO's etc.

Modulator: device or units which change timbre or signals

Module: term for an interchangeable function or equipment unit, constructed as a plug-in or push-in unit. It serves as an extension to a main system

Module Synthesizer: →Synthesizer, A which is built up of individual, interchangeable components. These components, →Modules, have certain functions. The modules (i. e. →Oscillators, →VCF, →VCA etc.) are connected together in the way required using a patch field

Monitor: term for control unit either as monitor

loudspeaker or screen

Monophone (mono): single channel

Mordent: grace, consisting of rapid alternation of written note with one immediately below it

Motive: short, melodic unit (usually consisting of only a few notes) e.g.

Moving Coil Microphone: →Microphone

Multi-Effect-unit: →Effect unit with several effect functions – e.g. →Echo, →Reverb and →Transposer

Multiplay: recording technique with a recording apparatus with at least two channels (stereo). Method involves playing signal onto second channel whilst simultaneously recording a new signal. A certain number of instruments and vocals can be recorded using this method

Multitrack Recording: recording procedure using a multi-channel recording apparatus upon which each channel can be matched with an individual instrument or voice. Each track can be processed subsequent to the recording with effect units and then mixed back with the other channel parts

Mute: function on mixing desk which silences individual channels

N

Natural harmonic series: →Overtone

Natural notes: The C major scale C, D, E, F, G, A, B

Natural notes series: →Natural notes

Natural tones: →Tones

Natural frequency or oscillation: the frequency at which an oscillatory material or system begins to oscillate, when affected by a signal

NG: abbr. for Noise Generator

Ninth: →Interval (Symbol number 9). The ninth corresponds in sound to an octave plus a second. A minor ninth has an interval distance of 13 half steps – e.g. C-Db' or C-C#'; a major ninth has 14 half steps – e.g. C-D'; and an augmented ninth has 15 half steps – e.g. C-D#'

Noise: sound made up of many frequencies which are located close together. a) White Noise contains all audible frequencies at the same volume. b) in Pink Noise the frequencies are dampened in the upper regions

Noise Filter: suppresses mainly the upper frequency range (above 5 kHz)

Noise Gate: electronic component to suppress interference. If a signal's level is below the threshold the transmission of the signal is interupted

Noise Generator: (NG) produces mostly white and pink sound for measurement purposes or for sound synthesis in synthesizers

Noise Reduction System: or Noise Limiter, a unit which suppresses interference noises in a transmission unit. The most famous processes: Dolby B, DBX, High Com. In studio use: Dolby A and/or TELCOM

Notation software: Computer program for writing notes. Is also often included in →sequencer software

Note-Off: →Note-On

Note-On: →MIDI command that is transmitted upon hitting a key on the keyboard. In other words: Come on, play the darned note! Of course, you shouldn't let the note continue for eternity and that's why there is also a Note-Off command when you let go of the key again.

Novatron: →Mellotron

O

Octave: →Interval distance of 12 half steps – e.g. C-C'. The octave and the →prime are the only intervals that exist solely in pure form. The frequency relationship between the two notes is 1: 2 (e.g. for a[1] and a[2] 440 Hz and 880 Hz)

Octaver: effect unit which can shift the key of a signal in octave steps either upwards or downwards

Octave switch: function on electric organ, Synthesizer, to raise or lower the key in octave steps

Off-beat: the non-emphasized beat or part of the bar, e.g. in Rock Music the "ands" (1 + 2 + 3 + 4)

Ohm: unit of measurement for electrical resistance (symbol: Ω)

Omnidirectional characteristic: →Directional Characteristic microphone

Omni-directional polar pattern: →Microphone

One-finger-automatic: →Auto-accompaniment

On Top: →Tight

Open voicings: Usually means →voicings in which the →thirds are exchanged for a →second or a →fourth; for example, the following chords: Cadd9/no3rd (C, D, G) or Csus4 (C, F, G). They are usually played in mid- to higher register (→powerchords).

Operator: function component unit in →Synthesizers which work with algorithmic →FM-synthesis. Can serve as sound producer or modulator

Operator Select: selection function on operator units

Options/Extensions: In modern chord theory for Jazz and Pop the notes that are added to a →triad (such as C-E-G) (e.g. B♭ (minor 7) – D (2 or 9) – A (6 or 13) are described as options/extensions. Some purists do not count the minor →seventh as an extension

Oscillation: (Vibration) periodic wave movement. The frequency indicates the number of oscillations per second. The amplitude indicates the volume and the phase indicates the condition of vibration/oscillation viewed from the zero point

Oscillator: generator which produces oscillations. One differentiates between High and Low frequency O., continuous Sound- and Transient Oscillator. Audible oscillations are produced by an Audio oscillator. L.C.-oscillators or Modulation-Oscillators deliver →Control Voltages, which can control individual modules or other oscillators in a synthesizer. The fre-

quency of an audio-oscillator in a synthesizer must be continually controllable. This is achieved by means of control voltages, through which a voltage controlled oscillator is obtained (→VCO). If instead of these voltages, digital signals are used we use the term digitally controlled oscillator (→DCO). Oscillators can usually produce various forms of →Oscillations, e.g. sinus, triangular, saw-toothed and pulse oscillations.

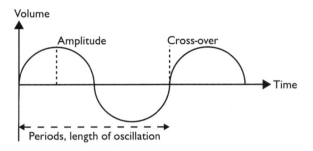

Ostinato: obstinant, a melodic phrase persistently reiterated in the same voice and pitch

Out of time: to play against the temporary basic structure of a piece of music

Out of tune: not correctly in key

Over-amplification: (saturation) occurs in amplifiers (usually at the input) when the amplifier levels are set too high. This leads to distortion of the signal

Overdrive: push too far, distort

Overdubbing: doubling or addition of a voice or instrument in multi-track recordings

Overhead Microphone: microphone usually positioned over a drum kit to record the cymbals and the complete sound

Overtone: Natural tone, partial tone (→Tone) When you strike a piano key or guitar string, you not only hear the note in question: you also hear a series (of often very quiet) notes that are pitched above the one you're playing and which are therefore called overtones. Many people are unable to distinguish them and hear them only in their sum as the characteristic harmonic coloring of the loud fundamental. There are myriads of such overtones: here are just the first ones: If you strike C on the piano two octaves left of middle C (the C in the major octave) you can hear the following overtones and in the following sequence: 1st: the C of the next octave; 2nd: the G above that; 3rd: the next C (= middle C) and then always the next note: E, G, Bß, C, D, E, F♯, G, Ab, B♭, B, C. This overtone series is basically the natural scale of all music and is therefore also called the natural harmonic series.

P

Pad: Drumming surface of electronic drums

Panorama Control: (Potentiometer) on the mixing desk to determine the position of a sound in the stereophonic sound image

Pan-Pot: abbr. for Panorama-potentiometer (→Panorama Control)

PA = Public Address: also Power amplification; term for the sound system used during concerts. Such a system is composed of →Microphones and →D.I. Boxes to receive/record the instruments and vocals on the stage. The signals are conveyed to a central mixing desk via a stage box and a special "multicore" cable, where they are processed accordingly (timbre, effects etc.). The mixed signal is then conveyed to a powerful →Power Amplifier and then to the loudspeakers

Parallel Key: Key, which uses the same key-signature as the departure key, e.g. C-major and A-minor

Parameter: constant quantity. The parameters of a note are, for example, pitch, length, volume and timbre etc.

Parametric Equalizer: →Equalizer, in general functions with band filters, in which three parameters can be set: Amplification or reduction of a frequency range, the range itself and the edge steepness, and the accentuation or lowering of the range

Paraphrase: Processing of a melody in free form. Usually attempt to disguise a stolen melody

Partialtone: →Overtone, →Tone

Passive speaker cabinet: Loudspeaker cabinet with no amplification

Patch board: connecting board on synthesizer, mixer etc.

Patch cord: connecting cable for synthesizer, mixer etc.

Patch panel: →Patch Board

Pattern: characteristic figure i.e. rhythmic or melodic pattern

PCM: Pulse Code Modulation; Process to convert analogous signals into digital information with the help of a code (→A/D converter, →Quantisation)

Peak: upper level, highest value

Pentatonic: scale based on five notes

Pedal point: stationary bass note, also in a chord change

Pedals: on an organ, the row of keys, played with the feet providing the bass voices

Pedalboard: foot-controlled effect switches

Pedal Synthesizer: mostly used for monophone synthesizers, the musical keys of which are controlled with pedals. Primarily used to play the bass voices

Percussion: instruments played by forcibly striking one body against the other (Drums, Congas, Maracas etc.)

Periphery: collective name for all additional apparatus which can be coupled with a main unit (synthesizer or computer e.g.). All kinds of effect units

PFL: abbr. for Pre Fader Listening. Monitoring facility on mixing desk

Phantom Powering: special kind of power supply in symmetrically arranged →Capacitor Microphones

Phase: indicates when a complete oscillatory process of an oscillation orwave begins e.g. from one crossover to the next. Phase reversal see diagr.

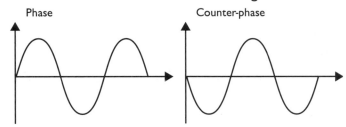

Phase | Counter-phase

Phase Modulation: term for the alteration of the Phase of an oscillation. Can be used as an effect or sound synthesis (Frequency Modulation, →Pulse Width Modulation)

Phaser: (also Phase Shifter) Effect unit based on periodic phase modulation. The phase-modulated signal is re-mixed with the "dry", non-modulated signal and has the effect of periodically deleting or amplifying partial oscillations in the signal

PhaseShifting: →Phase modulation

Phasing: effect produced by a phaser

Phon: measure for volume, which takes the frequency related sensitivity of the ear into account. This unit has been superseded by the unit →dB

Phone: →headphone

Phrasing: the division of a piece of music into sensible music units of mostly 2, 4 or 8 bars (Phrases). Without phrasing, a piece of music is like a text without punctuation. Often a phrasing slur or a small dash, indicates how the piece is phrased

Phrygian: ecclesiastical mode

Pianissimo: →Dynamics

Piano: →Dynamics

Pick-up: converts mechanical oscillations into electrical oscillations, used on guitars and pianos etc.

Pink Noise: →Noise

Pitch: the acuteness or gravity of all the tones of a given instrument with reference to some standard. Vibrations per second of one note

Pitch Bender: modulation wheel or similar unit to influence the pitch →synthesizer

Pitch Control: fine setting for the rotational speed of a record player or the tape transport speed on tape recorders or the tuning of electronic instruments

Pitchshifting: When recording on a →hard disc or with →sequencer software, you can change the pitch of an instrument or of a voice after the recording. Usually done because the singer didn't hit the pitch

Pitch to Voltage Converter: converts the pitch of an audio signal into a current. Using this one can, for example, determine the frequency of a voltage controlled oscillator (VCO)

Pitch Transposer: →Transposer

Pitch wheel: Control on the keyboard for turning the pitch up or down while playing

Pizzicato: Notes on string instruments that are plucked instead of being played with a bow

Plagal Ending: when a piece or a song ends with the **chord succession:** Sub-dominant-Tonic

Plagiarism: the unlawful use of copyright protected melodies or texts

Plate Reverb: →Reverb

Playback: replaying of part of a recording to be able to play the remaining voices and instruments during recording or at a concert simultaneously. In addition to this, a full playback is often used for television appearances where the artists only mime their parts

Plug: form of connector

Plug (and Socket) Connections: 1. Jack Plug (microphones, instruments, headphones); 2. Diode, DIN or Five-pin-plugs (microphones, tape recorders); 3. Cinch (HiFi); 4. XLR (Professional Audio-technology)

Plug-In: Software program that expands an existing computer program

Polar pattern: →Microphone

Polyphone: several voices (opposite of →Monophone, homophone)

Polysynthesizer: term for polyphone synthesizer. Usual types 4-, 6-, 8- and 16-voice polyphone synthesizers

Popular music: Dumb, mostly negative description for pieces of music and styles from the areas of Folklore, Blues, Country, Rock, Soul, Pop, Reggae, House, Hiphop, etc. Meant as the opposite to serious music (Verdi operas, Beethoven symphonies, Bach cantatas, etc.). The idea behind this classification is that Pop music is bad and has no value, whereas "Classical" music is deeply moving and valuable. This definitional stupidity of the united German high school teachers league completely misses the simple fact that there are also a lot of rather uninteresting and musically inferior operas, piano concertos and oboe quartets

Portable: unit which can be transported easily, possibly not dependent on mains supply

Portamento: term for gliding continuously from one pitch to another in a manner intermediate between →Legato and →Staccato (→Synthesizer)

Portato: →Articulation

Post Fader Listening: monitoring facility on →Mixers

Potentiometer: variable electrical resistance. Usually in the form of rotary or sliding controls

Power Amplifier: amplifies all sound signals in an amplifier system, providing the necessary power to drive the loudspeakers

Power Attenuator: also Power soak: Is connected between the →Power Amplifier and the →Loudspeakers to diminish the volume of a signal

Powerchords: →Open voicings that are usually played in lower register, in which musicians like to completely omit the 3rd of a triad. In this way, they lose their typical major or minor character ... Examples: C^5 (C, G) or G^5 (G, D)

Power Soak: →Power Attenuator

Power Supply Unit: equipment providing necessary power to system

Power Supply Unit: Mains Supply Unit; delivers the necessary current for an electronic unit by transforming the mains current to the correct level and then converting it

Preamp: abbr. for Pre-Amplifier

Preamplifier: primary amplification which amplifies the signal so that it can be amplified in the power amp.

Pre Fader Listener: (PFL) Monitoring facility on →Mixer

Preset: 1. a register to pre-selected items (channels etc.); 2. a permanently set or memorized sound programme in synthesizers or the fixed register on an

organ

Presto: →Tempo

Prime: →Interval distance of zero half steps – e.g. C-C (i.e. the same key on the piano)

Processor: collective term for a programmable control facility in digital equipment

Programme: sequence of instructions for a computer. In synthesizers term for memorized sounds

Progression: A (generally felt "logical") progression of harmonies. The progression usually starts from the →tonic and also returns there. The return to the tonic is very often not noted. Typical progressions (play each for half a tact): C-Am-F-G⁷ (can be infinitely repeated). Or C-Dm-G⁷-C. Progressions are often noted as →(ADD FUNCTIONARY SYMBOLS), irrespective of key

PROM: abbr. for Programmable Read Only Memory. Term for a permanent store/fixed memory which has to be programmed with a special programming unit. The contents are stored even after the computer has been switched off

Proximity Effect: Noise that occurs when you speak too close to the microphone

PU: abbr. for Pick-up

Pulse-width: size of the pulse wave

Pulse-width modulation: term for modulation of the pulse width of a pulse wave

Pulse Wave: oscillation produced by an Oscillator with rectangular lines and vertical sides. With a ratio of 50:50 between wave crest and wave trough one refers to →Square waves. During pulse-width modulation this ratio is periodically changed. Floating sounds are created by the constant alteration of the over-tone composition of the oscillations

Punch in (Punch out): term for the direct switching of Playback and Record functions on a tape player without tape stop

Pushing the beat: Playing the emphasized part of a bar earlier than notated, playing it as long as notated. →Syncope

P-VC: Pitch to Voltage Converter

PWM: →Pulse Width Modulation

Q

Q-factor: term for the size of a →Filter, →VCF

Quadruplets: are created if four notes of equal size are played instead of three. (Diagram)

Quantization: separation of an analogous signal into a certain number of stages in digital processing

Quintuplets: are created if five notes are played instead of four. (Diagram)

R

Rack: transport box, into which the power amp, effect units and similar equipment is permanently fixed

Ragtime: piano style originating from the end of the 19th century intended to imitate the banjo-style

Rallentando: abbr. rall. →Agogics

RAM: Random Access Memory, for quick storage of computer or synthesizer data. The data is lost if the unit is switched-off

Random Generator: →Random Voltage Generator

Random Voltage: Random Voltage Generator, Sample Hold Generator

Random Voltage Generator: unit in which random control voltages are produced which could, for example, influence a →VCO, with the effect of creating random changes in pitch

Rate: size and speed of an effect

Ratio: division of the pitch on the keyboard

Real Time: melodies are played into a →Sequencer or Rhythmic beats into a Rhythm-machine as if onto a sound tape (Opposite →Step-by-Step)

Real Time Analyzer: Spectrum Analyzer

Recitative: spoken vocals; section in a song where the singer has had enough of singing and reverts to talking

Real time messages: →MIDI messages

Record: →(Grammaphone) record

Reed Instrument: wind instrument, played with reeded mouthpiece (i.e. Oboe etc.)

Regeneration: →Feed Back

Register: Slider in organ controlling set of pipes used to set the sound

Rehearsal: practice (especially theatre/music)

Remote Keyboard: keyboard which is worn around the neck on a strap like a guitar and which is connected to a stationary →Synthesizer which is, in fact, the true sound producing unit

Repertoire: The songs which a band is able to perform

Reprise: the repeating of a musical section (sometimes in varied form)

Requiem: special mass for repose of souls of the dead

Resistance: offering hindrance to current

Resistor: electrical component offering resistance

Resonance: oscillation of air or other bodies when a note is produced. Also term for the special function of a →Filter on a synthesizer, responsible for the free oscillation of a →VCF

Resonance Frequency: →Resonance

Reverb: 1. acoustic process, reflexion of sound Echo; 2. Effect unit used to produce echos a) with metal springs, b) reverb plates and c) with digital process

Reverb(eration): a form of echo

Reverse: Changing of direction of musical tape on Sequencers and Composers, term for the playing a memorized melody backwards

Revival: re-introduction of an old musical style, for example

Rhapsody: form of free composition, usually with folklore quotes

Rhythm and Blues: rhythmically emphasized Blues-music with hard accentuated beats. Forerunner of Rock'n'Roll

Rhythm Computer: →Rhythm Machine

Rhythm Machine: unit designed to electronically imitate drum/percussion sounds or to automatically play rhythms which have either been determined by the manufacturer or which can be programmed freely. These are occasionally built into Electric Organs

Ride Cymbal: cymbal used to play rhythmical parts

Riff: short melodic or rhythmical theme which is often repeated

Rim Shot: term for a drum strike on the rim of the snare drum

Ring Modulator: sound module on a synthesizer, which mixes two different sound sources (especially frequencies) so as to produce most non-harmonic, metallic sounds

Ritardando: →Agogics

ROM: abbr. for Read Only Memory, fixed memory, where data can be called up but not changed

Rotating Loudspeakers: loudspeaker system using the →Doppler principle. The loudspeaker contains rotating horns or drums which turn the sound around. The sound effect created is a swaying, circling sound.

Rotating Sound: term for the effect produced with rotating loudspeakers and imitated by chorus and flanger, which results in the periodic changing of the pitch (→Vibrato) or the timbre (→Phasing). The special rotating loudspeakers were originally constructed by the Leslie Company for Hammond Electric Organs

Rough Mix: the first basic mix of a piece of music in a Sound studio

Rubato: →Agogics

S

Sample and Hold Generator: abbr. S/H-Random generator in synthesizers which removes some samples from control voltages (i.e. Keyboard voltages) and "Holds" them for a moment. This causes "Stepped-Melodies"

Sampler: A device that records digital and analog sounds. Samplers come in the form of both →hardware and →software

Sampling: random, digital sampling of an analogous signal e.g. an oscillation

Sampling Frequency/Rate: the frequency with which a signal (digital) is sampled

Sampling Rate: the speed/frequency with which an analogous signal is sampled by a sampler to give digital samples

Saw-tooth generator: →oscillator which produces saw-tooth waves

Saw-tooth, Ramp Waves: oscillations produced in

the form of a saw-blade. Rich in overtones

Scale: An ascending or descending series of notes. The most important scales are the →chromatic scale, the →whole tone scale, the →diatonic scale and the pentatonic scale (→pentatonic)

Score: note text, containing all instrumental and vocal voices. In Pop and Rock music usually Lead Sheet

Second: (symbol no. 2) Minor second → Interval with 1 half step distance - e.g. C-D♭ or C-C♯; major second: interval with 2 half steps – e.g. C - D; augmented second: interval with 3 half steps – e.g. C-D♯

Self Oscillation: state of self-vibration in a →Filter or →VCF

Semiconductor: material, the electrical resistance of which lies between non-conductor and conductor

Sempre: always

Send (Line): output terminal on mixers or effect units

Sensitivity: the input sensitivity of amplifiers has to be correctly set to enable optimal, distortion-free amplification

Sensitivity: responsiveness to slight changes

Sequencer: independent unit or component of a →Synthesizer which can memorize and repeatedly repeat a stored note or succession of chords or rhythms. Tempo and pitch can be varied. There are digital and analogue sequencers

Sequencing software: Computer programs that can make multitrack recordings from digital and/or analog sources. They thus replace a multitracking recording machine and/or a mixing console. The basic version can usually be expanded via →plug-Ins

Set: group of instruments, i.e. Drum Set

Seventh: (symbol no. 7) Minor seventh → Interval with distance of 10 half steps – e. g. C - B♭; major seventh: Interval distance of 11 half steps – e.g. C-B

Sex, Drugs & Rock 'n Roll: That's what its all about, folks!

Sextuplet: sextuplets are created when 6 notes of the same value are played instead of 4

S/H: abbr. for Sample and Hold Generator
Shanty: seaman's song

Shape: form of (oscillation) etc. →Envelope Generator

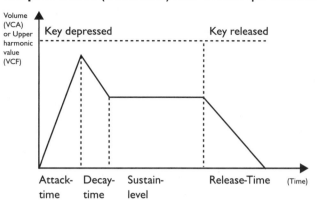

ADSR

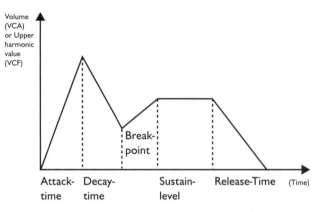

ADBSSR

Sharp: above true pitch, raising of a note
Shatter Echo: effect →Echo
Shuffle: rhythmical division into three of the Metre triplet style used in Blues, Rock and Jazz

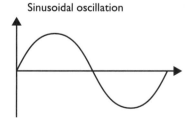

Side Fill Monitor: monitor used on the stage
Signal to Noise Ratio: →Unweighted Signal to Noise Ratio
Sine Generator: an oscillator which produces sine waves
Sine wave: an oscillation produced by an →Oscillator in the form of a sinus curve. Contains only the keynote and no overtones, also called "pure" note

Sinusoidal oscillation

Sixteenth feel: →Microtiming

Sixth (symbol no. 6) Minor sixth → Interval with distance of 8 half steps – e.g. C-A♭; major sixth: interval distance of 9 half steps – e.g. C-A

Skip: to leave out one part and go onto another

Slapback: →Effect Unit, throw back

Slave: Instrument or other type of device that is connected to the →master keyboard and controlled by it

Slope: the ascent or descent e.g. the envelope curve process

Slowly: →Tempo

Snare Drum: small drum with wires under the lower resonance skin or snare head

Software: programmes, data and contents used in the computer world

Solo: Italian for alone: part of a piece of music which is played by one instrument or sung by one voice

Soprano: highest female or boys voice, treble

Sostenuto pedal: (mainly found on concert pianos) Works in a similar way to the →sustain pedal, but it doesn't allow all notes to be sustained upon taking your hands from the keys. It only allows those notes to sustain that are played while the sostenuto pedal is pressed. Notes that are played after the pedal has been pressed will not sustain, i.e. they will sound "normal"

Sound: term for all mechanical oscillations and waves in any medium (air, wood, metal etc.)

Sound Check: testing the correct sound settings on a stage set-up (System)

Sound Memory: for the correct setting of the electronic equipment (Synthesizer, E-Organ, Mixer etc.)

Sound module: Device with preprogrammed sounds that can be connected as a →slave to a →master keyboard, →synthesizer or computer

Sound Sampling: the process of conversion and storage of natural sounds or other instruments. This means that analogous signals are divided into digital samples at a certain sampling rate with the help of an A/D-Converter. The digitalized sounds can then be extended using loops if the sample time is only very short. The sound can then be changed in analogous processes (→VCF, →VCA) before or after it has been made audible again by means or a D/A-Converter. The sound can then be played using the keyboard

Sound Sampling Unit: Digital Sound Memory; digital unit on a synthesizer which can record and store any desired sound and process it further (→Sound Sampling)

Sound Studio: room used to record and play back music or speech for the production of records, tapes or cassettes. The Sound Studio is usually divided into recording room, in which the musicians play together "live" or one after the other (→Multi-track Recording), and the central control room with mixing desk into which the musical signals are all fed. Here the signals are processed further and mixed. For this part of the procedure many effect units can be used (→Delays, →Reverb, →Noise Gate, Equalizers etc.). Before the final mixing is carried out it is usual practice to produce a rough mix, which contains a basic mixed version and provides a preliminary basic idea of how the piece sounds. Subsequent to this the music is mixed for the last time and recorded onto a normal two-track tape in stereo

Sound Synthesis: term for all kinds of electronic sounds. There are three main forms 1. subtractive, this is where mostly various wave forms are changed by filters and envelope generators; 2. Additive Synthesis; 2.1. Fourier's Synthesis; 2.2. FM synthesis. Here a →Carrier Frequency is modulated with other frequencies thus creating a new overtone composition; 3. Digital synthesis via computer controlled natural sound analysis or Sound Sampling (see →Synthesizer)

Sound Track: 1. track on a recorded tape; 2. recorded film music

Source: the origin of a sound

Split Point: dividing point (key) when using →Keyboard splitting

Square Wave: special form of oscillation

Square Wave Generator: →Oscillator which produces square waves

Staccato: →Articulation

Stack: →Top

Stacking: combination of pieces of equipment, usually in a rack

Stage Box: connection box on the stage by means of which all microphones, DI-Boxes and amplifiers on the stage are connected together and which itself is connected to the mixing desk by means of multicore-cable. The Stage Box is the electronic connection between stage and mixer

Stand Alone: A device that is not incorporated into anything else, is independent of any other parts, and can function without any other devices. CD players, for example, are alternatively available as stand-alones or built into a stereo unit

Steady Beat: →Tempo

Steady Tempo: Tempo

Step-by-Step: progressive entry of data for sequencers →Rhythm machines and computers

Storage: memorizing of data →Store

Store: instruction to memorize data

Subdominant: The triad formed on the fourth note of a major or minor scale

Subgroup: sub-classes of channels on a mixing desk

Suboscillator: an →Oscillator which is dependent on a main oscillator unit which usually produces oscillations up to two octaves below those from the main unit

Subtractive Sound Synthesis: →Sound Synthesis

Suite: 1. succession of instrumental pieces, usually dances; 2. dance parts in ballet and film etc.

Summation: the collection point for all sound signals in a mixing desk

Sustain: 1. on an organ, the continuation of a note; 2. abbr. for the sustain level on an envelope curve

Sustain Level: →Envelope Curve

Sustain pedal: If you depress the sustain pedal after striking a beat, it will continue unhindered, even if you take your hands from the keys

Swing: Jazz style which originated at the beginning of the 1930's with loose, advancing rhythms (Glenn Miller, Benny Goodmann)

Symphony: usually a four-movement musical work for a full orchestra

Sync: abbr. for →Synchronisation

Synchronisation: simultaneous controlling of processes, e.g. the simultaneous functioning of tape machines

Synchronizer: enables the synchronisation of several tape machines in a →Sound Studio

Syncope: the emphasizing of a part of a bar which is normally not emphasized

Sync to tape: a process during multi-track recordings which synchronizes various pieces of equipment and instruments

Synthesizer: electronic machine which produces noises, sounds and notes which can be played using a keyboard. The most important synthesis processes are: subtractive synthesis, algorithmic, additive synthesis, Fourier's Synthesis, digital analysis and re-synthesis process, and soundsampling. There are also differences in the form of the keyboard i. e. whether it is monophone or polyphone. 1. subtractive synthesis: here the →VCO's deliver the oscillation required to produce sounds, which are then modulated by →VCF's and →VCA's. 2. Algorithmic-additive synthesis: this uses the principle of →FM-synthesis. An oscillation is modulated using a second frequency (Thus producing new oscillations with new overtone structures). The basic components are coupled in certain orders (algorithms). 3. Fourier's synthesis: Here sound is produced with a combination of sinus oscillations. 4. Other synthesis processes are usually major systems requiring considerable computer technology and major investment

System exclusive messages: →MIDI messages

System messages: →MIDI messages

T

Take: a recorded unit

Take five: Stage jargon for "Take five minutes of rest". Also a well-known Jazz piece in the seldom-used 5/4 tact by Dave Brubeck

Talk back: command facility on mixing desk

Tape Echo: →Echo

Tempered tuning: The division of the →octave into 12 →half steps creates a problem: Apart from the octave, none of the intervals one can play on an octave divided in this manner corresponds to the pure original intervals from its overtone series. The division into twelve is thus a compromise between perfection and playability. But most people can hardly hear the difference and we can enjoy the comfort of the tuning known as well temperament that was developed by Andreas Werckmeister in 1691 – it is only this that makes the →enharmonic change possible because the distance between C-F♯ is actually slightly different to the distance C-G♭, something that fellow musicians who play string instruments without frets know.

Tempo: everything which refers to the speed in music,

Largo = broad, dignified, slow, MM = 40-59

Larghetto = more flowing than largo, MM = 60-65
Adagio = slow, peaceful, MM = 66-75
Andante = (movement) moderately slow, MM = 76-107
Moderato = moderately quick, MM = 108-119
Allegro = quickly, MM = 120-167
Presto = very quickly, MM = 16-199
In Pop and Rock music the following terms are usually used: Bright, Fairly slow, Lazily, Medium Tempo, Moderately, Moderately bright, Slowly, Slowly-strong beat, Steady beat, Steady tempo, very lively and bouncy

Tenor: →Voice Mode

Tenth: →Interval. A tenth corresponds in tone to that of an octave plus a third. A minor tenth has an interval distance of 15 half steps, e.g. C-E♭'; a major tenth has an interval distance of 16 half steps, e.g. C-E'

Tenuto: →Articulation

Ternary rhythm: → Binary rhythm

Third: (Symbol no. 3) Minor third: →Interval with distance of three half steps – e.g. C-E♯; major third: interval distance of four half steps - e.g. C-E

Thirteenth: →Interval (symbol no. 13). The thirteenth corresponds to an octave plus a sixth in terms of sound. Minor thirteenth: Interval distance of 20 half steps – e.g. C-A♭'; major thirteenth: interval distance of 21 half steps - e.g. C - A'

Threshold: a certain level at which a piece of electronic equipment starts or ceases to function

Tight: A method of playing in which most notes are played exactly on the tacts of the →microtimings. Alternative terms: on top, funky. Opposite: →laid back

Timbre: characteristic quality of sound produced by each particular instrument or voice

Time: →Tempo, beat

Time Lag: →Delay

Time stretching: During a → hard disk recording, or recording with → sequencer software, you can stretch or reduce the time that a song takes, within limits, without the →Micky Mouse effect setting in

Timer: provides timing to synchronize processes

Timpani: kettle drum, hollow brass or copper hemisphere, over edge of which parchment is stretched and tuned to a definite note

Tom-Toms: drums 14-60 cm high

Tone: periodical osciallation with a certain frequency. Generally a tone consists of a fundamental oscillation and a series of →Overtones (Partial tones, Natural tones), which determine the particular sound of a tone.

Natural harmonic row (for Keynote C)
Overtones

Tone Control: rotational or sliding switch which controls the Tone

Top: An amplifier, usually with built-in effects and corresponding adjustment controls, that is placed on top of a loudspeaker. A top and a loudspeaker are also called a stack (comes from "to stack up"). See also →amp and →amplifier

Touch Response: the ability to be able to influence the volume of a note or the timbre thereof through the strength of a strike (more accurately: the speed of the strike); other terms: Touch Control, Magic touch, Touch Sensitive

Tracking Filter: (also Keyboard Tracking) controlling of the cut-off frequency of a filter (→VCF) using a keyboard

Traditional: folklore melody which has been handed down. Composer or author is usually unknown

Transient Vibrato: delayed use of →Vibrato

Transistorized amplifier: as opposed to →Tube Amplifier. Amplifies using transistors

Transmitting: conveyance of information using →MIDI

Transposer: (also Pitch Transposer, Harmonizer) Function used to choose the key on →Electric Organs and →Synthesizers – used to place the whole keyboard in the same key. Pitch Transposers and Harmonizers as independent units enable notes to be transposed into virtually any interval required

Treble Filter: →Filter – suppresses treble frequencies i.e. Noise interference

Tremolo: (vibration) periodically become louder and then quieter

Triangle: round metal bar bent to form a triangle. This musical instrument sounds when struck with a bar

Triangle wave: form of oscillation waves; →wave

Triangular wave: →wave

Trigger: release signal, short impulse of current which signalsto start electronic processes (in Synthesizers the trigger starts the →Envelope Generator)

Triple Feeling: playing in triplet mood

Triplet: Triplets are formed if you play three notes of the same value instead of two

Tritone: augmented fourth = three whole-tone steps away from the keynote e.g. the interval c-f

Trombone: large musical instrument of the trumpet family with sliding tube or with valves

Tuba: very deep sounding giant trumpet

Tube Amp: amplifies a signal with the aid of electric valves (opposite: →Transistorized Amplifier)

Tubular Bells: hanging steel or brass pipes which when played with a hammer produce notes

Tuner: 1. device for tuning instruments (mainly string instruments) and 2. the receiver on a stereo unit

Tuning: term for the determination of the pitch of a musical instrument. Usually concert pitch "a" = 440 Hz is used as tuning pitch

Turntable: High quality record player without amplifier or loudspeakers - also suitable for DJs

Twelfth: →Interval. The twelfth corresponds in terms of sound to an octave plus a fifth. A diminished fifth corresponds to an interval distance of 18 half steps – e.g. C-Gb; a perfect fifth has an interval distance of 19 half steps – e.g. C-G'; an augmented fifth has an interval distance of 20 half steps e.g. C-G♯'

U

Unbalanced: not symmetrical

Unisono: one single voice, also a term for monophone operation of otherwise polyphone synthesizers

Unweighted Signal to Noise Ratio: relationship between the wanted signal and distortion noise signals measured in dB

Up beat: incomplete bar at the beginning of a piece of music

Upright piano: Piano

V

Valse: French for waltz

Vamp: Improvised (or sounding as though they were improvised) song intros, endings or accompaniments. Often found instead of a bridge or at the end of a song, where elements of the chorus (= Refrain) are mostly varied

VC: abbr. for Voltage Control

VCA: abbr. for Voltage Controlled Amplifier or Attenuator. Module or component unit of a →Synthesizer with which by means of →Voltage Controls the volume (amplitude) of a signal is influenced. In general the VCA, in doing this, controls the amplitude envelope curve of the signal

VCF: abbr. for →Voltage Controlled Filter. Usually a low pass filter (lets deep frequencies through and filters high ones out). Changes the timbre (overtone content) of a signal by filtering out the overtones which are over and above the settings for its cut-off frequency. By providing →Voltage Controls the way in which the cut-off frequency of a VCF functions can be influenced. If the filter is controlled using keyboard voltage controls (→Keyboard Tracking, →Filter Tracking) the deep notes sound darker and the high notes brighter. If a sine wave from a LFO is used as control voltage, a Wah-Wah effect is produced

VCO: abbr. →Voltage Controlled Oscillator. Produces oscillations in an analogous synthesizer which are then processed by →VCF and →VCA. Usually the VCO's have various forms of oscillations such as →Sinus Oscillation, →Triangular Oscillation, →Saw-tooth Oscillation, →Pulse and square-wave oscillation. Usually increases by 1 V per Octave. The frequency of the VCO can in addition also be controlled using the voltage from a →LFO which produces a vibrato effect, for example

Velocity Touch Control: →Touch Response

Very lively and bouncy: →Tempo

VFO: abbr. for →Variable Frequency Oscillation. Oscillators upon which it is possible to set the frequency

Vibrato: slight frequency modulation (usually with a vibrato frequency of between 5 Hz and 10 Hz)

Vibraphone: built like a →Marimbaphone but with metal instead of wooden bars

Viola: stringed instrument, somewhat larger than a violin, tuned a fifth deeper: somewhat nasal sound

Virtual analog: Digital reproduction of a synthesizer to sound like an analog device

Virtuoso: skilled in the mechanical side of an art, masterly

Vocalizer: A really brilliant device: You sing one part, select the matching chord on your keyboard, and it produces several parts of sound to your music. Newer devices sound really good. Vocalizer functions can already be found in electronic organs with a microphone input

Vocoder: term originating from VOice and CODER. Effect unit with which two different signals can be combined e.g. Vocals and Synthesizer. The V. processes the human voice for a connected synthesizer so that typical speech articulation is carried in the synthesizer sound (Robot voices etc.)

Voice Initialize: determining basic voice sound

Voice messages: →MIDI messages

Voice modes:

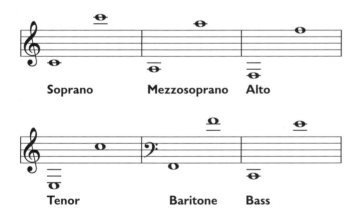

Voicing: the ordering of the intervals in a chord (or in a succession of chords)

Volt: (abbr. V) Unit of measurement for electronic force/currents

Voltage: electrical measure (measured in volts = V) for the potential difference between two oppositely charged poles

Voltage Control: = VC. Principle for controlling electronic processes e.g. synthesizers. Certain parts of the synthesizer are voltage controllable, →VCO, → VCF, →VCA

Voltage Controlled Amplifier: VCA

Voltage Controlled Attenuator: →VCA,

Voltage Controlled Filter: →VCF,

Voltage Controlled Oscillator: →VCO

Volt/Octave Characteristic: relationship between control voltage and frequency of a →VCO. If the control voltage changes by 1 V, the VCO frequency changes by one octave

Volume pedal: Softens the beat that's just been played, making it either quieter, or muting it completely

VU-Meter: Volume Unit Meter-used to set level controls

W

W: abbr. for →Watt

Wah-Wah: term used for a filter effect in which the cut off frequency of the filter is periodically or rhythmically changed. Used by guitarists as a foot pedal

Walking Bass: typical figure in Boogie Woogie and Jazz

Waltz: dance in triple time with graceful flowing melody and usually one harmony to each bar

Watt: unit of electrical power

Wave: vibration or stirring of a medium with sinuous or sweeping motion. Ridge and trough oscillation

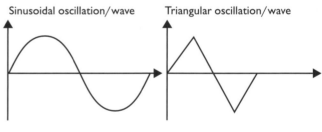

Sinusoidal oscillation/wave   Triangular oscillation/wave

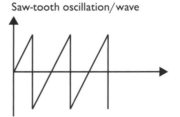

Saw-tooth oscillation/wave

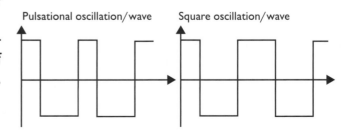

Pulsational oscillation/wave   Square oscillation/wave

Waveform: the shape of a →Wave

Wavelength: frequency of a →Wave

Wedge Monitor: floor monitor used on stage

Well-tempered tuning: →Tempered tuning

White Noise: →Noise

Whining/Wow: occurs when two oscillations which are slightly different are superimposed

Whole tone: →Half tone

Whole-tone scale: scale consisting purely of whole tones

Wire or Rhythm Brush: consists of thin steel wires, used for playing particular percussion styles

Working/main memory: →RAM or Random Access Memory

Workstation: →Synthesizer that also has a →sequencer for recording and/or a →sampler and other useful accessories

Woodwind instruments: Clarinette, Saxophone etc.

X

XLR plug: 3-pin plug in the professional and semi-professional areas. Is often used, e.g. for microphones

Yo! Belongs, with the expressions "Mother ..." and "Say What," to the most important words in Hiphop texts

Xylophone: Instrument similar to a "Glockenspiel" with wooden bars

13 CONTENT OF THE CD

Listening examples of strike patterns and rhythms (Tracks 1-27)

Improvisation lessons (Tracks 28-38)

Main songs from the chapter Keyboard Styles (Tracks 39-46)

Easy Chords Keyboard

The most important scales and chords for keyboard. Standard notation, combined with easy-to-understand diagrams makes using this book a breeze, even for the beginning keyboarder. Plus useful hints and tips on chord-voicings, drop-techniques, chord inversions and more ...

80 pages
Format: DIN A6 / 4.1" x 5.9" (pocket size!)

Bessler/Opgenoorth
Keyboard Guide

This practical overview o chords, keys and harmo nic relationships has bee especially designed wit the Jazz, Rock and Po keyboarder in mind.
It features a new struct re that makes it useful fo beginners as well as ad vanced musicians. Th enables you to improve your musical understanding.

104 pages
Format: DIN A5 / 5.8" x 8.3"

Bessler/Opgenoorth
Electronic Keyboard-SONGBOOK Classic

This songbook contains a selection of some of the most popular classical pieces. It is carefully structured according to the level of difficulty. It can be combined with almost any keyboard method on the market or used as a stand-alone songbook.
The notation of each song features standard notation, fingering suggestions, chord diagrams and even information on automation and factory presets.
The appendix contains helpful advice on "how to practice", explanations on some of the most important symbols in tempo and expression notation and an index of the essential terms and chords in "single finger mode", making this book a great learning tool for all keyboarders.

104 pages
Format: DIN A4 / 8.3" x 11.7"